Investing in Young Children

KEDLESTON ROAD

Investing in Young Children

An Early Childhood Development Guide for Policy Dialogue and Project Preparation

Sophie Naudeau
Naoko Kataoka
Alexandria Valerio
Michelle J. Neuman
Leslie Kennedy Elder

THE WORLD BANK
Washington, D.C.

ISBN: 978-0-8213-8526-5
eISBN: 978-0-8213-8528-9
DOI: 10.1596/978-0-8213-8526-5

Library of Congress Cataloging-in-Publication Data
Investing in young children : an early childhood development guide for policy dialogue and project preparation / Sophie Naudeau ... [et al.].
    p. cm. — (Directions in development)
Includes bibliographical references and index.
    ISBN 978-0-8213-8526-5 (alk. paper) — ISBN 978-0-8213-8528-9
    1. Child development—Developing countries. 2. Early childhood education—Developing countries. 3. Child welfare—Developing countries. I. Naudeau, Sophie. II. World Bank.
    HQ792.2I58 2011
    305.23109172'4—dc22

                                                                        2010036025

Cover photograph: Edwin Huffman/The World Bank
Cover design: Naylor Design

Contents

Boxes

Figures

Tables

Foreword

Investing in young children is the responsible thing to do. All children deserve a chance to grow into healthy, educated, and competent people, no matter where and when they were born. While parents bear most of the responsibility for raising their children, especially in the early years of life, governments also have an important role during this critical time of human capital accumulation. For example, governments can ensure that all expectant mothers and young children have access to quality health services and nutrition. They can support parents and other caregivers in providing a positive and stimulating environment for children from birth on by promoting parenting information programs, investing in direct services such as home-based visits, funding daycare centers and preschools, or providing financial incentives to access good quality programs for infants and children.

Investing in young children is also the smart thing to do. In the short term, early childhood development (ECD) investments translate into considerable cost savings and efficiency gains in the health and education sectors because the children who benefit from ECD services are more likely to be healthy, ready to learn upon entering primary school, stay in school longer, and perform well throughout their schooling. In the long term, ECD investments yield socially well-adjusted and productive adults who contribute to a country's economic growth and help break the intergenerational cycle of poverty, as demonstrated by higher wages, lower dependence on social assistance programs, greater asset accumulation, and healthier families. These benefits not only level the playing field for children from disadvantaged backgrounds but also make for better, more equitable, and more prosperous societies.

Clearly, ECD should be a prominent priority on a country's development agenda. Unfortunately, the majority of poor children in low- and middle-income countries do not have access to high-quality ECD programs that offer early opportunities for stimulation and learning. And this inadequate access persists despite strong evidence that early learning gaps between disadvantaged children and those from better-off families widen quickly in the first few years of life and that making up for these gaps becomes difficult and costly later in a child's life.

This ECD guide presents lessons and experiences that have been useful in informing the policy debate about ECD interventions and the design of such programs across the world. Whether the user of this guide is at the initial stage of deciding whether to expand an ECD portfolio or already in the program design stage, the content offers a range of evidence-based options to inform policy and investment choices.

It is my sincere hope that *Investing in Young Children* will stimulate a vigorous discussion with governments, development partners, and civil society on the tremendous benefits of investing in young children and the options that exist to set up high-quality programs. I look forward to the continued collective work of policy makers, development partners, and other key stakeholders to give tomorrow's adults a strong foundation to lead happy, healthy, and productive lives.

Tamar Manuelyan Atinc
Vice President, Human Development Network
The World Bank
August 2010

Acknowledgments

This guide was prepared by the core team of Sophie Naudeau (human development specialist, Human Development Network, Children and Youth Unit [HDNCY], World Bank; Naoko Kataoka (consultant); Alexandria Valerio (senior economist, HDNCY); Michelle J. Neuman (ECD specialist, Africa Region Education Department, World Bank); and Leslie Kennedy Elder (senior nutrition specialist, Health, Nutrition and Population Department, World Bank); with contributions from Jonathan Cohen Miles (consultant). The team benefited from the general guidance of Wendy Cunningham (lead specialist, HDNCY) and Ariel Fiszbein (chief economist, Human Development Network).

Helpful peer-review comments were provided by Caroline Arnold (Aga Khan Foundation); Judith Evans (University of Victoria, BC, Canada); Hiro Yoshikawa (Harvard University); and by the following World Bank colleagues: Harold Alderman, Felipe Barrera, Amanda Beatty, Simeth Beng, Luis Benveniste, Carla Bertoncino, Christian Bodewig, Mariam Claeson, David Evans, Deon Filmer, Emanuela Galasso, Marito Garcia, Rebekka Grun, Peter Holland, Susiana Iskandar, Wendy Jarvie, Venita Kaul, Christop Kurowski, Martha Laverde, Yi-Kyoung Lee, Arianna Legovini, Mattias Lundberg, Alessandra Marini, Aleksandra Posarac, Laura Rawlings, Norbert Schady, Meera Shekar, Renos Vakis, and Andrea Vermehren.

Abbreviations

AIID	Amsterdam Institute for International Development
ASQ	Ages and Stages Questionnaire
BMI	body mass index
CB	cost benefit
CBCL	Achenbach Child Behavior Checklist
CCT	conditional cash transfer
CDD	community-driven development
CE	cost-effectiveness
CEPAL	Comisión Económica para América Latina y el Caribe
CES-D	Center for Epidemiologic Studies
CIS	Caregiver Interaction Scale
DAP	Developmentally Appropriate Practices in Early Childhood Program
DHS	Demographic and Health Surveys
DQ	development quotient
DTP3	combined diphtheria-tetanus toxoid and pertussis vaccine
ECC	Early Childhood Commission (Jamaica)
ECCD	early childhood care and development
ECCE	early childhood care and education

ECD	early childhood development
ECE	early childhood education
ECERS-R	Early Childhood Environment Rating Scale
ENDEMAIN	Ecuador Demographic and Maternal and Child Health Survey
EPPE	Effective Provision of Pre-school Education Project
FCCERS-R	Family Child Care Environment Rating Scale-Revised
FDCRS	Family Day-Care Rating Scale
GDP	gross domestic product
GNP	gross national product
HIPPY	Home Instruction Program for Preschool Youngsters
HOME	Home Observation for Measurement of the Environment
ICD	Integrated Child Development Services
IE	impact evalution
IEA	International Association for the Evaluation of Educational Achievement
IEC	information, education, and communication
IMR	infant mortality rate
IRB	Institutional Review Board
IRI	interactive radio instruction
IRR	internal rate of return
ITERS-R	Infant-Toddler Environment Rating Scale
IUGR	intrauterine growth restriction
LBW	low birthweight
MCH	mother and child health
MDI	mental development index
MICS	Multiple Indicator Cluster Survey
MIS	management information system
NAEYC	National Association for the Education of Young Children
NGO	nongovernmental organization
NICHD	National Institute for Child Health and Development
OECD	Organisation for Economic Co-operation and Development
OEI	Organización de Estados Iberoamericanos para la Educacion, Ciencia y Cultura
OLS	ordinary least squares
PIDI	Proyecto Integral de Desarrollo Infantil
PPVT	Peabody Picture Vocabulary Test

PRSP	Poverty Reduction Strategy Paper
RISE	Radio Instruction to Strengthen Education project
SAR	Special Administrative Region
SMS	short message services
TVIP	Test de Vocabulario en Imagenes Peabody
U5MR	under-5 mortality rate
UNESCO	United Nations Educational, Scientific and Cultural Organization
UNICEF	United Nations Children's Fund
USAID	United States Agency for International Development
WHO	World Health Organization

Overview

Objective

The World Bank created this early childhood development (ECD) guide in response to growing demand from project managers for advice and support to facilitate the policy dialogue on the topic of ECD and to help clients make and implement relevant choices on how to best invest in ECD in the context of their country's economy and national priorities. This guide fills a gap in the literature by (1) distilling existing information in a user-friendly format of short notes, (2) providing practical information on recently relevant ECD topics, such as measuring child development outcomes through the identification and adaptation of relevant instruments, conditional cash transfers for families with young children, and so on, and (3) assessing the quality of the latest evidence on each topic and identifying the knowledge gaps for which additional experimentation and evaluation are required.

Methodology for Selecting the Evidence

The notes in this guide contain references to the findings of research studies. These studies were selected in an extensive literature review using the following criteria, unless otherwise noted:

1. Studies that assess the impact of interventions or incentives that are consistent with the definition of ECD (see introduction).
2. Studies that focus on measuring outcomes in at least one domain of child development or measure variables expected to play a mediating role in these outcomes.
3. Studies that describe the results of:
   a. Rigorous impact evaluations that identify a valid counterfactual[1] through experimental or quasi-experimental techniques,
   b. Large-scale cohort studies, or
   c. Process evaluations that focus on identifying critical elements of quality interventions across multiple sites (including meta-analyses).

Summary of Contents

This ECD guide is presented in a series of short notes grouped in thematic sections. The notes are not intended to be comprehensive, but rather to summarize the main debates in the field. Each note is designed to be read independently, so information is sometimes repeated across notes.

This guide contains the following sections:

Introduction. The introduction includes (1) a definition of ECD, (2) elements of ECD background and rationale, and (3) a conceptual framework, including a discussion of the various domains of child development and the critical windows of opportunity for specific interventions within the early childhood time frame.

Section 1: Initiating the policy dialogue on investing in ECD. The three notes in this section cover questions considered in the decision to invest in ECD: Should a given society invest public resources in ECD? Are ECD investments cost-effective and worthwhile compared to alternative allocations of public resources? Each note is designed to make an argument that would resonate with each of the main counterparts in the policy dialogue for ECD: ministers of finance, planning, and social affairs; ministers of health; and ministers of education, respectively.

Once the decision to invest in ECD has been made, several questions immediately follow and lay the groundwork for a project. Common questions include: What beneficiaries should be targeted? How can data be collected on the needs of this population and on their developmental outcomes? What specific services should be offered? What are the cost implications and financing options? These "second-generation" questions are addressed in sections 2, 3, and 4.

Section 2: Assessing needs, measuring outcomes, and establishing policy frameworks. The two notes in this section include information on the indicators, tools, and instruments that can be used to conduct ECD situation analyses as well as monitoring and impact evaluations in low-income settings, including collecting information on (1) the specific needs of children from conception to age 6 and their families, (2) the supply (scope and quality) of ECD services, (3) the demand for ECD services, and (4) the legal environment and institutional framework for ECD.

Section 3: Strategic entry points for ECD investments. The four notes in this section discuss options for strategic entry points: (1) center-based ECD programs that focus on school readiness; (2) home-based ECD programs for behavior change in health, nutrition, and parenting; (3) communication/media campaigns for families with young children; and (4) "conditional cash transfers" (CCTs) for families with young children.

Although integrated ECD interventions that address the health, nutrition, and early stimulation/learning needs of young children; until they transition to primary school are likely to yield the greatest positive results across domains of child development (Grantham-McGregor et al. 2007), such integrated interventions throughout early childhood are not always possible, especially in the initial stage of a client's engagement in ECD.

Each strategic entry point for investment is discussed in a separate note and can be used as a stand-alone tool or in combination with others. The notes aim to strike a balance between providing evidence-based recommendations (when evidence is available) and conventional wisdom or "best practice." They also identify the knowledge gaps for which additional experimentation and evaluation are required.

Section 4: Costing and financing ECD programs. Finally, both the decision to invest in ECD and the types of strategic entry points that are prioritized depend to a large extent on the financial opportunities and constraints in a given context. Accordingly, the two notes in this section include information on (1) types of costs to take into consideration when planning ECD interventions and (2) options for financial sources and financing mechanisms.

Appendix: Summary table of programs and evaluations. The appendix provides more details on the interventions and evaluation studies referenced throughout the notes.

Note

1. Counterfactual refers to a group of people who are as similar as possible in both observable and unobservable dimensions to those who participated in the intervention under discussion.

Reference

Grantham-McGregor, S., Y. Bun Cheung, S. Cueto, P. Glewwe, L. Richer, B. Trupp, and the International Child Development Steering Group. 2007. "Developmental Potential in the First 5 Years for Children in Developing Countries." *The Lancet* 369 (9555): 60–70.

Introduction

Definition

The field of early childhood development (ECD)[1] is framed by the United Nations Convention on the Rights of the Child, General Comment 7 (UN 2006) and refers to the physical, cognitive, linguistic, and socio-emotional development of young children until they transition to primary school (typically around age 6 or 7).[2] The first phase of human development (starting during pregnancy), ECD is an integrated concept that cuts across multiple sectors, including health and nutrition, education, and social protection.

Background and Rationale

Children who reach the end of early childhood should be developing well in the physical, cognitive, linguistic, and socio-emotional areas in order to fully benefit from further opportunities in the education and health sectors and to become fully productive members of society. They should be (1) healthy and well-nourished, (2) securely attached to caregivers and able to interact positively with extended family members, peers, and teachers, (3) able to communicate in their native language with both peers and adults, and (4) ready to learn throughout primary school.

Poor and otherwise disadvantaged children are least likely to reach these important milestones because they are often exposed to the cumulative effects of multiple risk factors,[3] including lack of access to basic water and sanitation infrastructures, lack of access to quality health services; inadequate nutritional inputs; parents with low education levels; and lack of access to quality daycare centers and preschools.

When compared to others, poor and otherwise disadvantaged children are less likely to enroll in school at the right age. They are also more likely to attain lower achievement levels or grades for their age and to have poorer cognitive ability (Vegas and Santibáñez 2010). A recent study (Grantham-McGregor et al. 2007) estimates that 219 million children under the age of 5 are disadvantaged.[4] While this number represents 39 percent of all children under 5 in the developing world, the prevalence is even higher in Sub-Saharan Africa and South Asia (61 percent and 52 percent of children, respectively).

Interventions in the early years have the potential to offset these negative trends and to provide young children with more opportunities and better outcomes in terms of access to education, quality of learning, physical growth and health, and, eventually, productivity. Better-off children also benefit from participation in quality ECD interventions. And because investing in ECD has ripple effects over the life span of beneficiaries, these interventions are among the most cost-effective investments a country can make in the human development and capital formation of its people (Heckman 2008).

Conceptual Framework

Development in early childhood is a multidimensional process in which progress in one domain often acts as a catalyst for progress in other domains. Conversely, delays in one area of development can trigger delays in other areas as well. For example, malnutrition in the early years not only leads to poor physical growth (including stunting), but also is highly predictive of delayed cognitive development and low academic achievement throughout the school years (Glewwe, Jacoby, and King 2001). In turn, lack of adult attention and stimulation in the early years not only leads to poor socio-emotional and cognitive development, but also is linked to poor health and physical growth.[5]

Domains of Child Development

The four interrelated domains of child development (see figure 1)—physical development, cognitive development, linguistic development, and socio-emotional development—are described as follows.[6]

Physical development is defined as an individual's rate of growth, physical fitness, fine motor skills, gross motor skills, and self-care abilities; it can be affected by the presence of chronic conditions such as diabetes, disability, and malnutrition. The prevalence of stunting (chronic undernutrition, as measured by height-for-age Z-score less than or equal to –2) in children between birth and age 2 is particularly important because it reflects the prevalence of undernutrition in a given population of children—which, in turn, is predictive of low cognitive and overall development in early childhood and later life (Grantham-McGregor et al. 2007).

Cognitive development encompasses progress in analytical skills, mental problem-solving, memory, and early mathematical abilities. For infants and toddlers, early cognitive development involves problem-solving, such as learning to stack or nest objects, and early understanding of arithmetic, demonstrated by such behaviors as sorting objects and knowing what "one" or "two" of something means. By age 3, children should be capable of solving simple puzzles and matching colors and shapes, as well as show awareness of concepts such as "more" and "less." As children approach school age, cognitive development broadens in scope to early knowledge

Figure 1   Integrated ECD

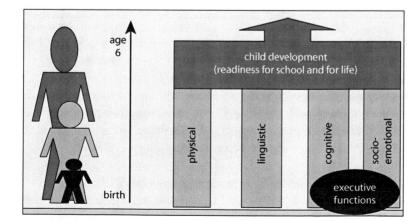

Source: Authors.

of numbers, including adding and subtracting, and familiarity with alphabet letters and printing. Indicators of cognitive development as children near school entry include knowledge of letters and numbers, ability to retain information in short-term memory, and knowledge of key personal information like one's name and address.

Language development manifests itself through babbling, pointing, and gesturing in infancy, the emergence of first words and sentences in toddlerhood, and an explosion of words between ages 2 and 3. It is important to note that the capacity to absorb language and to differentiate between sounds peaks at around 9 months of age (see Note 3.1), well before the child can actually talk, thus indicating that it is critical for parents/caregivers to verbally interact with children from birth onward. As children move into the preschool years, indicators of language development include production and understanding of words, abilities to tell stories and identify letters, and comfort and familiarity with books.

Social and emotional development, in the first 2 years of life, centers on children's relationships with caregivers and learning how much they can trust those around them to meet their needs. In the preschool years, social and emotional development builds upon previous acquisitions and expands to include social competence (getting along with others, including peers and teachers), behavior management (following directions and cooperating with requests), social perception (identifying thoughts and feelings in oneself and others), and self-regulatory abilities (having emotional and behavioral control, especially in stressful situations).

Some of these skills involve both socio-emotional and cognitive processes and have been called "executive function processes" (Fernald et al. 2009). They include impulse control, the ability to initiate action, the ability to sustain attention, and persistence, all of which are likely to significantly influence an individual's capacity to succeed in life. The more cognitive executive function processes have been called "cool" processes, such as remembering arbitrary rules and other non-emotional aspects of a given task, while "hot" executive function processes usually refer to the more emotional aspects of executive function, such as those involving inhibition or the capacity to delay gratification.

Windows of Opportunity for Intervention in Early Childhood
Development across the four ECD domains is cumulative throughout early childhood. Yet, some interventions are particularly critical during specific subperiods (or windows of opportunity) and should therefore be prioritized in decisions on appropriate interventions for different age

Figure 2   Timing Matters: The Most Important ECD Interventions Vary with Child's Age

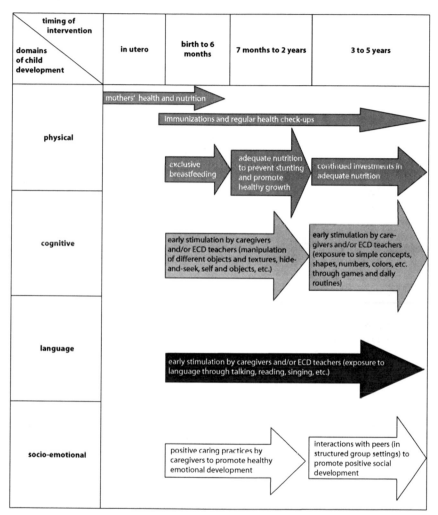

Source: Authors.

groups. Figure 2 summarizes the types of interventions that are most relevant during different subperiods within early childhood. For example, it is critical that young children receive adequate nutrition between conception and the age of 2 years through proper prenatal nutrition, exclusive breastfeeding in the first 6 months of life, and the addition of adequate complementary foods to continued breastfeeding from 6 months to 2 years (World Bank 2006). Similarly, it is critical that children up to age 2 are in the nurturing environment they need to develop strong bonds (or attachment) with their caregivers, thus laying the foundation for further development in all areas (Naudeau 2009). Therefore, ECD programs that show parents how to positively interact with their infants and toddlers through both touch and verbal communication are particularly important in these early years. Failure to provide children with adequate nutrition and stimulation during this window of opportunity damages human potential (Grantham-McGregor et al. 2007).

As children age from 3 to 5 years old, interactions with peers (for example, in the context of center-based ECD programs) and more advanced forms of linguistic and cognitive stimulation by parents and ECD teachers become increasingly important, along with continued investment in health and nutrition.

Notes

1. ECD is also known as early childhood care and development (ECCD) and encompasses early childhood education (ECE), early childhood care and education (ECCE), and other designations.
2. While the definition of ECD includes children up to age 8—on the premise that a successful transition to primary school depends not only on the child's school readiness, but also on the readiness of schools to adapt to the specific needs of young learners in the early grades—this guide focuses on ECD services up to primary school entry.
3. Risk factors are defined as "personal characteristics or environmental circumstances that increase the probability of negative outcomes for children" (Cole and Cole 2000).
4. In this study, children are considered disadvantaged if they are stunted, living in poverty, or both.
5. For a review of articles on this topic, see Naudeau (2009).
6. Much of the information contained in this section is adapted from Fernald et al. (2009).

References

Cole, M., and S. R. Cole. 2000. *The Development of Children* (4th ed.). New York: Worth.

Fernald, L., P. Kariger, P. Engle, and A. Raikes. 2009. *Examining Early Child Development in Low-Income Countries: A Toolkit for the Assessment of Children in the First Five Years of Life*. Washington, DC: World Bank.

Glewwe, P., H. G. Jacoby, and E. M. King. 2001. "Early Childhood Nutrition and Academic Achievement: A Longitudinal Study." *Journal of Public Economics* 81 (3): 345–68.

Grantham-McGregor, S., Y. Bun Cheung, S. Cueto, P. Glewwe, L. Richer, B. Trupp, and the International Child Development Steering Group. 2007. "Developmental Potential in the First 5 Years for Children in Developing Countries." *The Lancet* 369 (9555): 60–70.

Heckman, J. 2008. "Schools, Skills, and Synapses." *Economic Inquiry* 46 (3): 289–324.

Naudeau, S. 2009. "Supplementing Nutrition in the Early Years: The Role of Early Childhood Stimulation to Maximize Nutritional Inputs." *Child and Youth Development Notes* 3 (1) (March) World Bank, Washington, DC.

UN (United Nations). 2006. "UN General Comment 7: Implementing Child Rights in Early Childhood." (40th session, 2005). U.N. Doc. CRC/C/GC/7/Rev.1. http://www1.umn.edu/humanrts/crc/crc_general_comments.htm

Vegas, E., and L. Santibáñez. 2010. "The Promise of Early Childhood Development in Latin America and the Caribbean." World Bank, Washington, DC.

World Bank. 2006. *Repositioning Nutrition as Central to Development: A Strategy for Large-Scale Action.* Washington, DC: World Bank.

Initiating the Policy Dialogue on Investing in ECD

Why Invest in ECD? The Economic Argument
(for Policy Dialogue with Ministers of Finance, Planning, and Social Affairs)

This note makes the case for public investment in early childhood development (ECD) by providing evidence that delays in cognitive and overall development well before a child enters primary school often have long-lasting and costly consequences for both families and societies. This note also demonstrates that well-targeted ECD interventions are a cost-effective strategy to help prevent or remedy these delays, thus allowing children living in poverty to be healthier, perform better in school, engage in less risky activities, and become more productive adults.

Failure to Invest in ECD Is Costly and Difficult to Compensate for Later in Life

The skills developed in early childhood form the basis for future learning and labor market success. ECD enhances a child's ability to learn, work with others, be patient, and develop other skills that are the foundation for formal learning and social interaction in the school years and beyond.

Failure to develop these foundational skills can lead to long-term, often irreversible effects on educational attainment, health, fertility, and productive earnings, which later result in significant costs for both

15

individuals and society (Heckman and Masterov 2007). Studies in Brazil, Indonesia, Jamaica, Peru, the Philippines, and South Africa, among others, have shown that inadequate nutrition between conception and age 2 leads to serious cognitive delays in school-age children (Grantham-McGregor et al. 2007). In addition, among preschool-aged children, linguistic and cognitive delays can accumulate rapidly if not addressed. For example, figure 1.1.1 shows that, while differences in age-adjusted vocabulary among 3-year-old Ecuadorian children are generally small, by age 6, children in less wealthy or less educated households have fallen far behind their counterparts in wealthier or more educated households. This pattern occurs in part because poor children tend to receive less speech directed toward them and because the speech they do hear tends to have reduced lexical richness and sentence complexity (Fernald et al. 2009).

Associations between poverty and multiple areas of child development (including cognitive, physical, and socio-emotional) were also recorded as early as 6 months of age in the Arab Republic of Egypt, 12 months in Brazil, 10 months in India, and 18 months in Bangladesh (Grantham-McGregor et al. 2007).

As they get older, children living in poverty are likely to experience poor school performance, including high rates of repetition and dropout,

Figure 1.1.1   Vocabulary Scores of Ecuadorian Children Aged 36–72 Months
wealth quartiles

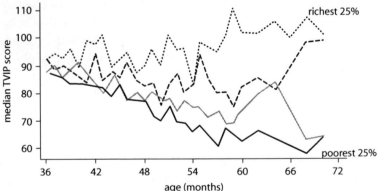

Source: Paxson and Schady 2007.
Note: TVIP (*Test de Vocabulario en Imagenes Peabody*) is a measure of Spanish receptive language based on the Peabody Picture Vocabulary Test—Revised. Y axis = standardized TVIP scores; mean of the reference population = 100; standard deviation = 15. Accordingly, children who score below 70 fall below the 5th percentile of the normative distribution. The four lines represent socioeconomic quartiles.

as well as high fertility and morbidity rates, which contribute to costly inefficiencies in the education and health sectors. They are also more likely to have low productivity and income, to provide poor care for their children, and to contribute to the intergenerational transmission of poverty (Grantham-McGregor et al. 2007), and they are less likely to contribute to the growth of their country's economy.

Developmental delays before age 6 are difficult to compensate for later in life because early childhood is a particularly sensitive period for brain formation. Indeed, neurological studies have shown that synapses (that is, connections or pathways between neurons in the nervous system) develop rapidly during this period, forming the basis of cognitive and emotional functioning for the rest of the child's life (Young and Mustard 2007). Both proper nutrition, especially from conception to age 2, and stimulation in the first 5 years of life play a critical role in the process of brain formation and development, mainly by supporting the multiplication of synapses and the myelination[1] process, both essential for the nervous system to function normally (World Bank 2006; Nelson, de Haan, and Thomas 2006). Conversely, lack of proper nutrition and stimulation in the early years can lead to dramatic abnormalities in brain development (Shonkoff and Phillips 2000).

There Is Strong Evidence That ECD Interventions Yield Significant Benefits in the Short and Long Term

Research increasingly demonstrates that cognitive abilities are as strongly affected by the quality of the environment and the amount of early stimulation and learning opportunities children are exposed to as they are by genetics, with genetic influences accounting for about half of the variance in cognitive abilities (Fernald et al. 2009). Similarly, children's socioemotional development and physical development are greatly influenced by their early environment.[2]

Environmental risk factors such as malnutrition, poor health, unstimulating home environments, and child maltreatment have all been shown to have a negative impact on children's development (Irwin, Siddiqi, and Hertzman 2007). These risk factors tend to be more concentrated among poor households with less educated parents, partly because of information failures (for example, parents' lack of knowledge on how to support children's growth and development) and partly because of supply-side constraints (for example, unequal distribution of resources and services for young children).

A number of ECD investments (detailed in Notes 3.1–3.4) have been shown to have significant and long-lasting benefits in three broad categories of interrelated outcomes.

- **Enhancing school readiness and related educational outcomes.** School readiness means a child possesses the cognitive and socio-emotional abilities necessary to learn and succeed in school (see Note 1.3.). Related educational outcomes include improved performance on standardized tests, reduced school dropout or failure, and increased grade retention (Lynch 2005). A number of different ECD interventions, including those that focus on early education and preliteracy, nutrition, and parenting skills and knowledge, have been shown to positively affect school readiness and academic achievement. For example, participants in a high-quality, active-learning preschool program, High/Scope Perry Preschool, had higher rates of high school completion than the control group (71 percent vs. 54 percent), which in turn resulted in higher monthly earnings (29 percent vs. 7 percent earned US$2000 or more per month) and rate of home ownership at age 27 (36 percent vs. 13 percent) (Schweinhart et al. 2005).

- **Improving physical and mental health and reducing reliance on the health care system.** While it is not surprising that programs that address nutrition, immunization, and hygiene have demonstrated significant health benefits, it is important to recognize that other types of ECD interventions, including those that promote opportunities for early stimulation and learning, also have a direct impact on children's health (see Note 1.2). Programs that strengthen young children's cognitive and socio-emotional abilities can lead to fewer health problems later in life, in part because they reduce the likelihood of mental health problems, and also because they lead children to make choices that have health benefits, such as increased use of seatbelts and reduced use of cigarettes, alcohol, and legal and illegal addictive drugs (Schulman 2005).

- **Reducing engagement in high-risk behavior.** High-risk behaviors common to children and youth include smoking, risky sexual behavior, substance use and addiction, and criminal and violent activity (Lynch 2005). These behaviors reduce a child's chance of making a successful transition to adulthood and increase the likelihood of negative outcomes such as illness, unemployment, adolescent pregnancy, sexually transmitted diseases, addictions, incarceration, and social exclusion (Cunningham et al. 2008). Programs that enhance cognitive and socio-emotional abilities improve children's ability to self-regulate their behavior and emotions. For example, an evaluation of a mother-child education program in Turkey showed that children whose families participated in the program had lower rates of delinquency than those whose families did not participate (Kagitcibasi et al. 2009). The Abecedarian Project, a randomized prospective trial of full-time quality child care from infancy to age 5 in the United States, found that, as they aged, participants were less likely to smoke, use marijuana, or become teen parents than children who had not participated in the program (Campbell et al. 2002).

Remedial interventions are possible later in a child's development—such as education equivalency degree programs for school dropouts or therapeutic interventions for violent youth—but the longer a society waits to intervene in the life cycle of a disadvantaged child, the more costly it is to remediate the disadvantage (Heckman 2008a). Indeed, ECD interventions have not only a high cost-benefit ratio, but also a higher rate of return for each dollar invested than interventions directed at older children and adults (see figure 1.1.2) (Heckman 2008b; Heckman, Stixrud, and Urzua 2006). Evidence suggests a potential return rate of 7–16 percent annually from high-quality ECD programs targeting vulnerable groups

Figure 1.1.2   Rate of Return to Human Development Investment across All Ages

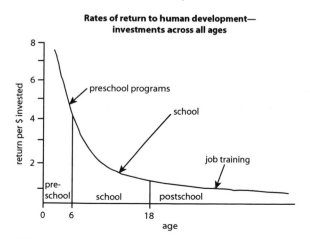

Source: Carneiro and Heckman 2003.

(Rolnick and Grunewald 2007; Heckman et al. 2009).[3] Accordingly, many countries invest public resources in ECD as both a rights-based service (UN 2006) and a sound financial investment.

Another economic advantage of ECD intervention is that it enhances both efficiency and equity,[4] in that it offers a cost-efficient way to produce a well-trained and capable workforce, and leads to better outcomes for those at greatest disadvantage (Heckman and Masterov 2007).

Depending on the political economy of a given country, public resources may be invested for the most vulnerable only or for larger segments of the population, with potential trade-offs between equity and universality of service provision, including implications for costing and financing (see Notes 4.1. and 4.2.).

ECD Investments Can Also Have a Positive Impact on Older Girls and Women

In addition to the direct impact of ECD interventions on young children, positive externalities can occur in the areas of girls' education and women's labor force participation. Indeed, evidence suggests that affordable child care for young children can increase the school enrollment rates of older female siblings to a greater extent than even an increase in maternal wages. For example, a Kenyan study showed that increasing maternal wages would likely lead to an 11 percent increase in the school enrollment of boys in the family but a decrease in school enrollment of girls by 10 percent, as adolescent girls took over more home responsibilities because their mothers worked outside the home. In contrast, the study showed that reducing the cost of child care increased school enrollment of girls in the family without having a measurable effect on boys' school enrollment in either direction (Lokshin, Glinskaya, and Garcia 2000).

Further evidence suggests that interventions that come with affordable child care can increase mothers' engagement in the workforce (Lokshin, Glinskaya, and Garcia 2000; Berlinski and Galiani 2007), particularly among more educated mothers (Schlosser 2005). For example, a study in Argentina looked at the effect of large-scale increases in the availability of free public preschools nationwide and estimated an effect on increased maternal employment of 7–14 percent (Berlinski and Galiani 2007). Another study of Argentine families estimated a 13 percent difference in workforce engagement in favor of mothers whose youngest child just made the age cutoff for preschool eligibility versus those whose youngest child just missed that age cutoff (Berlinski, Galiani, and McEwan 2008).

Notes

1. Myelination is the production of a coating of myelin (an electrically insulating material) around the axon of a neuron (nerve cell), which maximizes the intensity of neural transmissions within the brain.
2. Evidence distinguishing between genetic and environmental factors comes primarily from industrialized nations. For a review, see Plomin 1994.
3. It is important to note that these high rates of return were observed for small-scale interventions that targeted vulnerable groups of children. Large-scale interventions that target a broader range of beneficiaries may yield smaller returns.
4. However, ECD may require complementary inputs at the primary school level for its learning achievement efforts to be sustained. Therefore, equity efficiency trade-offs might be necessary for low-income children as they get older.

Key Readings

Grantham-McGregor, S., Y. Bun Cheung, S. Cueto, P. Glewwe, L. Richer, B. Trupp, and the International Child Development Steering Group. 2007. "Developmental Potential in the First 5 Years for Children in Developing Countries." *The Lancet* 369: 60–70.

Heckman, J. J., and D. V. Masterov. 2007. "The Productivity Argument for Investing in Young Children." *Review of Agricultural Economics* 29 (3): 446–93.

Heckman, J. J., S. H. Moon, R. Pinto, P. A. Savalyev, and A. Yavitz. 2009. "The Rate of Return to the High/Scope Perry Preschool Program." Working Paper 200936, Geary Institute, University College Dublin. http://www.ucd.ie/geary/static/publications/workingpapers/gearywp200936.pdf.

Shonkoff, J. P., and D.A. Phillips (eds.). 2000. *From Neurons to Neighborhoods: The Science of Early Childhood Development.* Washington, DC: National Academy Press.

References

Berlinski, S., and S. Galiani. 2007. "The Effect of a Large Expansion of Pre-primary School Facilities on Preschool Attendance and Maternal Employment." *Labour Economics* 14 (3): 665–80.

Berlinski, S., S. Galiani, and P. J. McEwan. 2008. "Preschool and Maternal Labor Market Outcomes: Evidence from a Regression Discontinuity Design." IFS Working Paper W09/05. The Institute for Fiscal Studies, London, UK.

Campbell, F. A., C. T. Ramey, E. P. Pungello, S. Miller-Johnson, and J. J. Sparling. 2002. "Early Childhood Education: Young Adult Outcomes from the Abecedarian Project." *Applied Developmental Science* 6 (1): 42–57.

Carneiro, P., and J. Heckman. 2003. "Human Capital Policy." NBER Working Paper 9495, National Bureau of Economic Research, Cambridge, MA.

Cunningham, W., L. M. Cohan, S. Naudeau, and L. McGinnis. 2008. *Supporting Youth at Risk: A Policy Toolkit for Middle-Income Countries*. Washington, DC: World Bank.

Fernald, L., P. Kariger, P. Engle, and A. Raikes. 2009. *Examining Early Child Development in Low-Income Countries: A Toolkit for the Assessment of Children in the First Five Years of Life*. Washington, DC: World Bank.

Grantham-McGregor, S., Y. Bun Cheung, S. Cueto, P. Glewwe, L. Richer, B. Trupp, and the International Child Development Steering Group. 2007. "Developmental Potential in the First 5 Years for Children in Developing Countries. *The Lancet* 369 (9555): 60–70.

Heckman, J. J. 2008a. "The Case for Investing in Disadvantaged Young Children." In *Big Ideas for Children: Investing in Our Nation's Future*, ed. First Focus, 49–58. Washington, DC: First Focus.

———. 2008b. "Schools, Skills, and Synapses." *Economic Inquiry* 46 (3): 289–324.

Heckman, J. J., and D.V. Masterov. 2007. "The Productivity Argument for Investing in Young Children." *Review of Agricultural Economics* 29 (3): 446–93.

Heckman, J. J., S. H. Moon, R. Pinto, P. A. Savalyev, and A. Yavitz. 2009. "The Rate of Return to the High/Scope Perry Preschool Program." Working Paper 200936, Geary Institute, University College Dublin. http://www.ucd.ie/geary/static/publications/workingpapers/gearywp200936.pdf.

Heckman, J. J., J. Stixrud, and S. Urzua. 2006. "The Effects of Cognitive and Noncognitive Abilities on Labor Market Outcomes and Social Behavior." *Journal of Labor Economics* 24 (3): 411–82.

Irwin, L., A. Siddiqi, and C. Hertzman. 2007. "Early Child Development: A Powerful Equalizer: Final Report for the World Health Organization's Commission on the Social Determinants of Health." WHO, Geneva. http://www.who.int/social_determinants/resources/ecd_kn_report_07_2007.pdf.

Kagitcibasi, C., D. Sunar, S. Bekman, N. Baydar, and Z. Cemalcilar. 2009. "Continuing Effects of Early Enrichment in Adult Life: The Turkish Early Enrichment Project 22 Years Later." *Journal of Applied Developmental Psychology* 30 (6): 764–79.

Lokshin, M. M., E. Glinskaya, and M. Garcia. 2000. "The Effect of Early Childhood Development Programs on Women's Labor Force Participation and Older Children's Schooling in Kenya." Working Paper 2376. World Bank, Washington, D.C.

Lynch, R. G. 2005. "Early Childhood Investment Yields Big Payoff." *Policy Perspectives*. San Francisco, CA: WestEd.

Nelson, C. A., M. de Haan, and K. M. Thomas. 2006. *Neuroscience and Cognitive Development: The Role of Experience and the Developing Brain.* New York: John Wiley.

Paxson, C., and N. Schady. 2007. "Cognitive Development among Young Children in Ecuador: The Roles of Wealth, Health, and Parenting." *Journal of Human Resources* 42 (1): 49–84.

Plomin, R. 1994. *Genetics and Experience: The Interplay Between Nature and Nurture.* Thousand Oaks, CA: Sage Publications.

Rolnick, A. J., and R. Grunewald. 2007. "The Economics of Early Childhood Development as Seen by Two Fed Economists." *Community Investments* 19 (2), Federal Reserve Bank of San Francisco.

Schlosser, A. 2005. "Public Pre-school and the Labor Supply of Arab Mothers: Evidence from a Natural Experiment." Unpublished manuscript, Hebrew University of Jerusalem.

Schulman, K. 2005. "Overlooked Benefits of Prekindergarten." National Institute for Early Education Research. Retrieved March 21, 2009, http://www.nieer.org.

Schweinhart, L. J., J. Montie, Z. Xiang, W. S. Barnett, C. R. Belfield, and M. Nores. 2005. *Lifetime Effects: The High/Scope Perry Preschool Study through Age 40.* Monographs of the HighScope Educational Research Foundation 14. Ypsilanti, MI: HighScope Press.

Shonkoff, J. P., and D. A. Phillips. 2000. *From Neurons to Neighborhoods: The Science of Early Childhood Development.* Washington, DC: National Academy Press.

UN (United Nations). 2006. "UN General Comment 7: Implementing Child Rights in Early Childhood." (40th session, 2005). U.N. Doc. CRC/C/GC/7/Rev.1. http://www1.umn.edu/humanrts/crc/crc_general_comments.htm.

World Bank. 2006. *Repositioning Nutrition as Central to Development: A Strategy for Large-Scale Action.* Washington, DC: World Bank.

Young, M. E., and F. Mustard. 2007. "Brain Development and ECD: A Case for Investment." In *Africa's Future, Africa's Challenge: Early Childhood Care and Development in Sub-Saharan Africa,* ed. M. Garcia, A. Pence, and J. L. Evans. Washington, DC: World Bank.

Why Invest in ECD? The Survival and Health Arguments
(for Policy Dialogue with Ministers of Health)

This note makes the case for public investment in early childhood development (ECD) as a critical contributor to healthy child growth and development from the earliest ages. It presents the evidence that many young children in low- and middle-income households continue to experience high mortality/morbidity from preventable causes, such as undernutrition, that have negative and costly effects on both short- and long-term development. The note also demonstrates the important synergies among early childhood stimulation,[1] nutrition, and health/hygiene, showing that all three are necessary for children to thrive and to achieve their full potential (see figure 1.2.1).

Despite Recent Progress, Many Poor Children Still Die of Preventable Causes

Child mortality is a sensitive indicator of a nation's development, representing multiple inputs to child well-being including nutrition, health and child-rearing knowledge of mothers and other caregivers; birth timing and spacing; access to health services, potable water, and sanitation; care-seeking during illness; and the general safety of the environment.

Figure 1.2.1   Early Stimulation, Adequate Nutrition, and Health/Hygiene Are Key in Promoting Optimal Child Health and Development

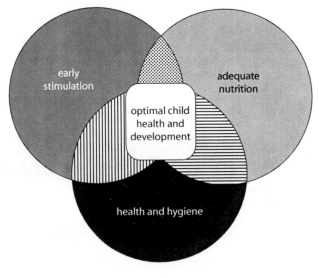

Source: Authors.

Recent UNICEF estimates (January 2010) of under-5 mortality show progress and positive trends (You et al. 2010). For example, between 1990 and 2008, the global under-5 mortality rate has dropped by 28 percent from 90 to 65 deaths per 1000 live births; the total number of deaths has similarly declined, from 12.5 million to 8.8 million. Yet, despite progress in many countries, under-5 mortality rates have stalled in eastern and southern Africa and worsened in central Africa and West Africa.

Infections are the primary killers of children, including pneumonia (20 percent of neonatal and child deaths); diarrheal diseases (18 percent for both neonatal and child deaths); and measles, malaria, and AIDS (combined, these three diseases cause 15 percent of under-5 deaths) (UNICEF 2008). Depending on the country context and the reductions in deaths to children over 1 month of age, neonatal disorders are claiming an ever-higher percentage of the deaths of children under 5, pointing to the urgent need to address the determinants of neonatal mortality. Finally, undernutrition is the underlying cause for as many as one-third of under-5 deaths, highlighting the critical importance of an integrated approach to health and nutrition (including through positive caring practices such as responsive feeding)[2] for promoting the survival of vulnerable children.

Estimates indicate that approximately two-thirds of under-5 deaths could be prevented by interventions that are currently available and feasible worldwide (Black, Morris, and Bryce 2003). The single most promising intervention strategy for improving child survival is the promotion of exclusive breastfeeding. For example, increasing the rate of exclusive breastfeeding during the first six months of life to 90 percent would help prevent up to 13 percent of children's deaths worldwide. Other effective preventive strategies to increase the likelihood of child survival include feeding children with nutritious complementary foods starting at age 6 months (including through responsive feeding strategies, as further discussed in Note 3.2.); provision of twice yearly vitamin A supplements; inoculation with vaccines; and the prevention and timely treatment of pneumonia, diarrhea, and malaria (Black, Morris, and Bryce 2003).

For Those Who Survive, Poor Health and Inadequate Nutrition and Stimulation in Early Childhood Often Lead to Long-Term Health and Development Issues That Are Costly for Societies

Ensuring that children survive the first five years of life is a high priority, especially in countries where UN Millennium Development Goal 4 (Reduce child mortality by two-thirds between 1990 and 2015) will not be met. However, survival alone is not sufficient for children to grow into healthy, competent, and productive members of society. A 2007 study (Walker et al. 2007) estimates that at least 200 million children under the age of 5 worldwide will most likely survive early childhood but will fail to reach their full potential in life because of poor health, undernutrition, and lack of stimulation in early childhood. For these children and the societies in which they live, early deficits will translate into long-lasting and costly consequences.

Inadequate Nutrition, Particularly before Birth through Age 2, Leads to Stunting

Health and hygiene in early childhood are closely interrelated with nutrition. Poor diet (quantity and quality), inadequate caring practices, and childhood infections can contribute to stunting. For example, a pooled analysis of nine studies showed that each episode of diarrhea increased the risk of stunting at age 24 months by approximately 2.5 percent (Humphrey 2009). Illness can suppress appetite as well as increase a child's nutritional requirements, while nutrient deficiencies can increase the risk of illness and the severity of disease (World Bank 2006).

A recent report also suggests a likely high contribution (previously not well-documented or discussed) of tropical enteropathy (a subclinical disorder of the small intestine caused by the ingestion of fecal bacteria by young children living in conditions of poor hygiene and sanitation) to child undernutrition, highlighting the important role that provision of toilets and adequate handwashing will have in reducing the prevalence of child undernutrition (Aboud, Shafique, and Akhter 2009).

Poor nutrition often begins in utero and leads to poor health outcomes later in life. Maternal undernutrition (including inadequate calories and deficiencies of iron and iodine) and untreated infections (for example, malaria and sexually transmitted infections) contribute to intrauterine growth restriction (IUGR), low birthweight (LBW, that is, weight at birth less than 2500 g), and stunting. Already facing disadvantage before birth, LBW children rarely fully recover the lost linear growth suffered in utero (Alderman and Behrman 2006).

Additional risks of LBW link small babies to later adult health problems. Evidence from observational studies supports the hypothesis of the fetal origins of adult disease. This theory proposes that LBW and stunted growth in early childhood, followed by compensatory weight gain at later ages (after age 2), are associated with hypertension, increased serum cholesterol, higher susceptibility to type 2 diabetes, and increased risk of coronary heart disease in adulthood (Barker et al. 2002).

In addition to the high likelihood of irreversible growth deficits, a recent analysis of children born during three years of famine in China (1959–61) points to an increased risk of mental health disorders (including schizophrenia) associated with nutritional deficits in the developing fetus (St. Clair et al. 2005). These findings align with earlier studies of the impact of the 1944 Dutch famine (Stein et al. 1975; Susser et al. 1996).

Undernutrition also leads to impaired brain development, cognitive delays, and reduced productivity. The associations between early childhood health and nutrition status and later outcomes for cognitive development and school progress are well-documented in cross-sectional studies (Grantham-McGregor et al. 2007). When compared to nonstunted children, those stunted before 24 months are less likely to be enrolled in school or they enter school late; they demonstrate lower levels of school readiness and exhibit lower school achievement, including lower grades and lower cognitive achievement scores. Iodine deficiency in pregnant women can lead to irreversible mental retardation in their offspring (Walker at al. 2007). Undernourished children, including those with anemia during the first 2 years of life, also have poorer psychomotor skills, lower activity levels, more apathy, less interaction with caregivers, and lower rates of exploration of their environments.

The long-term effects of early undernutrition also include reduced adult productivity resulting from fewer overall years of education and less learning per year in school (Walker at al. 2007), with the clear economic costs of less education for the individual and the workforce. In addition to the association between stunting and educational outcomes, evidence also links early stunting with short adult stature and reduced lean body mass, which negatively affect physical work capacity and productivity (Haas et al. 1995). For instance, one study estimated that adults who were stunted in early childhood earn between 22.2 percent and 30.1 percent less than adults who were not stunted (Grantham-McGregor et al. 2007). In Guatemala, the results of a recent study show that boys given a nutritional supplement[3] between birth and 24 months (1969–77) earned on average 46 percent higher wages as adults than those in the control group (who were more likely to be stunted) (Hoddinott et al. 2008).

Finally, there is also a high risk of intergenerational transmission of poor nutrition, health, and development as stunted, underweight girls are at greater risk of giving birth to stunted and small babies than are their well-nourished peers.

The double burden of under- and overnutrition. While many low- and middle-income countries continue to deal with the problems of infectious disease and undernutrition, they are also experiencing a surge in obesity and overweight—risk factors for noncommunicable diseases. In more and more countries, communities, and households, the double burden of under- and overnutrition is evident.

The prevalence of overnutrition in the young has increased substantially, with the global estimate of numbers of overweight children under the age of 5 at over 42 million.[4] Nearly 35 million of these children live in developing countries. Overweight and obese children are likely to stay obese into adulthood and more likely to develop noncommunicable diseases like diabetes and cardiovascular diseases at a younger age.

According to the World Health Organization, the rise of overweight and obesity in low- and middle-income countries, particularly in urban settings, likely results from a combination of increased intake of energy-dense foods high in fat and sugars and decreased physical activity (WHO 2006).

Lack of Stimulation in Early Childhood Also Contributes to Poor Growth and Impairs Children's Overall Development[5]

Young children cannot reach their full potential through good health and nutrition alone. Indeed, children who have access to adequate nutrition sometimes fail to eat and grow properly because they lack stimulation and attention at an early age. These cases may lead to a spectrum of conditions called "failure to thrive" (Lozoff 1989; Tanner 1990).

Stimulation also plays a critical role in the process of brain formation, and developmental delays before age 6 are difficult to compensate for later in life because early childhood is a particularly sensitive period for brain formation. Indeed, neurological studies have shown that synapses (connections or pathways between neurons) are developed rapidly during this period and form the basis of cognitive and emotional functioning for the rest of the child's life (Young and Mustard 2007).

Therefore, both adequate nutrition, especially from conception to age 2, and early childhood stimulation in the first 5 years of life play critical roles in the process of brain formation and development, mainly by supporting the multiplication of synapses and the myelination[6] process, which are essential for the nervous system to function normally (World Bank 2006; Nelson, de Haan, and Thomas 2006).

There Is Strong Evidence That ECD Interventions Focusing on Health, Nutrition, and Early Stimulation (Rather Than on Health and Nutrition Alone) Yield the Greatest Benefits in Terms of Children's Health and Overall Development

Evidence from a study in Jamaica demonstrates the cumulative effects of nutrition and child stimulation. Among 9- to 24-month-old children who were stunted, those receiving both nutritional supplements and stimulation scored higher on developmental tests than children receiving only one or neither of the interventions (see figure 1.2.2) (Grantham-McGregor 1997). After two years of intervention (1 kg of milk-based formula per week and 1-hour weekly home visits by community health workers to improve mother-child interactions through play),

Figure 1.2.2   Development Quotient (DQ) of Stunted Children Receiving Nutrition Supplement Only, Early Stimulation Only, or Both

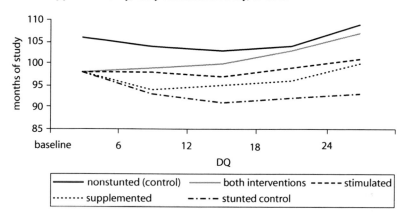

Source: Grantham-McGregor et al. 1997.
Note: DQ at baseline age (between 9 to 24 months) and at 6-month intervals to 24 months.

the development quotient (DQ) gap between stunted and non-stunted children was nearly erased among the malnourished children receiving both nutrition and stimulation interventions.

Follow-up of a substantial portion of the original study cohort at ages 7–8, 11–12, and 17–18 found that children receiving stimulation maintained improved cognitive and educational performance over time. Among children who received the nutritional supplement but not the stimulation, the positive cognitive effects were evident at age 7, but not at ages 11 and 17 (Walker et al. 2007).

A study in Vietnam yields similar findings. Staged interventions (nutrition between ages 0 and 3 years and a stimulation intervention between ages 4 and 5 years) produced improved cognitive outcomes compared to children who received only the nutrition intervention (Watanabe et al. 2005). There was even greater impact on stunted children, demonstrating that stimulation activities can mitigate the negative consequences of linear growth failure for cognitive development.

Accordingly, planning paradigms that support the delivery of integrated ECD services, including health, nutrition (starting during pregnancy), and early child stimulation (starting at birth), will ensure maximum returns for human capital investments at later ages while also promoting significant efficiencies in the public health system.

Notes

1. Early childhood stimulation is defined as providing young children with constant opportunities to interact with caring people and to learn about their environment from the earliest age. In practice, stimulation is about parents and other family members and caregivers being responsive to the emotional and physical needs of children from birth onward, playing and talking with them (even before children can respond verbally), and exposing them to words, numbers, and simple concepts while engaging in daily routines.

2. Responsive (or active) feeding refers to "positive behaviors by caregivers during feeding (e.g., encouraging the child to eat, offering more servings, smiling and talking to the child) and to feeding practices that are attuned to the child's psychomotor abilities (e.g., ability to pick up food with fingers, handle a spoon or a cup, and so on)." See Aboud, Shafique, and Akhter 2009.

3. The nutritional supplement (Atole) consisted of dry skimmed milk, vegetable protein (cornmeal), and sugar. It was given twice a day to participating children.

4. Extracted from WHO website, May 2010.

5. Much of the information contained in this section comes from Naudeau (2009).

6. Myelination is the production of a coating of myelin (an electrically insulating material) around the axon of a neuron, which maximizes the intensity of neural transmissions within the brain.

Key Readings

Heckman, J. J., S. H. Moon, R. Pinto, P. A. Savalyev, and A. Yavitz. 2009. "The Rate of Return to the High/Scope Perry Preschool Program." Working Paper 200936, Geary Institute, University College Dublin. http://www.ucd.ie/geary/static/publications/workingpapers/gearywp200936.pdf.

Naudeau, S. 2009. "Supplementing Nutrition in the Early Years: The Role of Early Childhood Stimulation to Maximize Nutritional Inputs." *Child and Youth Development Notes* 3 (1) (March), World Bank, Washington DC.

Victora C. G., L. Adair, C. Fall, P. C. Hallal, R. Martorell, L. Richter, and H. S. Sachdev. 2008. "Maternal and Child Undernutrition: Consequences for Adult Health and Human Capital." *The Lancet* 371 (9609): 340–57.

World Bank. 2006. *Repositioning Nutrition as Central to Development: A Strategy for Large-scale Action.* Washington, DC: World Bank.

References

Aboud, F. E., S. Shafique, and S. Akhter. 2009. "A Responsive Feeding Intervention Increases Children's Self-Feeding and Maternal Responsiveness But Not Weight Gain." *Journal of Nutrition* 139 (9): 1738–43.

Alderman, H., and J. R. Behrman. 2006. "Reducing the Incidence of Low Birth Weight in Low-Income Countries Has Substantial Economic Benefits." *World Bank Research Observer* 21 (1): 25–48.

Barker, D. J., J. G. Eriksson, T. Forsén, and C. Osmond. 2002. "Fetal Origins of Adult Disease: Strength of Effects and Biological Basis." *International Journal of Epidemiology* 31 (6): 1235–39.

Black, R. E., S. S. Morris, and J. Bryce. 2003. "Where and Why Are 10 Million Children Dying Every Year?" *The Lancet* 361 (9376): 2226–34.

Grantham-McGregor, S., Y. Bun Cheung, S. Cueto, P. Glewwe, L. Richer, B. Trupp, and the International Child Development Steering Group. 2007. "Developmental Potential in the First 5 Years for Children in Developing Countries. *The Lancet* 369: 60–70.

Grantham-McGregor, S. M., S. P. Walker, S. M. Chang, and C. A. Powell. 1997. "Effects of Early Childhood Supplementation With and Without Stimulation on Later Development in Stunted Jamaican Children." *American Journal of Clinical Nutrition* 66 (2): 247–53.

Haas, J. D., E. J. Martinez, S. Murdoch, E. Conlisk, J. A. Revera, and R. Martorell. 1995. "Nutritional Supplementation During the Preschool Years and Physical Work Capacity in Adolescent and Young Adult Guatemalans." *Journal of Nutrition* 125 (4): 1068–77.

Hoddinott, J., J. A. Maluccio, J. R. Behrman, R. Flores, and R. Martorell. 2008. "Effect of a Nutrition Intervention During Early Childhood on Economic Productivity in Guatemalan Adults." *The Lancet* 371 (9610): 411–16.

Humphrey, J. H. 2009. "Child Undernutrition, Tropical Enteropathy, Toilets, and Handwashing." *The Lancet* 374 (9694): 1032–34.

Lozoff, B. 1989. "Nutrition and Behavior." *American Psychologist* 44: 231–36.

Naudeau, S. 2009. "Supplementing Nutrition in the Early Years: The Role of Early Childhood Stimulation to Maximize Nutritional Inputs." *Child and Youth Development Notes* 3 (1) (March), Washington DC.: World Bank.

St.Clair, D., M. Xu, P. Wang, Y. Yu, Y. Fang, Z. Feng, X. Zheng, et al. 2005. "Rates of Adult Schizophrenia Following Prenatal Exposure to the Chinese Famine of 1959–61." *Journal of the American Medical Association* 294 (5): 557–62.

Stein, Z., M. Susser, G. Saenger, and F. Marolla. 1975. "Famine and Human Development." In *The Dutch Hunger Winter of 1944–1945*. New York: Oxford University Press.

Susser, E., R. Neugebauer, H. W. Hoek, A. S. Brown, S. Lin, D. Labovitz, and J. M. Gorman. 1996. "Schizophrenia after Prenatal Famine: Further Evidence." *Archives of General Psychiatry* 53 (1): 25–31.

Tanner, J. M. 1990. *Fetus into Man: Physical Growth from Conception to Maturity* (2nd ed.). Cambridge, MA: Harvard University Press.

UNICEF (United Nations Children's Fund). 2008. "The State of the World's Children 2008: Child Survival." UNICEF, New York.

Walker, S. P., T. D. Wachs, J. M. Gardner, B. Lozoff, G. A. Wasserman, E. Pollitt, J. A. Carter, and the International Child Development Steering Group. 2007. "Child Development: Risk Factors for Adverse Outcomes in Developing Countries." *The Lancet* 369: 145–57.

Watanabe, K., R. Flores, J. Fujiwara, and L. T. H. Tran. 2005. "Early Childhood Development Interventions and Cognitive Development of Young Children in Rural Vietnam." *Journal of Nutrition* 135 (8): 1918–25.

WHO (World Health Organization). 2006. "Overweight and Obesity." Fact Sheet 311, from http://www.who.int/mediacentre/factsheets/fs311/en/index.html.

World Bank. 2006. *Repositioning Nutrition as Central to Development: A Strategy for Large-Scale Action*. Washington, D.C.: World Bank.

You, D., T. Wardlaw, P. Salama, and G. Jones. 2010. "Levels and Trends in Under-5 Mortality, 1990–2008." *The Lancet* 375: 100–03.

Why Invest in ECD? The School Readiness and School Achievement Arguments
(for Policy Dialogue with Ministers of Education)

This note makes the case for public investment in early childhood development (ECD) by presenting evidence that poor children who do not benefit from quality ECD interventions are often not prepared to learn once they enter primary school, which leads to inefficiencies in the public education system that are costly to both families and societies. This note also provides evidence that well-targeted ECD interventions are a cost-effective strategy to promote school readiness, school achievement, and school completion (including among older girls in the family), thus maximizing further investment in public education and allowing poor children to become productive adults.

Poor Children Are Often Not Ready to Learn by the Time They Enter Primary School

School readiness is the degree to which a child is prepared to learn and succeed in school (Ackerman and Barnett 2005). Research has increasingly shown that children's school readiness depends not only on their cognitive skills upon primary school entry, although these skills are crucial, but also on their physical, mental, and emotional health, as well as ability to relate to others (Hair et al. 2006) (see table 1.3.1).

Research also demonstrates that cognitive abilities are as strongly affected by the quality of the environment and the amount of stimulation and learning opportunities children are exposed to from birth onward as they are by genetics (with genetic influences accounting for about half of the variance in cognitive abilities) (Fernald et al. 2009). Similarly, children's socio-emotional development and physical capacity are strongly influenced by their early environment.[1]

Table 1.3.1   Dimensions of Children's School Readiness

Physical health and motor development	Social and emotional development	Approaches to learning	Language development	Cognitive development and general knowledge
Rate of growth; physical fitness; chronic conditions such as diabetes, disability, malnutrition; fine motor skills; gross motor skills; and self-care abilities.	Ability to form positive relationships with teachers and peers; aspects of self-concept and self-efficacy, ability to express feelings appropriately, and sensitivity to others' feelings.	Openness and curiosity to tasks and challenges, task persistence, imagination, attentiveness, and cognitive learning style (e.g., better at processing information by listening than observing/reading).	*Verbal language:* listening, speaking, social uses of language (e.g., using social conventions and manners), and spoken vocabulary. *Emergent literacy:* Interest in books and stories, emergent writing (scribbling to imitate writing), print awareness (understanding that text represents spoken words), and sequencing (stories follow a standard sequence).	Knowledge of the properties of objects (e.g., color, weight, and movement); understanding the relationships between objects, events, or people (e.g., determining how two objects are different); learning social conventions or school-learned knowledge (e.g., knowing one's name and address or being able to count).

Source: Kagan, Moore, and Bredekamp 1995.

Environmental risk factors such as malnutrition, poor health, un-stimulating home environment, and child maltreatment have all been shown to have a negative impact on the development of a child's capac-ities and ability to learn and succeed in school (Irwin, Siddiqi, and Hertzman 2007). These risk factors tend to be more concentrated among poor households with less-educated parents, partly because of informa-tion failures (for example, lack of parental knowledge about the critical importance of supporting children's growth and development from con-ception on) and partly because of supply-side constraints (for example, unequal distribution of resources and services for young children).

A 2007 analysis of data from children in developing countries reveals that more than 200 million children under 5 years of age are exposed to multiple risks that detrimentally affect their development (Grantham-McGregor et al. 2007). The consequences can be dramatic. For example, while differences in age-adjusted vocabulary among 3-year-old Ecuadorian children are generally small, steep socioeconomic "gradients" appear in the following years. By age 6, children in less wealthy house-holds and children born to mothers with low education levels have fallen far behind their counterparts in wealthier or more educated households (see figure 1.1.1 in Note 1.1) (Paxson and Schady 2007).

This pattern occurs in part because poor children tend to receive less speech directed toward them and because the speech that they do hear tends to have reduced lexical richness and sentence complexity (Fernald et al. 2009). Associations between poverty and multiple domains of child development (including cognitive, physical, and socio-emotional) were also recorded as early as 6 months of age in Egypt, 12 months in Brazil, 10 months in India, and 18 months in Bangladesh (Grantham-McGregor et al. 2007).

For all these poor or otherwise disadvantaged children, early gaps in phys-ical, linguistic, cognitive, and socio-emotional development seriously jeop-ardize their capacity and motivation to learn upon primary school entry. As they age, these children are more likely to have poor academic performance, to repeat grades, and to drop out of school than those whose cognitive skills and overall school readiness were higher upon primary school entry (Feinstein 2003; Pianta and McCoy 1997; Currie and Thomas 1999).

Lack of School Readiness among Poor Children Leads to Costly Inefficiencies in the Public Education System

When more than just a few students enter primary school with low lev-els of school readiness, even the best schools struggle to maintain an environment conducive to learning (Wentzel and Wigfield 1998), and children are more likely to score poorly, to repeat grades, and to drop out of school before they complete the primary cycle (Reynolds et al. 2001; Heckman and Masterov 2007). These phenomena naturally undermine the social and economic benefits expected from the investment that parents and governments, in the case of publicly funded education, make in children. Moreover, these phenomena raise a fundamental question about the quality of human resources available in the employment market and their capacity to make an effective contribution in the face of the challenges of competitiveness and overall development of the country.[2]

Remedial interventions such as special education or equivalency degree programs for school dropouts are possible. However, these interventions are usually costly and they are often much less effective than preventive interventions in early childhood (Heckman 2008a).

There Is Strong Evidence That ECD Interventions Yield Significant Benefits in Terms of School Readiness and Achievement, Particularly among Poor Children

Many brain functions are particularly sensitive to change early in life and become less plastic (malleable) over time (Heckman 2008). In fact, much of a child's brain architecture is "wired" in the first 5 years of life (Shonkoff and Phillips 2000), which leaves little room for adjustment later on. As shown in figure 1.3.1, even functions that continue to have a high degree of sensitivity in later childhood (for example, numerical ability and peer social skills) have their peak sensitivity levels in the first 4 to 5 years of life. Other functions such as emotional control and habitual response patterns not only peak in the first few years but typically reach a high stability level before age 5. This suggests that those patterns cannot easily be modified afterward, which is why early stimulation and learning opportunities before primary school entry are essential.

Several studies have shown that investing in quality ECD programs helps bridge the gap between poor and otherwise disadvantaged children and those from more privileged backgrounds, thus preparing them for a successful transition to primary school and for quality lifelong learning. More specifically, participation in quality ECD programs has been linked to higher school attainment and completion (Kagitcibasi, Sunar, and Bekman 2001); improved attention and better learning outcomes (Vegas and Petrow 2008; Berlinski, Galiani, and

Figure 1.3.1   Sensitive Periods in Early Brain Development

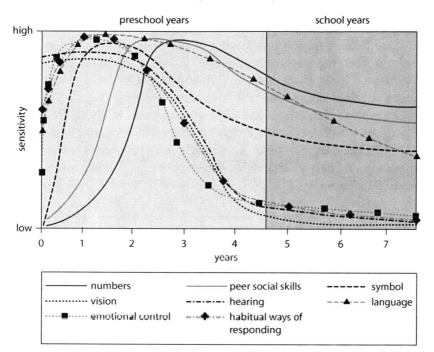

Source: Council for Early Child Development (2010).

Gertler 2009); and increased exposure to the official schooling language early on.

As an example of ECD benefits, Bangladeshi children who received some form of organized preschool education outperformed their peers in the control group by 58 percent on a standardized test of school readiness (Aboud 2006). In Colombia, children who received a comprehensive community-based ECD intervention were 100 percent more likely to be enrolled in third grade, thus indicating lower dropout and repetition rates for program children than for those in the control group (Young 1995). In Argentina, one year of preschool was estimated to increase the average third-grade test grade in mathematics and Spanish by 8 percent (Berlinski, Galiani, and Gertler (2009). In Turkey, children who attended a mother-child education program providing cognitive enrichment to children and training and support for mothers were more likely to be in school during their teenage years than those in the control group (86 percent vs. 67 percent) (Kagitcibasi, Sunar, and Bekman 2001). And in the United

States, children who received high-quality, comprehensive ECD services were 50 percent more likely to finish secondary school than those not receiving those services (Schweinhart et al. 2005).

Thus, ECD interventions have a higher rate of return per dollar invested than interventions directed at older children and adults (Heckman 2008b; Heckman, Stixrud, and Urzua 2006). Evidence suggests a potential return rate of 7–16 percent annually from high-quality ECD programs targeting vulnerable groups—that is, those from low-income or otherwise disadvantaged settings (Rolnick and Grunewald 2007; Heckman et al. 2009).[3] Accordingly, many countries invest public resources in ECD as both a rights-based service (UN 2006) and a sound financial investment.

ECD Investments Can Also Have a Positive Impact on the Education of Older Girls

In addition to the direct impact that ECD interventions have on young children, positive externalities (or benefits not directly connected to the cost of a service) can occur in girls' education. Indeed, evidence suggests that affordable child care for young children can increase the school enrollment rates of older female siblings to a greater extent than even an increase in maternal wages. For example, a Kenyan study shows that increasing maternal wages would likely lead to an 11 percent increase in the school enrollment of boys in the family but would decrease enrollment of girls in the family by 10 percent as adolescent girls took over more home responsibilities because their mothers engaged in more out-of-home work. In contrast, the study shows that reducing the cost of child care increased school enrollment of girls without having a measurable impact on boys' school enrollment in either direction (Lokshin, Glinskaya, and Garcia 2000).

Notes

1. Evidence distinguishing between genetic and environmental factors comes primarily from industrialized nations. For a review, see Plomin (1994).
2. See Marouani and Robalino (2008) for an example of these dynamics in Morocco.
3. Note that these high rates of return were observed for small-scale interventions that targeted vulnerable groups of children. Large-scale interventions that target a broader range of beneficiaries may yield smaller returns.

Key Readings

Grantham-McGregor, S., Y. Bun Cheung, S. Cueto, P. Glewwe, L. Richer, B. Trupp, and the International Child Development Steering Group. 2007. "Developmental Potential in the First 5 Years for Children in Developing Countries." *The Lancet* 369 (9555): 60–70.

Heckman, J. J., and D. V. Masterov. 2007. "The Productivity Argument for Investing in Young Children." *Review of Agricultural Economics* 29 (3): 446–93.

Heckman, J. J., S. H. Moon, R. Pinto, P. A. Savalyev, and A. Yavitz. 2009. "The Rate of Return to the High/Scope Perry Preschool Program." Working Paper 200936, Geary Institute, University College Dublin. http://www.ucd.ie/geary/static/publications/workingpapers/gearywp200936.pdf.

Shonkoff, J. P., and D. A. Phillips (eds.). 2000. *From Neurons to Neighborhoods: The Science of Early Childhood Development.* Washington, DC: National Academy Press.

References

Aboud, F. E. 2006. "Evaluation of an Early Childhood Preschool Program in Rural Bangladesh." *Early Childhood Research Quarterly* 21 (1): 46–60.

Ackerman, D. J., and W. S. Barnett. 2005. "Prepared for Kindergarten: What Does 'Readiness' Mean?" New Brunswick, NJ: National Institute for Early Education Research.

Berlinski, S., S. Galiani, and P. Gertler. 2009. "The Effect of Pre-primary Education on Primary School Performance," *Journal of Public Economics* 93 (1–2): 219–34.

Council for Early Child Development. 2010. "The Science of Early Child Development." CECD, Vancouver, Canada. Accessed August 3, 2010, http://www.councilecd.ca/files/Brochure_Science_of_ECD_June%202010.pdf.

Currie, J., and D. Thomas. 1999. "Early Test Scores, Socioeconomic Status and Future Outcomes." NBER Working Paper 6943. National Bureau of Economic Research, Cambridge, MA.

Feinstein, L. 2003. "Inequality in the Early Cognitive Development of British Children in the 1970 Cohort." *Economica* 70 (1): 73–97.

Fernald, L., P. Kariger, P. Engle, and A. Raikes. 2009. *Examining Early Child Development in Low-Income Countries: A Toolkit for the Assessment of Children in the First Five Years of Life.* Washington, DC: World Bank.

Grantham-McGregor, S., Y. Bun Cheung, S. Cueto, P. Glewwe, L. Richer, B. Trupp, and the International Child Development Steering Group. 2007.

"Developmental Potential in the First 5 Years for Children in Developing Countries. *The Lancet* 369 (9555): 60–70.

Hair, E., T. Halle, E. Terry-Humen, B. Lavelle, and J. Calkins. 2006. "Children's School Readiness in the ECLS-K: Predictions to Academic, Health, and Social Outcomes in First Grade." *Early Childhood Research Quarterly* 21 (4): 431–54.

Heckman, J. J. 2008a. "The Case for Investing in Disadvantaged Young Children." In *Big Ideas for Children: Investing in Our Nation's Future*, ed. First Focus, 49–58. Washington, DC: First Focus.

———. 2008b. "Schools, Skills, and Synapses." *Economic Inquiry* 46 (3): 289–324.

Heckman, J. J., and D. V. Masterov. 2007. "The Productivity Argument for Investing in Young Children." *Review of Agricultural Economics* 29 (3): 446–93.

Heckman, J. J., S. H. Moon, R. Pinto, P. A. Savalyev, and A. Yavitz. 2009. "The Rate of Return to the High/Scope Perry Preschool Program." Working Paper 200936, Geary Institute, University College Dublin. http://www.ucd.ie/geary/static/publications/workingpapers/gearywp200936.pdf.

Heckman, J. J., J. Stixrud, and S. Urzua. 2006. "The Effects of Cognitive and Noncognitive Abilities on Labor Market Outcomes and Social Behavior." *Journal of Labor Economics* 24 (3): 411–82.

Irwin, L., A. Siddiqi, and C. Hertzman. 2007. "Early Child Development: A Powerful Equalizer: Final Report for the World Health Organization's Commission on the Social Determinants of Health." WHO, Geneva. http://www.who.int/social_determinants/resources/ecd_kn_report_07_2007.pdf.

Kagan, S. L., E. Moore, and S. Bredekamp, eds. 1995. "Reconsidering Children's Early Development and Learning: Toward Common Views and Vocabulary." Report of the National Education Goals Panel, Goal 1 Technical Planning Group. Government Printing Office, Washington, DC. http://ceep.crc.uiuc.edu/eecearchive/digests/ed-cite/ed391576.html.

Kagitcibasi, C., D. Sunar, and S. Bekman. 2001. "Long-Term Effects of Early Intervention: Turkish Low Income Mothers and Children." *Journal of Applied Development Psychology* 22 (4): 333–61.

Lokshin, M. M., E. Glinskaya, and M. Garcia. 2000. "The Effect of Early Childhood Development Programs on Women's Labor Force Participation and Older Children's Schooling in Kenya." Working Paper 2376. World Bank, Washington, DC.

Marouani, M. A., and D. A. Robalino. 2008. "Assessing Interactions among Education, Social Insurance, and Labor Market Policies in a General Equilibrium Framework: An Application to Morocco." Policy Research Working Paper 4681. World Bank, Washington, DC.

Paxson, C., and N. Schady. 2007. "Cognitive Development among Young Children in Ecuador: The Roles of Wealth, Health, and Parenting." *Journal of Human Resources* 42 (1): 49–84.

Pianta, R. C., and S. J. McCoy. 1997. "The First Day of School: The Predictive Validity of Early School Screening." *Journal of Applied Developmental Psychology* 18 (1): 1–22.

Plomin, R. 1994. *Genetics and Experience: The Interplay Between Nature and Nurture.* Thousand Oaks, CA: Sage Publications.

Reynolds, A. J., J. A. Temple, D. L. Robertson, and E. A. Mann. 2001. "Long-Term Effects of an Early Childhood Intervention on Educational Achievement and Juvenile Arrest—A 15-Year Follow-Up of Low-Income Children in Public Schools." *Journal of the American Medical Association 285* (18): 2339–46.

Rolnick, A. J., and R. Grunewald. 2007. "The Economics of Early Childhood Development as Seen by Two Fed Economists." *Community Investments* 19 (2), Federal Reserve Bank of San Francisco.

Schweinhart, L. J., J. Montie, Z. Xiang, W. S. Barnett, C. R. Belfield, and M. Nores. 2005. *Lifetime Effects: The High/Scope Perry Preschool Study Through Age 40.* Monographs of the HighScope Educational Research Foundation 14. Ypsilanti, Mich.: HighScope Press.

Shonkoff, J. P., and D. A. Phillips. 2000. *From Neurons to Neighborhoods: The Science of Early Childhood Development.* Washington, DC: National Academies Press.

UN (United Nations). 2006. "UN General Comment 7: Implementing Child Rights in Early Childhood." 40th session, 2005. U.N. Doc. CRC/C/GC/7/Rev.1. http://www1.umn.edu/humanrts/crc/crc_general_comments.htm.

Vegas, E., and J. Petrow. 2008. *Raising Student Learning in Latin America—The Challenge for the 21ˢᵗ Century.* Washington, DC: World Bank.

Wentzel, K. R., and A. Wigfield. 1998. "Academic and Social Motivational Influences on Students' Academic Performance." *Educational Psychology Review* 10 (2): 155–75.

Young, M. E. 1995. "Investing in Young Children." World Bank Discussion Paper 275. World Bank, Washington, DC.

Assessing Needs, Measuring Outcomes, and Establishing Policy Frameworks

Data Collection for Designing, Monitoring, and Evaluating ECD Interventions

This note provides an overview of data collection for designing, monitoring, and evaluating ECD interventions. First, to design ECD interventions to fit a country's national economy and priorities, it is important to conduct a situation analysis or needs assessment that includes data on the socioeconomic, demographic, health, nutrition, and education status of the population, as well as data on the quality and availability of existing services. By identifying population needs and service gaps, the situation analysis is the first step in developing a national ECD policy (see Note 2.2). Second, data are collected to track and monitor the implementation of ECD services. Third, governments may wish to measure outcomes of a specific ECD intervention to determine the impact of a program and its need for improvement. Impact evaluations can also guide future investments by providing data for estimating the cost-effectiveness of interventions. Collecting these data should be a cyclical process (see figure 2.1.1). Ideally, governments and partners will assess and reassess their population's needs over time and adjust the provision of ECD services accordingly. As needs are met, the interventions can be refocused to prioritize the next set of issues. In turn, approaches that work best can be scaled up.

The first section of this note provides a list of priority indicators for assessing the needs of young children, taking into consideration the typical

Figure 2.1.1   Cycle of Data Collection for Designing, Monitoring, and Evaluating ECD Interventions

Source: Authors.

time, funding, and logistical constraints on accessing information from administrative data and household surveys. The second section focuses on the supply-side and demand-side indicators for monitoring the scope and quality of ECD services. The third section focuses on outcome data, specifically on children's development (physical, cognitive, language, and social and emotional) and the issues related to selecting, adapting, and using data collected with standardized child assessment instruments.

Assessing the Needs of Young Children for Situation Analyses and Monitoring

A comprehensive assessment of young children's needs is an important component of a situation analysis, complementing data on existing policies, resources, and services. The indicators most helpful in assessing these needs and the service gaps that need to be filled in a given country or region can be divided into three categories:

- **General socioeconomic and demographic indicators** provide an overview of the subgroups of young children who may be particularly at risk and who are most likely to benefit from ECD services. In many developing countries, there are steep socioeconomic "gradients" in cognitive development among preschool-age children, with children from poorer households showing significantly worse outcomes by age 5 or 6 (see Note 1.1).

- **Health/nutrition indicators** can be used to assess: (1) the general health and hygiene conditions in which young children are raised and (2) whether malnutrition is an important issue, both at the national level and for specific subgroups of children.
- **Education indicators** can be used to assess the overall level of children's "school readiness" (as defined in Note 1.3) upon primary school entry and the efficiency of the education system.

Table 2.1.1 provides a short list of the indicators for conducting a complete ECD situation analysis that can inform project design and program implementation.

Depending on the country, data on all or part of these socioeconomic, demographic, health/nutrition, and education indicators may be available through Demographic and Health Surveys (DHS), typically supported by the United States Agency for International Development (USAID), through the country's ministries of health and education (for example, MIS [management information systems] data), or through the Multiple Indicator Cluster Survey (MICS) supported by UNICEF (United Nations Children's Fund).[1] In addition, the UNESCO (United Nations Educational, Scientific and Cultural Organization) Institute for Statistics annually reports standardized cross-national data on ISCED (International Standard Classification of Education) for level 0 (preprimary education for children from age 3) and above.[2] To the extent possible, all data should be disaggregated by age group (that is, 0–2, 3–4, 5–6 years) and by the following variables: ethnicity, languages, special needs, urban vs. rural, wealth quintiles, parental education/literacy rates, and household information such as gender and family status (for example, single-parent household, female-headed household).

In addition, data on child development outcomes can be collected either by direct assessment of the child or by report from a knowledgeable adult. Issues involved in collecting and using these data are presented later in this note.

Assessing the Scope and Quality of Existing ECD Services for Situation Analyses and Monitoring

For both situational analysis and ongoing monitoring purposes, it is important to assess the ECD service gaps in a given country or region by collecting data on the scope and quality of existing ECD services. Given that services may vary widely for different groups of children, it is useful

Table 2.1.1 Indicators for Conducting an ECD Situation Analysis

Indicator description	Indicator definition
Socioeconomic and demographic indicators	
Absolute size of early childhood population	Total children under age 6
Relative size of early childhood population	Percent of total population under age 6
Young child poverty rate	Percent under age 6 in households with less than 50% of median income
Parental education	Highest education level completed by each parent
Parental literacy	Percent of population age 15 years and older who can both read and write (understand short, simple, everyday-life sentences). Generally, "literacy" also encompasses "numeracy," the ability to make simple arithmetic calculations.
Parent employment rates	Percent of adults who have children under age 6 and participate in the labor force
Prevalence of orphans	Percent of children under age 6 who have lost one or both parents
Prevalence of single-parent households	Percent of households led by one parent
Prevalence of teen-parent households	Percent of households led by a parent under age 20
Birth registration	Percent of children under age 6 with a birth certificate
Health and nutrition indicators	
Mother's age at birth of first child	Median age of mother at birth of first child
Mother's use of focused prenatal care	Percent of pregnant women who used prenatal care provided by skilled health personnel at least four times during pregnancy
Exclusive breastfeeding rate	Percent of infants birth through 5 months who were given only breast milk in the last 24 hours
Incidence of low birth weight (2500 g)	Percent of births of weight less than 2500 g out of the total number of live births in the same time period
Prevalence of stunting (too short) in children	Percent of children of a specific age (for example under age 2) with height- or length-for-age less than –2 Z-score
Prevalence of underweight (too small) in children	Percent of children of a specific age with weight-for-age less than –2 Z-score
Prevalence of wasting (too thin) in children	Percent of children of a specific age with weight-for-height less than –2 Z-score

Body mass index (BMI)—estimate of body fat	Calculated by using an individual's weight in kg/height in meters[2]
Prevalence of overweight/obese (too heavy)	Percent of children of a specific age with BMI-for-age at 85th percentile (overweight) or at or above 95th percentile (obese)
Infant mortality rate (IMR)	Probability of a child born in a specific year or period dying before reaching age 1 year, subject to age-specific mortality rates of that period, expressed per 1,000 live births
Under-5 mortality rate (U5MR)	Probability of a child born in a specific year or period dying before reaching age 5 years, subject to age-specific mortality rates of that period, expressed per 1,000 live births
Prevalence of anemia in young children	Percent of children age 6–59 months with hemoglobin less than 11 g/dL
Consumption of iodized salt to prevent iodine deficiency disorders	Percent of children age 0–23 months living in a household with adequately iodized salt (15 ppm or more)
Immunization rate: coverage of children with DTP3 (combined diphtheria-tetanus toxoid and pertussis vaccine)	Percent of children age 1 year who have received three doses of DTP3 in a given time period
Access to safe drinking water	Percent of population using an improved drinking water source
Access to hygienic latrines	Percent of population using an improved sanitation facility

Education indicators

Percent of new entrants in grade 1 with Early Childhood Care and Education (ECCE) program experience	Number of new entrants to primary grade 1 who have attended some form of organized ECCE program for the equivalent of at least 200 hours, expressed as a percentage of total number of new entrants to primary grade 1
Gross intake ratio at grade 1	Number of new entrants to primary grade 1, regardless of age, expressed as a percentage of the population at the official age for primary school entrance
Proportion entering grade 1 on time	Number of new entrants to primary grade 1 who are of official eligible school age, expressed as a percentage of the corresponding population
Gross enrollment ratio in grade 1	Total enrollment in grade 1, regardless of age, expressed as a percentage of official eligible school-age population corresponding to the same level of education in a given school year
Net enrollment rate in grade 1	Enrollment of the official age group for grade 1, expressed as a percentage of the corresponding population

(continued)

Table 2.1.1 Indicators for Conducting an ECD Situation Analysis *(continued)*

Education indicators

Indicator description	Indicator definition
Repetition rates in grades 1 and 2	Percent of pupils from a cohort enrolled in a given grade at a given school year who study in the same grade in the following school year
Dropout rates in grades 1 and 2	Percent of pupils from a cohort enrolled in a given grade at a given school year who are no longer enrolled in the following school year
School wastage (absenteeism)	Average number of days children were absent from school in the last month
Primary completion rate	Ratio of the total number of students successfully completing (or graduating from) the last year of primary school in a given year to the total number of children of official graduation age in the population

Source: Authors.

to disaggregate the following data by age group (ages 0–2, 3–4, 4–5) and, where possible, by socioeconomic background and other risk factors.

Provision of Existing ECD Services

Before designing a new ECD intervention, existing resources and services must be mapped and the extent to which they serve the needs of the population must be assessed. Most countries have some services for young children—government-organized health services for mothers and young children, public daycare facilities or preschools, and privately run daycare facilities or preschools and private health services, or some combination of these.

The following questions can guide the mapping of existing services, focusing on supply-side and demand-side indicators:

Supply-side indicators

- What is the coverage rate for different types of services (center-based, home-based, and so on)[3]; for different segments of the population (rich vs. poor, urban vs. rural, children with disabilities); and for different regions within a country?
- Are relevant services available in the most vulnerable communities?
- Are existing services mostly public or private, or a combination of both?
- Which ministry/agency/department is responsible for policy implementation and quality monitoring?
- Which ministry/agency/department is responsible for financing?

Demand-side indicators

- What is the take-up rate (enrollment rate) for existing services?
- What are the financial constraints (direct and opportunity costs) that may prevent the poorest families from using existing services?
- Do the most disadvantaged groups have access to existing services and use them?
- Are there any other constraints that prevent at least some families from using existing services? Possible constraints could include: (1) long distances and lack of transport between home and service location; (2) lack of parental awareness of the need to take an active part in their children's development; (3) cultural constraints, as in the case of minority families who feel that existing services are not sensitive to their child-rearing beliefs and practices or their language or religion.

Quality of Existing ECD Services

An assessment should also be made of the quality of existing ECD services in order to monitor implementation of the service and to determine which ECD services (1) appear particularly promising and could be scaled up, (2) need improvement in specific areas, and (3) are potentially detrimental to the children's development and should be discontinued.

Quality of a service is a contextually determined concept that can be defined and measured in various ways (see Notes 3.1 and 3.2). Yet, there are common structural, organizational, and process elements of "quality" that predict child development outcomes, including their physical, cognitive, linguistic, and socio-emotional development (Myers 2004; 2006). These process elements are as follows:

- **Structural variables:** adult-child ratios, group size, physical environment, and availability of equipment and pedagogical materials.
- **Caregiver variables:** initial education, training, mentoring/supervision, and wages.
- **Program variables:** program intensity, parent involvement, language of instruction, curriculum, daily routine, and health/nutrition inputs.
- **Process variables:** caregiver-child and child-child interactions.

To measure the quality of an early childhood environment, several standardized observation tools have been developed, often as part of a national quality assurance and monitoring framework, as in Australia, Chile, Costa Rica, Ecuador, Indonesia, Mexico, Panama, Pakistan, Singapore, and Vietnam (National Research Council 2008). Some tools are self-assessment instruments[4] that can be used by service providers to evaluate quality and identify areas for improvement. Others are designed for external evaluations, including, for example, the widely used Early Childhood Environment Rating Scale (ECERS-R, for $2\frac{1}{2}$- to 5-year-olds), Infant-Toddler Environment Rating Scale (ITERS-R, from birth to 30 months), and Family Child Care Environment Rating Scale (FCCERS-R, for in-home/family daycare, from birth to primary school starting age). Evaluation items included in these instruments are physical environment, basic care, curriculum, interaction, schedule and program structure, and parent and staff education (Harms, Clifford, and Cryer 1998). These scales have been adapted for use in multiple countries, including Bangladesh (Aboud 2006), Brazil, and East Africa (Kenya, Zanzibar, and Uganda) (Malmberg, Mwaura, and Sylva, forthcoming), to name a few. They can also be used to undertake a needs assessment, although care must always be taken to assess how relevant the subscales and items are to the local context.

These instruments for quality assessment can also serve as a useful complement to the analysis or interpretation of impact evaluations that aim to assess whether a given ECD intervention results in better health and nutrition status or higher levels of school readiness, or both, among beneficiary children (see next part of this note). For example, quality assessment tools may provide monitoring data that can shed light on whether the intervention was implemented as planned or whether there was any variation in the quality of service delivery across intervention sites that could help explain any impact evaluation results.

Measuring Child Development Outcomes

Within the context of World Bank support to clients, the three main reasons for collecting data on child development outcomes are as follows:

- **To establish a baseline and document the magnitude of the problem.** Before implementing an intervention, it is important to collect data on child development outcomes as a baseline from which change can be measured. These data also document service delivery gaps. For example, the baseline of an evaluation of a community-based ECD program in rural Mozambique highlighted the extensive cognitive and language delays of disadvantaged children compared to their more advantaged peers, as well as the need for ECD interventions to help close the gap as much as possible before children begin school and disparities increase further.

- **To evaluate the impact of existing ECD interventions.** While it is important to know how many children are reached by a given ECD project, or how many ECD teachers or providers are trained, among other factors, that information by itself is not enough. Projects that do not show a measurable positive impact on child development outcomes that contribute to school readiness and to long-lasting health benefits cannot be considered successful and may, in fact, be a waste of resources. Similarly, measuring only the quality of interventions is not enough since "quality" interventions may be ineffective or inappropriate for certain settings.

- **To assess the specific types of ECD interventions that are most effective and cost-effective in a given context or for specific populations**

and to inform the policy dialogue for future planning. The relative feasibility and cost-effectiveness of different ECD interventions may vary in different contexts, depending on the types of services and infrastructures already in place. The evidence base is still relatively limited in this area, but several World Bank–supported impact evaluation studies are currently under way to address this question. For example, an impact evaluation in Cambodia aims to assess the relative cost-effectiveness of three types of ECD interventions (formal preschools, community-based preschools, and home-based programs) to inform scaling-up activities.

Selecting the Domains of Child Development to be Measured

The commonly used indicators differ within each of the four domains of child development described in the introduction to this guide. The domains and specific indicators within each are as follows:

- **Physical development indicators** cover growth and general health (see health and nutrition indicators in table 2.1.1), gross motor development (for example, walking, running, jumping), and fine motor development (for example, picking up objects and holding eating utensils in infants and toddlers, holding a pencil to draw and write in preschool-age children).

- **Cognitive development indicators** include problem-solving skills (for example, stacking and nesting objects), memory, and early math skills (for example, sorting objects and knowing what is meant by "one" or "two" of something). As children near school entry, indicators include knowledge of letters and numbers, ability to retain information in short-term memory, and knowledge of key personal information like one's name and address.

- **Language development indicators** include babbling, pointing, and gesturing in infancy, the emergence of first words and sentences in toddlerhood, and an explosion of words between ages 2 and 3 years. For preschoolers, indicators include production and understanding of words, abilities to tell stories and to identify letters, and comfort and familiarity with books.

- **Social and emotional development indicators** include infants' relationships with caregivers in terms of trust and confidence. For preschoolers, indicators include getting along with peers and teachers, behavior management (following directions and cooperating with requests), social perception (identifying thoughts and feelings in themselves and others), and self-regulatory abilities (emotional and behavioral control, especially in stressful situations).

- **Executive function** is a mix of cognitive and socio-emotional skills that can also be measured.

The domains of child development to be measured depend on the original intent of the intervention and the research questions to be addressed. For example, in the case of a nutritional intervention, it would be relevant to measure both physical and cognitive development outcomes among children who benefit from this intervention, but it may be less directly relevant to measure language and socio-emotional development.

During a child's early years, however, new capacities emerge continuously and often in close succession. Development in one domain often acts as a catalyst for development in another. For example, after learning to walk, children are faced with new demands on self-control, as parents are more likely to restrict their behavior and expect that a "no" command will be obeyed. Similarly, children who are slow to develop in one domain (for example, understanding language) may have limited capacity to display the skills that they possess in other domains (for example, cognitive tasks that require language skills).[5] Further, several recent studies have shown that noncognitive skills play a significant role in school achievement, productivity, and the likelihood of engaging in risky and criminal behaviors later in life (Heckman 2008). Therefore, development in young children should be assessed as comprehensively as possible whenever feasible.

When selecting domains to measure, it is also important to consider the relationship between the length of the intervention and the sustainability of the development gain. In other words, it is important to look at which outcomes can be expected to change as a result of an intervention at the time the evaluation data are collected. For example, height-for-age is not very malleable after age 2, so it is probably not a very good indicator of the impact of a project focused on 3–5-year-olds (Glewwe and King 2001).

Selecting and Adapting Child Development Instruments for Use in Low- and Middle-Income Countries

Most child development instruments have been developed, validated, and normed in the developed world. While it can be useful to use some of these "western" (that is, originated in OECD countries) tests in different contexts—such as when there is no local test available to assess a specific child-development outcome or for cross-country comparisons—the extent to which these tests can be used and adapted for low- and middle-income countries varies widely. Indeed, some tests are simply too culturally biased. Others are intended mainly for screening purposes (for example, to identify children who could benefit from special services such as remedial education), and still others require extensive amounts of testing time or must be administered by a trained child psychologist. Furthermore, some tests are not equally effective at assessing children at all levels in the range of abilities or characteristics being evaluated. It may be necessary to adapt scales for some populations, such as by adding or dropping questions designed to assess one end or the other of the scores' distribution, in order to capture the full range. Table 2.1.2 provides examples of child development tests used in recent impact evaluations supported by the World Bank.

The following are considerations to keep in mind in selecting and adapting tests for use in low- and middle-income countries (see Fernald et al. 2009 for a comprehensive review):

Selecting tests. It is preferable to use tests that:

- Allow for the interpretation of data at the population level rather than the level of the individual child. Indeed, the main objective of data collection in the context of World Bank support to clients usually is to assess developmental trends among groups of children (for example, to compare children in a treatment group with children in a control group) and not to conduct developmental screenings for individual children.
- Provide continuous scores rather than a cutoff point under which children may be considered at risk of development delays. Continuous measures are often more useful in the context of impact evaluations (that is, measuring score differences across treatment and control groups).

It is also important to consider some of the specific constraints under which the data collection will take place. In low- and middle-income countries, the most common constraints include:

- A limited budget to purchase and administer tests. The price of tests, as well as the cost to administer them, varies widely. The copyright requirements of some tests may require new kits to be purchased for each data collection team.

Table 2.1.2   Examples of Child Development Tests Commonly Used in ECD Impact Evaluations

Test name	Age range (years)	Domains of child development	Type of measurement	Country examples[a]
Peabody Picture Vocabulary Test (PPVT) and TVIP (equivalent Spanish version)	2½ and above	Language development (receptive language)	Direct assessment of the child	Cambodia Ecuador[b] Madagascar Mozambique Nicaragua[c]
Ages and Stages Questionnaire (ASQ)	0–6	Multiple domains of child development	Ratings and reports (by parent or caregiver) and direct assessment of the child	Cambodia Chile[d] Ecuador[e] Mozambique
Woodcock - Johnson III Memory for Names test	2½ and above	Cognitive development (associative memory)	Direct assessment of the child	Cambodia Ecuador[f]
Stanford-Binet Intelligence Scales	2½ and above	Cognitive development	Direct assessment of the child	Madagascar
Achenbach Child Behavior Checklist (CBCL)	1½ to 6 (5 years 11 months)	Socio-emotional development	Ratings and reports (by parent or caregiver)	Brazil China[g] Turkey
Stroop test (adapted as day/night test)	3 to 6	Executive function	Direct assessment of the child	Madagascar
Strengths and Difficulties Questionnaire	3 and above	Socio-emotional development	Ratings and reports	Madagascar
Early Development Instrument (EDI)	4–7	Multiple domains/school readiness	Ratings and reports (by preschool or grade 1 teachers)	Mozambique, Kosovo Mexico Indonesia

Source: Fernald et al. 2009.
Notes: a. This list provides representative examples and is not intended to be exhaustive. Also, several of these studies are ongoing at the time of publication, so specific references cannot yet be provided. Please contact the first author of this guide for further information.
b. Paxson and Schady (2010).
c. Macours, Schady, and Vakis (2008).
d. Urzúa and Veramendi (forthcoming).
e. See complete references in Fernald et al. (2009).
f. Paxson and Schady (2007).
g. See complete references in Fernald et al. (2009).

- The need to collect child development data within a short period of time, especially if household data are also collected from the caregiver or another adult during the same visit. Keeping it short (that is, no more than 30 minutes for direct child testing) will help prevent respondent fatigue, especially in younger children.
- The lack of available child development specialists or child psychologists to administer the tests. In such cases, it may be necessary to choose tests that do not require extensive professional training to administer.
- The presence of multiple official and vernacular languages. Translating tests into multiple local languages can be time-consuming, and ensuring the proper translation across languages can be difficult. Therefore, tests that do not rely too extensively on language are often more reliable and easier to use in such contexts.

Adapting tests. Once relevant child development tests have been identified, several steps must be taken to ensure that these tests are as valid[6] and reliable[7] as possible in the context of a given data collection exercise. Ideally, the whole adaptation process should be conducted jointly with local professionals—pediatricians, child development specialists/psychologists, social and community health workers, ECD specialists, and so on—to ensure that the final tests and administration protocols are appropriate and effective for the local context. The adaptation process typically includes the following steps:

- Providing an accurate translation, which requires the following: (1) producing an accurate translation in the local language, (2) having a different translator or group of translators do a back translation, and (3) assessing and addressing any discrepancies in meaning.
- Adapting the test content to fit the contexts where the tests will be used. Specific items may need to be dropped (for example, if they are not relevant or cannot be tested) or modified (for example, if the required props are not readily available).
- Adapting the test administration protocol to the cultural context where the tests will be used to ensure both optimal testing conditions in a given setting and consistency across households. For example, many young children are unfamiliar with "test" taking and will be wary of a stranger coming to their house for this purpose. Protocols can encourage data collectors to play simple games with children prior to collecting data, to help "break the ice."

- Conducting a pilot test. Once the test is translated and adapted and the protocol written, both need to be extensively field-tested in real conditions to (1) ensure that the materials are relevant for the population, (2) serve as an additional training opportunity for the data collectors, and (3) obtain pilot data that can be used to conduct preliminary analysis and to verify the validity and reliability of the adapted tests.[8]
- Further adapting the test and administration protocols as needed. Based on the result of the pilot, further adaptations are often needed to refine the instruments and protocols, and additional pilot testing may be necessary.

This iterative adaptation process can be both time-consuming and expensive, but it is a necessary investment to ensure that quality data will eventually be collected. Box 2.1.1 provides a concrete example of this process in Mozambique.

Box 2.1.1

Adapting Child Development Instruments in Mozambique

The World Bank is currently conducting several impact evaluations of ECD interventions across various countries (including Cambodia, Indonesia, Mozambique, Brazil, Chile, and Nicaragua). In the Gaza province of Mozambique, for example, a randomized study aims to assess whether a low-cost, community-based ECD program implemented by Save the Children can significantly improve child development outcomes and school readiness among participants.

Before collecting baseline data in 2008, the team spent time selecting and adapting child development instruments to ensure their relevance to the local context and that the data collected would be useful for answering the main research questions. The instruments selected included the TVIP (direct assessment of the child's receptive language); the Ages and Stages Questionnaire (ASQ) (combination of direct assessment mother's report of the child's competencies across domains, including fine-motor, gross-motor, problem-solving, communication, and personal-social) for children ages 3–5 years; and the EDI (first-grade teacher's report of the child's competencies across domains) for first-grade students. The team also collected anthropometric data (through direct

(continued)

Box 2.1.1 *(continued)*

measurement), family-level socioeconomic data (through household surveys), and data on feeding and early stimulation patterns at the household level (through mothers' questionnaires).

The child development instruments were adapted as follows:

- They were translated first into Portuguese and then into Changana (the main local language in the Gaza province) by a team of local professionals, including a Mozambican child psychologist, and then back-translated.
- Some items were dropped. For example, a question about whether young children could climb stairs (as part of the gross-motor section of the ASQ) would have been difficult to answer since most children in the target communities live in single-level huts with no access to staircases. Therefore the question was not included.
- Other items were modified to be more relevant to the local context and to facilitate the data collection process. For example, a question about whether young children could place a book on top of a chair and then under a chair (to assess whether children understood the concepts of "on top of" and "under," as part of the communication section of the ASQ) was inappropriate since there were neither books nor chairs in most target households. Simply replacing "book" and "chair" by familiar items (that is, plate and straw mat) solved the problem.
- The revised instruments were pilot tested several times, first by the core evaluation team and then by the data collectors (after they received training from the local child psychologist), and additional adaptations of the instruments and administration protocols were made before the actual data collection process began.

Measuring Mediating or Moderating Variables

Variables such as the quality of the home environment, frequency of parental stimulation, maternal depression, breastfeeding, and complementary feeding patterns, can be impacted by ECD interventions, and may play an important *mediating* role (that is, act as a transmission mechanism) toward better child development outcomes. ECD impact evaluation studies collect data on these variables as well in the context of a household survey and/or mother-child questionnaires. For example, the Home Observation for Measurement of the Environment (HOME) can be used cross-culturally to assess the quality of the home environment and parent-child interactions, and the Center for Epidemiologic Studies (CES-D) scale can be used to assess the maternal depression level (Fernald et al. 2009).

Other variables (for example, mother's education level and cognitive development, number of siblings in the household, number of adults in the household, among others) are not likely to be affected by the ECD intervention, but they nonetheless can play an important *moderating* role in child development outcomes. For example, some ECD interventions may be particularly effective for mothers with low education levels and others for those with higher education levels. Information on these family background variables should also be collected in the study, either by including specific questions in the household survey or through specific tests for assessing mothers' cognitive development, and used as controls in the analysis. Caution should be exercised to ensure selection of measures that are appropriate to distributions of these factors in particular countries, and to variation across regions within a country.

Finally, before the data collection process can begin, it is important to keep in mind several important ethical considerations (see box 2.1.2).

Box 2.1.2

Ethical Considerations for Collecting and Managing Human Development Data

In some countries, proposed research must go through an Institutional Review Board (IRB) process before researchers can collect human development data, which ensures that (1) participants (the child or caregiver) are given a choice in participating in the study; (2) the data will be kept confidential, (3) the data collection process will not harm the participants in any way, either physically or psychologically, and (4) participants are referred to specific services when further problems are detected (for example, children identified as anemic referred to iron-supplementation programs; mothers identified as depressed referred to counseling services).

Many countries do not have a well-established IRB system, and some of the above requirements may be difficult to fulfill in contexts where follow-up services are not available. However, the research team remains responsible for ensuring that data are collected in a way that is respectful of participants' rights.

Considerations for Interpreting Data

Even after spending time and resources selecting and adapting a given test for use with a specific population, researchers must cautiously interpret the results. While results can be relevant if used to compare different groups of children within a given environment (for example, to say that a treatment group scored higher than a control group on a given test, or to identify the most vulnerable children within a community), it is much more difficult to draw comparisons across cultural and socioeconomic contexts. For example, the fact that 40 percent of a sample of low-income children in Cambodia score at the level of the 5th percentile of a test developed and norm-referenced in the United States does not necessarily mean that this group is developmentally delayed. Indeed, it could be that the adapted test is still not fully valid and reliable for this population, or that the way in which the data were collected in Cambodia did not allow for optimal performance among respondents.

In conclusion, collecting multisectoral data on the specific needs of young children and on the scope and quality of existing ECD services provides important background information that can be used to design new ECD services or to modify existing ones in the most relevant ways. A complete situation analysis will also document the policies (see Note 2.2) and the type of financing (see Note 4.2) in place. The categories of data included in the situation analysis also provide the framework for strengthening MIS capacity to monitor progress toward meeting these identified needs. Finally, a range of tools can be used to measure child development outcomes to establish a baseline for new interventions and to evaluate the impact and cost-effectiveness of existing ECD interventions. Several ongoing impact evaluations of diverse ECD programs will generate information to guide future national and international investments.

Notes

1. Results from the MICS, including national reports, standard sets of tabulations, and micro-level datasets, can be found at http://www.childinfo.org.
2. Customized data tables can be created using the following website: http://www.uis.unesco.org.
3. See notes in Section 3 for a description of service types.
4. For example, the Association for Childhood Education International has developed "global guidelines" and a companion assessment tool (available at http://www.acei.org). Other tools are listed in Myers (2006).

5. Fernald et al. (2009) provide a comprehensive description of each of these tests (and others), including purpose and age range, norms, administration and testing, training needed, time needed for administration, cost, and publisher information.

6. Validity means the instrument in fact measures what it is intended to measure.

7. Reliability refers to both inter-rater reliability (that is, the extent to which two data collectors would give the same score to a given child) and test-retest reliability (that is, the extent to which the same data collector would give the same score to a given child if the child were assessed several times within a short period, such as a week or so).

8. Ideally, both the inter-rater and test-retest reliability would be around .8 or above. In addition, tests that contain scales (that is, several items grouped under one heading) should be checked for their Cohen Alpha Reliability, that is, the extent to which individual items within this scale behave in a consistent way.

Key Readings

Fernald, L., P. Kariger, P. Engle, and A. Raikes. 2009. *Examining Early Child Development in Low-Income Countries: A Toolkit for the Assessment of Children in the First Five Years of Life*. Washington, DC: World Bank.

Myers, R. G. 2006. "Quality in Programs of Early Childhood Care and Education. Paper commissioned for the *Education for All Global Monitoring Report 2007: Strong Foundations: Early Childhood Care and Education*. United Nations Educational, Scientific and Cultural Organization, Paris. Accessed April 22, 2010: http://unesdoc.unesco.org/images/0014/001474/147473e.pdf.

National Research Council. 2008. *Early Childhood Assessment: Why, What, and How?* National Research Council of the National Academies. Washington, DC. National Academies Press.

References

Aboud, F. E. 2006. "Evaluation of an Early Childhood Preschool Program in Rural Bangladesh. *Early Childhood Research Quarterly* 21 (1): 46–60.

Fernald, L., P. Kariger, P. Engle, and A. Raikes. 2009. *Examining Early Child Development in Low-Income Countries: A Toolkit for the Assessment of Children in the First Five Years of Life*. Washington, DC: World Bank.

Glewwe, P., and E. M. King. 2001. "The Impact of Early Childhood Nutritional Status on Cognitive Development: Does the Timing of Malnutrition Matter?" *The World Bank Economic Review* 15 (1): 81–113.

Harms, T., R. Clifford, and D. Cryer. 1998. *Early Childhood Environment Rating Scale* (rev. ed.). New York: Teacher College Press.

Heckman, J. J. 2008. "Schools, Skills, and Synapses." *Economic Inquiry* 46 (3): 289–324.

Macours, K., N. Schady, and R. Vakis, 2008. "Cash Transfers, Behavioral Changes, and Cognitive Development in Early Childhood: Evidence from a Randomized Experiment." World Bank Policy Research Working Paper 4759. World Bank, Washington, DC.

Malmberg, L. E., P. Mwaura, and K. Sylva. Forthcoming. "Effects of a Preschool Intervention on Cognitive Development among East-African Preschool Children: A Flexibly Time-Coded Growth Model." *Early Childhood Research Quarterly.*

Myers, R. G. 2004. "In Search of Quality in Programmes in Early Childhood Care and Education." Paper commissioned for the *Education for All Global Monitoring Report 2005: The Quality Imperative.* United Nations Educational, Scientific and Cultural Organization, Paris.

———. 2006. "Quality in Programs of Early Childhood Care and Education. Paper commissioned for the *Education for All Global Monitoring Report 2007: Strong Foundations: Early Childhood Care and Education.* United Nations Educational, Scientific and Cultural Organization, Paris. Accessed April 22, 2010: http://unesdoc.unesco.org/images/0014/001474/147473e.pdf.

National Research Council. 2008. *Early Childhood Assessment: Why, What, and How?* National Research Council of the National Academies. Washington, DC: National Academies Press.

Paxson, C., and N. Schady. 2007. "Cognitive Development among Young Children in Ecuador: The Roles of Wealth, Health, and Parenting." *Journal of Human Resources* 42 (1): 49–84.

Urzúa, S., and G. Veramendi. Forthcoming. "The Impact of Out-of-Home Childcare Centers on Early Childhood Development." Background paper for Inter-American Development Bank.

A Policy Framework and Institutional Arrangements for Integrated Services

This note provides an overview of the rationale for and process of developing a national ECD policy framework.[1] Given the multisectoral nature of ECD programs, which encompass areas of health, nutrition, education, and social protection, as well as the fact that government involvement often has limited precedent, constructing a policy framework can raise the visibility of a nation's vision and goals for young children, clarify the respective responsibilities of different actors and agencies, and provide critical guidance for public and private investments.[2] Closely linked to policy development are the country's institutional arrangements for and governance of ECD. However, there is no one-size-fits-all approach.

This note describes the rationale for creating an ECD policy framework and its development phases. Three case studies in Ghana, Indonesia, and Jamaica show how effective cross-sectoral ECD policy development and program implementation can be achieved across diverse political, economic, and cultural contexts. The Jamaica case exemplifies a strategic approach to collaboration across ministries and political parties, taking a strong private sector into account. Indonesia's example shows how ECD coordination mechanisms at national, provincial, and district levels can support decentralized, community-driven development (CDD) in the delivery of integrated ECD services in poor and underserved rural areas.

Ghana's case illustrates the importance of consensus-building over time to adopt and implement a multisectoral policy. The note concludes with cross-national lessons for policy development and implementation.

Rationale for Creating an ECD Policy Framework

A National Policy Framework for ECD Presents Vision and Goals for Young Children and Families
The policy framework raises the visibility of ECD for young children and their families and identifies strategies to address their needs. In fact, young children are often omitted or their needs inadequately addressed in sectoral policies and in key documents like the Poverty Reduction Strategy Papers (PRSPs).

A policy framework typically includes both a policy statement and a description of institutional and administrative structures to implement the policy. The policy statement includes a vision of where the ECD is heading, a set of goals or objectives that the government would like to achieve, and strategies for achieving them (CARICOM Secretariat 2008). It is important for the ECD policy to be coherent with other related sectoral policies.

The ECD Policy Framework Clarifies the Responsibilities of Different Actors and Agencies
The policy framework identifies the lead agency and the entities that will implement, manage, monitor, and evaluate ECD programs (CARICOM Secretariat 2008). Government responsibility for the provision or supervision of ECD services is often scattered across ministries, often according to the age of the child. Typically, the ministry of health is responsible for infants and young children under the age of 2 and the ministry of education plays a role from preschool through basic education. An ECD policy framework can help harmonize the goals and strategies of these institutions *horizontally*. A policy can engage new ministries that have not traditionally been engaged in ECD, such as agriculture and finance. Furthermore, responsibility may also be distributed *vertically* among multiple levels of government, such as the national/central, provincial, district, and community levels (see box 2.2.1), as in Indonesia. A policy framework can help maximize scarce financial, human, and material resources by reducing duplication of effort (Neuman 2007).

Box 2.2.1

ECD in Indonesia: Special Considerations for Decentralization

Indonesia's government is one of the most decentralized in the world. Most spending on education, health, and infrastructure is district-based, and the districts employ three-quarters of the civil service. In recent years, for example, 90 percent of the Ministry of National Education (MoNE) annual budget has been shifted from the central government to the districts in the form of block grants channeled directly to the education and training units, including schools. In the past, districts were carrying out the implementation, financing, and supervision of early childhood education and development (ECED) services, often without an ECED unit, a clear legal mandate, or implementation capacity. To address these concerns, the Indonesian government, with support from the World Bank, developed a community-based approach for the provision of ECD services, including center-based programs, home-based daycare programs, and home-visit or parent education and support programs. The design was informed by a pilot project in 12 districts, which revealed that centralized service delivery was not best suited to the needs of poor communities. In the new model, community-driven development (CDD) grants channel funds directly to the village level for about 738,000 children ages 0 to 6 and their parents/caretakers who live in approximately 6,000 poor communities in 3,000 villages within 50 impoverished districts throughout Indonesia.

Indonesia has developed institutional structures within this highly decentralized context to ensure that ECED services are provided in a sustainable and integrated manner. First, before implementing ECED services, districts are asked to show evidence of (1) budget allocation for ECED programs, (2) a unit and staff with a clear and comprehensive mandate for managing ECED, (3) existence of an ECED forum that allows for coordination among a wide range of stakeholders, (4) an action plan to support the integration of early education, health, nutrition, and parenting education aspects of ECED; and (5) readiness to finance some of the activities after the project period to sustain ECED services over time. Second, to ensure that local governments do not focus too much on education at the expense of other sectors, communities are given a menu of services to provide with the funds they receive, and district-level capacity building has expanded. Third, to support coherence, these decentralized structures are supported centrally by an Early Childhood Directorate within MoNE and a National ECED Forum of practitioners, academics, and bureaucrats.[3]

A Policy Framework Should Clarify the Degree to Which ECD Is a Public or Private Responsibility

In a purely private-sector approach, services might be fee-paying and limited to those who can afford them. The government's role might be more regulatory, ensuring the quality of services provided. A purely public-sector approach might envision that all children, or at least some broad group such as the most vulnerable children, should have access to ECD services, with assistance available for those who cannot afford the fees. Most often, there will be a balance of both private- and public-sector approaches. To establish services in areas that are not financially attractive to the private sector, the government can initiate ECD services and gradually transfer some responsibilities to the private sector, while keeping some key roles, such as financing of teachers. To address quality issues, the government may also subsidize private inputs into service delivery in exchange for improvements in quality indicators (see Note 4.2).

Elements of an ECD Policy Framework

A policy framework comprises a policy statement and a description of institutional structures. The policy statement should conform to national guidelines and format requirements that govern policy papers and should include the following elements:

1. **Vision**—a statement of the long-term national goal for the ECD program and the children's outcomes that should be achieved once the program becomes successful.
2. **Goals and objectives**—should grow out of the vision and describe measurable outcomes that can be evaluated over time.
3. **Leading strategies**—general description of the activities envisioned as a way of achieving the goals and objectives.

Usually the decision to implement an ECD framework is driven by a detailed *situational analysis* (see Note 2.1), or needs assessment, of the status, problems, and needs of children and their families. It is good practice to include a brief summary of the findings of the situational analysis as the introduction to the policy statement, to provide a context for the vision, goals, objectives, and strategies.

The description of the institutional structures should include:

- **Organizational structures**—a description of the administrative and coordinating structures operating at all levels of government and the private sector, including organizational structure and responsibilities.

- **Investment plans**—a description of how human, institutional, financial, and material resources will be allocated and mobilized, including the balance of public and private resources.
- **Communication strategies**—a description of how communication will flow among administrative structures and other stakeholders, including communication such as policy advocacy.
- **Partnerships**—particularly partnerships between funders/donors and implementers, including NGOs and community-based organizations, and responsibility for liaison between them.
- **Monitoring and evaluation processes**—a description of the accountability systems that will measure, monitor, and evaluate progress toward the policy goals.

Process Phases in Developing a Policy Framework

The process of developing a policy framework comprises five phases (Vargas-Barón 2005) described as follows:

1. **Preparation**—though often overlooked, this phase can ensure that the following phases run smoothly. During this phase, leaders and key stakeholders are identified and engaged; a planning committee may be organized to take the lead on the ensuing phases; lines of communication and authority are established; a work plan, schedule, and budget are developed; and sources of financing are confirmed. Discussions begin during this phase about the lead agency for ECD.

2. **Situation analysis**—similar to a needs assessment (see Note 2.1.), this study provides the foundation for the policy statement. It should be comprehensive and thorough, and the task of developing it, while often overseen by the planning committee, may be assigned to an external entity with particular expertise.

3. **Community and stakeholder consultation**—engaging stakeholders at this stage generates awareness, enthusiasm, and a sense of ownership for the ECD initiative, making it much more likely that it will reflect the needs and priorities of the beneficiaries. Consulting with partners also builds trust, provides feedback about feasibility of the policy plan, identifies issues early enough to more easily resolve them, and creates a network of partners to provide support as the process moves forward.

4. **Policy drafting and consensus building**—from the feedback generated by the previous phase, a first draft of a policy document can be generated, discussed, and finalized.

5. **Policy approval and adoption**—involves presenting the proposed policy and plan of action to the decision-making authority, gaining approval, and building on momentum by beginning the implementation process quickly. To ensure sustainability over time, the policy will need to be interpreted into long-term programs, services, or actions, and steps taken to build it into the annual operation plan and budgets.

Identifying an Institutional Anchor Is Essential to Engaging Different Sectors and Overcoming Turf Issues

There needs to be early agreement within a country on a lead agency or institutional anchor to coordinate policy development and implementation. One of the line ministries—social welfare or education—generally takes the lead. Since the late 1980s, more and more countries, including Brazil, Kenya, New Zealand, Norway, Sweden, Spain, and Vietnam, have designated the education ministry as the lead agency to provide continuity between the early childhood and primary years. Alternatively, engaging the ministry of planning, the ministry of finance, the office of the president or prime minister, or creating an independent commission (for example, as in Chile, Colombia, and Jamaica) as the institutional anchor can minimize competition among line ministries. Debates over the lead agency in Ghana (box 2.2.2) delayed the policy development process, but were eventually resolved in a way that supports intersectoral coordination. Intersectoral coordination mechanisms (for example, ECD commissions) work best when a strong agency leads and when the commission has the power to make funding decisions (UNESCO-OREALC 2004).

Elements of Successful Policy and Institutional Frameworks

The three case studies described here support lessons from cross-national reviews about the main elements of successful ECD policy and institutional frameworks that include the following:

- Seek high-level political endorsement to secure ECD on the national agenda.
- Define an institutional anchor, preferably early on in the policy development process.
- Involve stakeholders from a range of sectors (including those outside the traditional child-focused agencies) in developing the policy and clearly delineate responsibilities.

Box 2.2.2

ECD in Ghana: the Journey Is as Important as the Destination

Ghana is one of 19 countries in Sub-Saharan Africa with a national ECD policy in place to promote the survival, growth, development, and protection of children from birth to age 8, so that they can develop to their full potential. The main policy objectives are to address the problem of poverty among children, streamline the activities of all stakeholders in ECD, and attract support from all stakeholders who have resources for the sector. The policy covers institutional arrangements, roles and responsibilities, implementation strategies, and cost and financial implications (Government of Ghana 2004).

The policy development process was long and not without challenges. A draft policy was developed in 1995 by a task force and used in consultations with stakeholders. The process encountered serious delays at various steps including in the long preparation of the initial document by the task force, multiple revisions and rewrites, and time-consuming community consultations. A major delay was caused by the ongoing indecision over which ministry should coordinate the ECD program. Although initially the Ghana National Children's Commission (GNCC) in the Office of the President was appointed as the lead coordinating body, by the time the draft was sent to the cabinet in 2000, the political administration had changed. The Ministry of Women and Children's Affairs (MOWC) then absorbed the GNCC as a department and became the lead agency (UNESCO 2006a). The final document, adopted in 2004, has encouraged expansion and improvement efforts, some of which were already under way (UNESCO 2006b). Two years of kindergarten are now part of basic education, with a set curriculum and early learning and development standards. Currently about 40 percent of 5-year-olds and 35 percent of 4-year-olds are covered. The government also created guidelines for establishing ECD centers and for addressing HIV-related issues, expanded training, and mobilized resources for implementation (Addison, Noyoru, and Kyei-Gyamfi 2007).

The Ghana program has also developed strong institutional coordination mechanisms. A National ECD Coordinating Committee and Secretariat advise the MOWC and coordinate implementation of the policy. The committee comprises five key government ministries, the Ghana National Association of Teachers, recognized associations of ECD practitioners, and any other co-opted individuals or organizations. This institutional structure is being replicated at regional and district levels. Regional education and social welfare officials have received an orientation on

(continued)

Box 2.2.2 *(continued)*

the ECD policy. Key stakeholders are being sensitized to ensure that ECD is incorporated into district plans (Pence et al. 2004).

Initiated almost 11 years ago, this process of ECD policy development has enabled multiple reviews and revisions to improve quality, encouraged a participatory process with community-level contributions, and improved stakeholder ownership, all of which increase the likelihood of successful implementation (Boakye et al. 2008). Ghana's experience reinforces the importance of selecting a strong lead agency for ECD to coordinate policy development, adoption, and implementation.

- Ensure bipartisan representation on inter-agency coordination bodies.
- Engage local governments to ensure ownership and sustainability.
- Support a participatory approach to encourage buy-in and relevance of the policy framework.
- Ensure adequate funding to support effective implementation.

Box 2.2.3

ECD in Jamaica: Institutional Arrangements to Govern across Sectors

In the late 1990s, Jamaican government agencies, including the ministries of health and education and the Planning Institute of Jamaica, recognized the need for a long-term plan for offering comprehensive, integrated services to Jamaican children that would benefit from synergies and complementarities between actors, reducing duplication and minimizing gaps in service delivery. In 2000, a strategic review of the ECD sector recommended the creation of a new Early Childhood Commission (ECC). An act of parliament established the ECC in 2003 to develop standards and licensing regulations for early childhood institutions, advise the minister of education on policy matters relating to early childhood, assist in the planning of and preparations for strategies and programs, and monitor the implementation of programs. Two years later, parliament passed the Early Childhood Act, which stipulated the regulations, standards, licensing, and policies governing

(continued)

Box 2.2.3 *(continued)*

ECD in Jamaica. The ECC has the authority to develop the systems and policies, including the ability to impose fines of up to JM$50,000 (US$560) for licensing noncompliance.

The Jamaican approach is significant in the way that it addresses the multisectoral nature of ECD by reaching across sectors and political parties in the formation of the ECC. As written in the ECC Act, the Board of Commissioners of the ECC includes:

- Executive director of the ECC, as an *ex officio* member
- Chairman appointed by the governor-general, who represents the king or queen of Jamaica, on the recommendation of the prime minister, after consultation with the leader of the opposition
- Representative of the opposition political party
- Permanent secretary (or nominee) of each of the ministries of education, health, labor, and social security, local government and community development, and finance and the public service.
- Executive director (or nominee) of the Child Development Agency; and the Planning Institute of Jamaica, and
- At least seven persons who "appear to the governor-general to be qualified as having experience of, and shown capacity in, matters relating to early childhood development, including child care, child psychology, nutrition, pediatrics and the field of nursing."

There are three ways this institutional structure has contributed to Jamaica's success in governing ECD across sectors. First, the presence of all key ministries, as well as nonpublic actors, on the ECC Board provides a standing forum for discussions of challenges and planning of the ECD sector. This is of paramount importance in Jamaica and other countries with a dominant private sector. Second, the inclusion of both political parties on the board and in the selection process for the chairman ensures a degree of bipartisan support for the sector. This proved crucial during the consultations and design of the National Strategic Plan for ECD. Although the government changed hands halfway through the planning, there were few disruptions to the process. Third, the fact that the ECC has legislative authority to enforce quality standards of service delivery and impose sanctions has facilitated its work.

Notes

1. A *policy* framework is distinct from a *regulatory* framework, which includes formal standards, regulations, and procedures for operating, licensing, and monitoring ECD institutions (CARICOM Secretariat 2008).
2. A tool for benchmarking national ECD policies against several dimensions and assessing the extent to which they are sectoral or comprehensive is currently being developed by the World Bank (see Vegas et al., forthcoming).
3. For more information, see World Bank (2006).

Key Readings

CARICOM Secretariat (Caribbean Community). 2008. *Guidelines for Developing Policy, Regulation, and Standards in Early Childhood Development Services.* Jamaica: Pear Tree Press.

Vargas-Barón, E. 2005. "Planning Policies for Early Childhood Development: Guidelines for Action." Paris: UNESCO/ADEA/UNICEF (United Nations Educational, Scientific and Cultural Organization/Association for the Development of Education in Africa/United Nations Children's Fund).

UNESCO–OREALC. 2004. "Inter-sectoral Co-ordination in Early Childhood Policies and Programmes: A Synthesis of Experiences in Latin America." Regional Bureau of Education for Latin America and the Caribbean, United Nations Educational, Scientific and Cultural Organization, Santiago, Chile.

References

Addison, R. O. Q., C. C. Noyoru, and S. Kyei-Gyamfi. 2007. "Overview of Ghana's National Early Childhood Care and Development Policy." Accessed October 18, 2009 from http://mowacghana.net/?q=node/30.

Boakye, J. K. A., S. Etse, M. Adamu-Issah, M. D. Moti, J. L. Matjila, and S. Shikwambi. 2008. "ECD Policy: A Comparative Analysis in Ghana, Mauritius, and Nambia." In *Africa's Future, Africa's Challenge: Early Childhood Care and Development in Sub-Saharan Africa*, ed. M. Garcia, A. Pence, and J. L. Evans, 169–86. Washington, DC: World Bank.

CARICOM Secretariat (Caribbean Community). 2008. *Guidelines for Developing Policy, Regulation, and Standards in Early Childhood Development Services.* Jamaica: Pear Tree Press.

Engle P. L., M. M. Black, J. R. Behrman, M. C. de Mello, P. J. Gertler, L. Kapiriri, R. Martorell, and M. E. Young, and the International Child Development Steering Group. 2007. "Strategies to Avoid the Loss of Developmental Potential in More Than 200 Million Children in the Developing World." *The Lancet* 369 (9557): 229–42.

Government of Ghana. 2004. "Early Childhood Care and Development Policy." Accra: Ministry of Women and Children's Affairs.

Myers, R. G. 2006. "Quality in Program of Early Childhood Care and Education." Paper commissioned for the *Education for All Global Monitoring Report 2007: Strong Foundations: Early Childhood Care and Education.* United Nations Educational, Scientific and Cultural Organization, Paris. Accessed April 22, 2010: http://unesdoc.unesco.org/images/0014/001474/147473e.pdf.

Neuman, M. J. 2007. "Good Governance of Early Childhood Care and Education: Lessons from the *2007 Education for All Global Monitoring Report.*" UNESCO Policy Briefs on Early Childhood 40. United Nations Educational, Scientific and Cultural Organization, New York.

Pence, A. R., M. Amponsah, F. Chalamanda, A. Habtom, G. Kameka, and H. Nankunda. 2004. "ECD Policy Development and Implementation in Africa." *International Journal of Educational Policy, Research, and Practice* 5 (3): 13–29.

UNESCO. 2006a. "Ghana: Early Childhood Care and Education Programmes." Country profile commissioned for the *Education for All Global Monitoring Report 2007: Strong Foundations: Early Childhood Care and Education.* United Nations Educational, Scientific and Cultural Organization, Paris. Accessed October 18, 2009 from http://unesdoc.unesco.org/images/0014/001471/147192e.pdf.

———. 2006b. *Education for All Global Monitoring Report 2007: Strong Foundations: Early Childhood Care and Education.* United Nations Educational, Scientific and Cultural Organization, Paris.

UNESCO–OREALC. 2004. "Inter-sectoral Co-ordination in Early Childhood Policies and Programmes: A Synthesis of Experiences in Latin America." Regional Bureau of Education for Latin America and the Caribbean, United Nations Educational, Scientific and Cultural Organization, Santiago, Chile.

Vargas-Barón, E. 2005. "Planning Policies for Early Childhood Development: Guidelines for Action." Paris: UNESCO/ADEA/UNICEF (United Nations Educational, Scientific and Cultural Organization/Association for the Development of Education in Africa/United Nations Children's Fund).

Vegas, E. et al. Forthcoming. "Roadmap of ECD Policies across the World." World Bank, Washington, DC.

World Bank. 2006. "Project Appraisal Document for the Indonesia Early Childhood Development Project." World Bank, Washington, DC.

Strategic Entry Points for ECD Investments

NOTE 3.1

Center-Based ECD Programs with a Focus on School Readiness

Center-based ECD programs can be provided in a range of locations, including classrooms, community centers, religious establishments (for example, churches, mosques, pagodas), private homes (that is, family-based daycare), or even under a tree. These centers can be owned, financed, and managed by a range of entities, for example, government, community, non-profit organizations, private businesses, religious institutions, or through partnerships among these entities. Depending on the context and age groups they serve, these programs may be called nursery schools, daycares, preschools, children's centers, or kindergartens. This diversity of settings and labels can be confusing. This note focuses on programs that share the following characteristics: (1) they aim to promote the development of young children (for all or part of the 0- to 6-year-old age range) and (2) they provide services in a group setting where children can interact with peers. Ideally, center-based programs provide services that meet the various needs of young children (that is, health, nutrition, education, and stimulation) in an integrated manner.

While the type and nature of center-based ECD programs may vary, existing evidence from both developed and developing countries suggests that children who participate in these programs tend to exhibit higher cognitive skills and overall school readiness (that is, comprehensive development, as defined in the introduction and in Note 3.1.) upon primary school entry than those who have not participated (Engle et al. 2007). For example, longitudinal evaluations of U.S.-based ECD projects for disadvantaged children, such as the High/Scope Perry Preschool Program and the Abecedarian Program, recorded not only gains in cognitive skills among children in the program, but also continued advantages compared to the control group in school performance and social behaviors later in life (Campbell et al. 2002; Schweinhart et al. 2005). Evaluations conducted in developing countries, such as Bangladesh, Cape Verde, Colombia, Guinea, and Vietnam, also showed a substantial effect of center-based programs on children's development (Engle et al. 2007). Further, center-based programs seem particularly effective at promoting the physical, cognitive, and socio-emotional development of at-risk children, that is, those who are from low-income families or are otherwise disadvantaged.

This note presents evidence on the impact of center-based ECD programs under various conditions and for various groups of beneficiaries, and indicates where research gaps exist. Program implementation will be discussed, including factors to consider and program details, such as targeting, frequency and duration of the sessions, child-to-staff ratio, staff qualifications, program content, and overall program quality. Several promising center-based programs in low- and middle-income countries are highlighted in box 3.1.4.

Targeting Considerations

The evidence in both developed and developing countries indicates that children with the poorest socioeconomic backgrounds are the most likely to benefit from center-based care, especially if they start between ages 2 and 3 years. The factors that need to be taken into account when implementing a program include: socioeconomic background, starting age, frequency and duration of sessions, and quality of the program as indicated by staff qualifications, program content, and adult-child ratio and interactions.

Socioeconomic Background
Children in many developing countries show steep "gradients" in cognitive development according to socioeconomic level; children from poorer households show significantly worse outcomes early on. In Ecuador, differences in age-adjusted vocabulary among 3-year-olds are generally

small. By age 6, however, children in less wealthy households and those born to mothers with low education levels have fallen far behind (that is, by 2.5 standard deviations) their counterparts in wealthier or more educated households (Paxson and Schady 2007). Since poorer children generally receive a lower quality school education, these differences are likely to be magnified even further as children enter school. Steep socio-economic gradients in cognitive development at early ages have also been found in Bangladesh, Brazil, Egypt, India, Mexico, and the Philippines (Grantham-McGregor et al. 2007).

Evidence from longitudinal studies conducted in the developed world, as well as nonexperimental studies from developing countries, consistently show that children with low socioeconomic status or whose mothers have lower levels of education particularly benefit from early interventions and center-based care. For example, data from the Uruguayan Household Survey, in which information about preschool attendance was retrospectively collected, show larger gains in education attainment at age 15 among children with less educated mothers (Berlinski, Galiani, and Manacorda 2008). In the United States, longitudinal studies found that disadvantaged children benefited the most from increased quantity (Loeb et al. 2007) and higher quality of services (Peisner-Feinberg et al. 2001). Therefore, while center-based ECD programs can also benefit children from middle-class families, ensuring access to the most disadvantaged children should be a priority for decisions on investing scare public resources.

Starting Age

Most center-based ECD programs focus on children ages 4 and 5, that is, one or two years before primary school entry. Yet, data from the U.S.-based Early Childhood Longitudinal Study show that the strongest cognitive benefits are experienced by those children who entered a center-based program between the ages of 2 and 3 (Loeb et al. 2007). A program evaluation conducted in the Philippines also found that the impact of integrated ECD services on cognitive, social, motor, and language development were higher for children who were exposed to the program for more than 12 months and among children ages 2 and 3. Indeed, the mean impact on outcomes such as cognitive development and motor skills was 90 percent of a standard deviation for 2-year-olds and 49 percent for 3-year-olds, but only 26- to 29 percent for 4–6-year-olds. Further, children aged 2 and 3 started demonstrating positive outcomes quicker (that is, after 4 to 12 months) than older children (Armecin et al. 2006).

In Colombia, while as little as 9 months of integrated center-based care (nutrition, health, and early education) prior to primary school entry produced significant gains in children's cognitive ability, significantly greater effects were observed among those who started younger, that is, at age of $3\frac{1}{2}$ (McKay et al. 1978). These studies seem to affirm the value of providing center-based ECD services to children as young as 2, especially among the most vulnerable groups. However, in doing so, it is important to ensure that the curriculum and overall program are appropriate to the specific needs of young children.

The evidence on the effects of center-based services for children younger than 2 is mixed. An analysis of the Early Childhood Longitudinal Study in the United States found that center-based programs had no positive effect on children under 2. In fact, the study found that attendance in center-based ECD services had a negative impact on children's behavior. These effects were even greater for children who started utilizing these services before turning 1 year old. (Loeb et al. 2007). On the other hand, when controlling for the total quantity of nonmaternal care that children were receiving, the National Institute for Child Health and Development (NICHD) study did not find any negative behavioral impact of center-based care among children who were enrolled before age 2 (as measured at age $4^1/_2$) (NICHD 2003).

Frequency and Duration of Center-Based Sessions

Center-based ECD services may be offered throughout the year (12 months) or only during the school year (9–10 months). The length of each session can vary from just 2–3 hours a day to 8–10 hours a day in centers that aim to provide full-time child care while parents work. Long hours in center-based ECD programs have been associated with negative effects on the behavior of children from high-income families in the United States (Loeb et al. 2007). However, analysis of data from the Early Childhood Longitudinal Study found that children from low-income households experienced more cognitive gains when attending center-based ECD programs for longer hours (30 hours or more per week), with no significant increase in behavioral problems. This study concluded that most children could experience cognitive gains when participating in center-based ECD programs for 15–30 hours a week (that is, 3–6 hours a day), during at least nine months of the year, and that children from lower-income families could benefit even further from more intensive programs (Loeb et al. 2007).

In contrast, the Effective Provision of Pre-school Education (EPPE) Project, a large-scale longitudinal study conducted in the United Kingdom, did not find any additional cognitive gains among children who attended preschool full-time compared to those who were in part-time programs, but the project did not analyze the possible difference in effect sizes among children from different family backgrounds and did not collect data on children's behavior (Sylva et al. 2003).

Generally speaking, the research indicates that center-based ECD services should offer at least 15 hours of weekly activities in order to yield significant effects.

Quality

Most of the experimental or quasi-experimental studies available on the impact of ECD assess the effectiveness of a given program in a particular setting, but few studies evaluate the relative impact of differential treatments. Therefore, there is little evidence regarding how different types and quality levels of center-based ECD programs influence early childhood outcomes (Karoly, Kilburn, and Canon 2005). The information on this topic comes from several large-scale longitudinal studies with nonexperimental designs in the United States and the United Kingdom. These studies point to the positive influence of quality programming (as evaluated by global standardized quality ratings outlined in box 3.1.1), on children's school readiness, performance in primary school, and language skills (see, for example, Flood et al. 2007). For instance, the NICHD early childhood study found that higher quality in center-based ECD services predicted better pre-academic and language skills among 4½-year-old children in the United States (NICHD 2002). The Cost, Quality and Outcomes Study in the United States found that the quality of center-based ECD services predicted higher language skills among children in kindergarten and higher math skills among children in second grade (Peisner-Feinberg et al. 2001). The EPPE Project mentioned earlier, a similar large-scale longitudinal study conducted in the United Kingdom, also linked quality of center-based ECD services (as measured by standardized rating scales) with positive outcomes among beneficiaries, including fewer behavioral problems upon school entry (Sylva et al. 2003). In Bangladesh, preschool quality (as measured by the ECERS-R) was significantly associated with children's cognitive skills and school readiness (Aboud 2006). Similar results were found among children who attend the Madrasa Resource Center preschools in East Africa (Malmberg, Mwaura, and Sylva, forthcoming).

Box 3.1.1

Quality of Center-Based ECD Programs

Quality refers to the characteristics of center-based ECD programs that influence child development outcomes (Flood et al 2007; see also Note 2.1 for more information on ECD outcomes). Most studies focusing on the quality of center-based ECD programs look at both structural quality and process quality. Structural quality includes such variables as child-to-adult ratio; class size; teachers' education level, experience, and specialized training; and staff wages. Process quality refers to variables that shape children's experience in a particular program, such as the types of activities being conducted, interactions with teachers, and overall program structure.

Two commonly used quality standards for evaluations and research are the following scales:

- Early Childhood Environment Rating Scale-Revised (ECERS-R, for ages $2^{1}/_{2}$–5), the Infant-Toddler Environmental Scale-Revised (ITERS-R, birth to 30 months), and the Family Child Care Environment Rating Scale-Revised (FCCERS-R, in-home/family daycare, from birth to start of primary school). These scales measure overall quality in multiple types of center-based early childhood programs (including family daycares) and include items such as physical environment, basic care, curriculum, interactions, schedule, program structure, and parent and staff education.

- Caregiver Interaction Scale (CIS) measures process quality and is used to rate caregivers' emotional tone and responsiveness toward children. Through observation, interactions are rated in the areas of sensitivity, harshness, detachment, and permissiveness.

Several other studies have assessed how indicators of structural quality, such as class size, child-to-adult ratio, staff qualifications, and program content/curriculum may affect the overall level of quality observed in the classroom as measured by global standardized quality ratings.

Staff qualifications and teacher-child interaction. Most studies indicate a strong correlation between staff qualifications and early childhood outcomes, between staff qualifications and classroom quality, or both. For instance, a cross-country study of nonexperimental data in seven countries found that teachers' education level was positively correlated with language scores among the children (Montie, Xiang, and Schweinhart

2006). Studies of nonexperimental data in the United States and Canada also found staff quality to be a good predictor of the quality of classroom interactions (Goelman, Forer, and Kershaw 2006; Burchinal, Howes, and Kontos 2002). The elements of ECD staff quality that have been studied include caregivers educational attainment (Montie, Xiang, and Schweinhart 2006), specialized training in early childhood education and care (Doherty et al. 2006); and commitment to child-care work (Doherty et al. 2006). The EPPE Project conducted an in-depth qualitative study of 12 ECD centers with high performance in terms of child outcomes and concluded that teachers' knowledge of the curriculum as well as their knowledge and understanding of child development were particularly important qualities (Siraj-Blatchford et al. 2003).

The level of financial compensation that ECD teachers receive also appears to be strongly correlated with the quality of care they provide. For example, teacher's wages were more strongly associated with classroom quality at daycare centers and preschools in the United States than any other structural indicators (such as adult-to-child ratio and teacher's education level) (Phillips et al. 2000; Phillipsen et al. 1997).

Along the same lines, Early et al. (2007) analyzed seven major studies of early childhood education in the United States and recommended a comprehensive approach to human resource development of the ECD sector. In particular, the report recommends that programs be designed to recruit, train, and retain qualified and motivated staff by providing (1) reasonable wages, (2) pre-service and in-service opportunities for training and professional growth, and (3) opportunities for support systems among teachers and caregivers, including opportunities for exchanges of best practices through networks of ECD providers.

Finding, training, and paying qualified teachers can be particularly challenging in developing countries, especially in view of human resource constraints and the many competing priorities governments face. A few center-based programs that have used paraprofessionals in developing countries, such as Madrasa Resource Center Preschools in East Africa (Mwaura and Mohamed 2008) and *Hogares Comunitarios de Bienestar Familiar* in Colombia (Vegas and Santibáñez 2009), have produced promising results. In addition, in-class assistance using communications technology (that is, interactive radio instruction; see box 3.1.2) may be a low-cost option to improve the quality of teaching. Further studies are needed to better understand what elements of quality matter most in low-income settings and how countries with limited resources can provide quality center-based care and education.

Box 3.1.2

Interactive Radio Instruction

Interactive Radio Instruction (IRI) is

> "a distance education system that combines radio broadcasts with active learning to improve educational quality and teaching practices. ... IRI programs require teachers and students to react verbally and physically to questions and exercises posed by radio characters and to participate in group work, experiments, and other activities suggested by the radio program." (Anzalone and Bosch 2005)

IRI has emerged as an important option to improve the quality of instruction and learning in low-income settings and has shown promising results in several large-scale projects in Africa and Latin America. Although evidence of the effectiveness of IRI is available mostly for primary and secondary education programs, some programs targeting younger children show encouraging results. For example, the Radio Instruction to Strengthen Education (RISE) project in Zanzibar produced child-friendly preschool, first-grade, and second-grade radio programs to engage children in learning Kiswahili, math, English, and life skills. Evaluation of the RISE program was conducted only for first-graders. It showed that children who were exposed to IRI in either formal or informal schools scored higher on standardized tests, on average, than their peers in the control group (Educational Development Center 2009). IRI for preschool children was also piloted in Bolivia, El Salvador, Honduras, and Indonesia (Ho and Thukral 2009).

Program content and curriculum. The best curriculum for early childhood programs appears to be one that focuses on the comprehensive development of children by nurturing not only their cognitive and linguistic skills but also their socio-emotional functioning, including motivation and capacity for self-regulation. Indeed, evidence suggests that children's social competence enhances other areas of development such as cognitive functioning—and eventually school success. Downer and Pianta's analysis of the NICHD data shows that better social skills among young children contribute to higher achievement in reading, mathematics skills, and phoneme knowledge among participants in first grade (Downer and Pianta 2006). Further, an evaluation of the High/Scope Perry Preschool Program in the United States showed that while the positive impact of the program on participating children's IQ scores gradually disappeared over the four years following the intervention, those children still performed better than children in the control group on achievement tests, attained higher levels of education, earned higher wages, and were less likely to be on welfare or in prison in early adulthood. Heckman suggests that these positive and long-lasting outcomes result from the positive impact the program had on participants' noncognitive skills (Heckman 2008).

To provide a framework for best practices in early childhood care and education, the U.S.-based National Association for the Education of Young Children (NAEYC) adopted the Developmentally Appropriate Practices (DAP) in Early Childhood Programs (see box 3.1.3). This framework is designed to guide policy makers, administrators, and teachers/caregivers to identify goals for children's development and to make

---

Box 3.1.3

Developmentally Appropriate Practices (DAP)

The National Association for the Education of Young Children defines DAP as "a framework of principles and guidelines for best practice in the care and education of young children" (NAEYC n.d.). Its core principles include fostering the comprehensive development of children by recognizing the importance of early childhood, the sequential development of children's skills and functions, individual differences, various ways that children learn (including through play); and the importance of developing secure child-to-caregiver and child-to-child relationships, in concurrence with theories and literature about child development (NAEYC 2009).

In practice, DAP involves (1) promoting positive relationships between all children and adults; (2) curriculum that is thoughtfully planned, challenging, engaging, developmentally appropriate, culturally and linguistically responsive, comprehensive, and likely to promote positive outcomes for all young children; (3) developmentally, culturally, and linguistically appropriate and effective teaching approaches that enhance each child's learning and development; (4) systematic, formal, and informal assessment approaches to provide information on children's learning and development; (5) the nutrition and health of children; and (6) a safe and healthful environment that provides appropriate and well-maintained indoor and outdoor physical environments, among others (NAEYC 2008).

intentional decisions on the curriculum that take into consideration the child's age (that is, age-specific characteristics that direct how a child learns), individual differences in development, and his/her social and cultural contexts (NAEYC 2009). A joint statement of NAEYC and the National Association of Early Childhood Specialists in State Departments of Education lists the indicators of effective curriculum as follows: "(1) children being active and engaged; (2) curriculum goals are clear and shared by all stakeholders; (3) evidence-based; (4) valued content is learned through investigation, play, and focused, intentional teaching; (5) builds on prior learning and experience; and (6) comprehensive (that is, physical, social and emotional, and cognitive development)," among other criteria (NAEYC and NAECSSDE 2003). The DAP is not free of criticism, even in the United States. However, it serves as a useful framework, and several cross-cultural studies have found that its core principles are supported by many ECD professionals outside the United States (Hoot et al. 1996; McMullen et al. 2005).

The evidence that supports the efficacy of the DAP approach is drawn mostly from experience in the United States among disadvantaged children, where some studies suggest that more active, child-initiated early learning experience is associated with better achievement among children, compared with academically focused programs (Marcon 2002; Huffman and Speer 2000). International experience also finds that curricula that are child-centered are most likely to promote positive outcomes among participating children. The IEA Preprimary project (International Association for the Evaluation of Educational Achievement), a longitudinal cross-country study of children's cognitive and language performance and their early childhood experience at age 7, collected data in Finland; Greece; Hong Kong SAR, China; Indonesia; Ireland; Poland; Spain; Thailand; and the United States. The study found that programs in which children spend most of their time in teacher-led whole group activities where all children engage in the same teacher-selected activity (such as reading stories to children, guiding all children to sing, or dancing together) tend to be less effective than those in which children can choose from a few structured activity options (Montie, Xiang, and Schweinhart 2006). The EPPE project's in-depth qualitative case study of high-performing centers, mentioned earlier, also found that the most effective learning environments are those where both adult-initiated group work and freely chosen play options are provided (Siraj-Blatchford et al. 2003).

Finally, the variety and quantity of learning materials available in the ECD center were also found to be positively correlated with children's cognitive development (Montie, Xiang, and Schweinhart 2006). In low-income settings where learning materials and educational toys may not be readily available, ECD teachers can be trained to make creative use of the natural resources and recycled materials available in their environment.

Class size and adult-to-child ratio. Class size seems to matter most for the youngest children (Montie, Xiang, and Schweinhart 2006). For example, a study in the United States found that compliance with state regulations on group size and adult-to-child ratio correlated more strongly with the overall quality of care for infant classes than for toddler and preschool classes (Phillips et al. 2000). Similarly, another study of infant and toddler classrooms in the United States found that a higher adult-to-child ratio was correlated with better overall quality of the program and that, in such situations, caregivers spent more time interacting with the children (NICHD 2002). In family-based care—ECD services provided to a group of young children age 0–6 by a trained caregiver in his or her home—some studies indicate that programs with lower proportions of infants and toddlers (in relation to the overall group size) tend to provide better quality of care (Phillipsen et al. 1997). The IEA Preprimary Project did not find associations between class size and children's cognitive development, and it concluded that the relationship between variables such as class size or adult-to-child ratio and child outcomes is specific to each country (Montie, Xiang, and Schweinhart 2006).

Ultimately, the ideal class size and adult-to-child ratio in a given setting depend on several factors, including (1) the age of the children, (2) whether ECD services are provided in mixed-age groups, and (3) the cultural context and behavioral expectations for children in a given age group. For example, the first phase of the IEA Preprimary Project studied various preprimary education settings in 15 countries[1] and found that the average group size for preschool classes for 4-year-olds ranged from 11 to 30 and tended to be larger in Asia and Africa.[2] Bolivia's PIDI (*Proyecto Integral de Desarrollo Infantil*) project provided in-home day care for up to 15 children per center, with an adult-to-child ratio of 1 to 5, and the project had a provision of additional staff in the centers with a higher proportion of infants. The Madrasa preschools in East Africa (Kenya, Uganda, and Zanzibar) enrolled 40 to 60 children per school on average, with a teacher-to-child ratio ranging from 12 to 17 children per teacher, depending on the country (Issa and Evans 2008).

Most developed countries have age-specific standards for class sizes and adult-to-child ratios. All of them specify smaller group sizes or higher adult-to-child ratios for younger children (OECD 2006). However, these regulations may be difficult to implement in low-income settings where the availability of trained teachers is often limited.

Overall quality assurance. Ensuring the quality of ECD services provided by both the public and private sectors can be a challenge, especially when limited resources are also spent to increase the supply (quantity) of such services. Generally speaking, quality assurance systems for ECD need to be designed within the context of prevailing legal frameworks and institutional and financing arrangements (see Notes 2.1 and 4.2), and there is no one-size fits all approach. Nevertheless, existing systems tend to rely on one of two approaches: (1) voluntary accreditation (for example, the NAEYC accreditation system in the United States)[3] or (2) a combination of public regulations, licensing, certification, and monitoring linked to public funding (for example, in New Zealand[4] and Australia[5]).

Value-Added of Including a Parenting Information Component

Many children who participate in center-based ECD services enroll at age 3 or older. Yet, as discussed in the introduction to this guide, the first two years of a child's life are particularly critical in terms of physical and overall development (that is, lack of proper nutrition and early stimulation during this period leads to stunting and reduced brain development).

Parents play the primary role in providing a strong foundation for their child's future development. Indeed, even after controlling for the quality and quantity of care children receive outside the home, family background variables, especially maternal education, continue to be among the strongest predictors of children's cognitive and socio-emotional development and of their academic performance in primary school (Montie, Xiang, and Schweinhart 2006; Downer and Pianta 2006). Almost all of the center-based ECD interventions that have been rigorously evaluated (that is, using random assignment or quasi-experimental design) and found effective in the United States included some parent education or home-visit component, along with the center-based care they provided (Karoly, Kilburn, and Canon 2005). And, in practice, several ECD programs in low- and middle-income countries have added a parenting component to their center-based interventions.[6]

Results of the NICHD study, which included observation of interactions between mothers and children, indicate that children who received more sensitive, stimulating, and supportive maternal care and engaged in

Box 3.1.4

Examples of Promising Center-Based Programs in Developing Countries

Argentina's public school system provides three-year preprimary education to 3- to 5-year-olds. The goals of the preprimary program are (1) to enhance educational achievements accomplished at home and develop new age-appropriate competencies, and (2) to provide early access to knowledge and skills that improve performance in the first years of primary education. The curriculum is focused on developing a range of skills including communications, personal autonomy and behavioral, social, logical and mathematical, and emotional. Children typically attend preprimary classes for three-and-a-half hours a day, five days a week, during the nine-month school year. The average class size is 25.

Following introduction of a new law in 1993 to expand compulsory education to include the last year of preprimary education, the government invested in construction of more than 3,500 new preprimary classes. As a result, the enrollment rate for preprimary education increased from 49 percent in 1991 to 64 percent in 2001. Analysis of nationally administered standardized test scores and teacher surveys estimated that one year of preprimary education increased the standardized third grade test scores in Spanish and mathematics by 8 percent of the mean or 23 percent of the standard deviation. It also found positive effects of preprimary education in areas of attention, effort, discipline, and class participation among third-graders (Berlinski, Galiani, and Gertler 2009).

Bolivia's PIDI (*Proyecto Integral de Desarrollo Infantil*) provides home-based, integrated services (full-time, family-based daycare, nutrition, and educational activities) to children aged 6 months to 6 years from poor families in urban areas. The goals of PIDI are to improve health and early cognitive/social development by providing children with better nutrition, adequate supervision, and stimulating environments. The children in the program are cared for in groups of 15 by two or three caregivers in the home of a local woman selected by the community. Under the program, the children receive two meals a day and a snack, about 70 percent of their caloric requirements, and participate in stimulating, structured, age-appropriate play and games. They also receive basic health services, including routine immunizations and growth monitoring. The project provides daycare providers with training in child development, as well as loans or grants to upgrade their homes. The results of the impact evaluation using quasi-experimental[7] data show the program's positive effects on bulk and

(continued)

Box 3.1.4 *(continued)*

fine motor skills, psychosocial skills, and language acquisition, particularly among children who participated in the program for at least seven months (Behrman, Cheng, and Todd 2004; Van der Gaag and Tan 1997).

India's Integrated Child Development Services (ICDS) program is one of the world's largest ECD programs. Each community under the program establishes an *anganwadi*, a community-wide daycare and maternal care center, staffed by a trained community worker and an assistant who is recruited from the community and who receives an honorarium from the government. The program serves children under the age of 6 and pregnant and lactating women with integrated services that include immunization, growth monitoring, supplementary nutrition, as well as preschool education for children aged 3 to 6. The goal of the preschool component is to provide a natural, joyful, and stimulating environment, with emphasis on necessary inputs for optimal growth and development. On average, 37 children are registered in each preschool program, where they engage in organized activities, such as singing and storytelling. They also receive supplemental nutrition during preschool sessions (Department of Woman and Child Development, n.d.).

Although this program has not yet been rigorously evaluated, a few nonexperimental studies show promising findings. For example, a survey of 16,000 children found that ICDS children were less likely to be severely malnourished and more likely to attend school than those who did not attend ICDS.[8] Another study in the three wealthier states found that ICDS children aged 3 to 5 years performed better on measures of child development (motor and cognitive skills) than the matched nonparticipants (Vazir and Kashinath 1999).

semi-structured play at home showed better academic, cognitive, and social outcomes. The effect size of parenting quality in this study and others (Pianta and Harbers 1996) is large because it includes both shared genes and environmental influence, and because the cumulative effect of good parenting (as opposed to a few years of experience in preschool or daycare) outweighs the impact of the care outside the home (NICHD 2002).

Indeed, parenting information sessions could be a powerful addition to center-based programs. For example, the Turkish Early Enrichment Project provided a two-year parenting information program to the mothers of three types of children: children who attended an educational preschool, those who attended a daycare where only custodial care was provided, and those who stayed at home. Although the children in educational preschools had a higher baseline IQ and significantly higher short-term gains in various cognitive and social-emotional measures than those in custodial daycare or home care, their earlier advantage in academic performance had dissipated by the fifth year of primary school. On the other hand, irrespective of attendance in center-based care, the effects of the parenting information program on children's school achievement and socio-emotional development and social adjustments were sustained throughout childhood (Kagitçibasi, Sunar, and Bekman 2001).

Therefore, it is strongly recommended that center-based ECD programs are complemented by quality parenting and home environments through either integrated or parallel initiatives (see Note 3.2 for more information on programs that focus on behavior change among parents and other caregivers).

Center-Based ECD Programs: Summary and Moving Forward

Key Implementation Considerations

- Start early, ideally with 2- or 3-year-olds, and ensure that the curriculum is age-appropriate.
- Target at-risk children, that is, children from low-income or otherwise disadvantaged backgrounds.
- Provide 15 hours or more of center-based ECD services per week, for at least 9 months a year.
- Recruit teachers who are committed to ECD and provide them with frequent training (both pre-service and in-service), acceptable financial rewards, and opportunities for professional growth and networking.
- Maintain group size and adult-to-child ratios appropriate to the children's ages and overall cultural context.
- Design a curriculum that focuses not only on developing cognitive and language skills, but also socio-emotional skills.
- Incorporate child-centered activities in which children freely choose from several structured play/learning corners and teachers adapt to the flow of children's choices.
- Train teachers to use a variety of learning materials.
- Complement center-based ECD activities with an outreach program that aims to provide parents with relevant information on how to nurture and promote their children's development, including through proper nutrition and early stimulation activities.

Areas for Further Research

- Relative effectiveness and cost-effectiveness of formal vs. community-based vs. family-based models in the developing world.
- Effects of various center-based models on children below the age of 2 years.
- Effects of center-based models on children's socio-emotional development in the developing world.
- Optimal intensity and duration of center-based programs for low-income children in developing countries.
- Relationship between program quality (including group size and adult-to-child ratio, staff qualifications, and curriculum) and children's outcomes in developing countries.
- Added value of parenting component in interventions that combine center-based services for children and parenting information.

Notes

1. The economies are Belgium (French-speaking areas); China; Finland; Greece; Hong Kong SAR, China; Indonesia; Ireland; Italy; Nigeria; Poland; Romania; Slovenia; Spain; Thailand; and the United States.

2. HighScope IEA Preprimary Project Web site; accessed May 10, 2010 from http://www.iea.nl/ppp.html.

3. Information on accreditation of programs for young children is provided by NAEYC at: http://www.naeyc.org/academy/.

4. Regulations, licensing criteria, and certification criteria are available from the Ministry of Education Web site: http://www.lead.ece.govt.nz/Management Information/RegulatoryFrameworkForECEServices/2008Regulatory Framework.aspx.

5. Australia recently introduced the National Quality Standard; details of the policy are available from the Department of Education, Employment and Workplace Relations Web site: http://www.deewr.gov.au/EarlyChildhood/ Policy_Agenda/Quality/Pages/home.aspx.

6. For an example of how this has been done in Chile, see Rolla et al. (2009).

7. Assignment to treatment was not random: control group children were selected among those with backgrounds similar to the program children using propensity score matching.

8. According to the NIPCCD national evaluation of ICDS, New Delhi 1992, as quoted in Engle et al. (2007).

Key Readings

Engle P.L., M. M. Black, J. R. Behrman, M. C. de Mello, P. J. Gertler, L. Kapiriri, R. Martorell, and M. E. Young, and the International Child Development Steering Group. 2007. "Strategies to Avoid the Loss of Developmental Potential in More Than 200 Million Children in the Developing World." *The Lancet* 369 (9557): 229–42.

Garcia, M., A. Pence, and J. Evans (eds.). 2008. *Africa's Future, Africa's Challenge: Early Childhood Care and Development in Sub-Saharan Africa.* Washington, DC: World Bank.

Karoly, L. A., M. R. Kilburn, and J. S. Canon. 2005. "Early Childhood Interventions: Proven Results, Future Promise." RAND Corporation, Santa Monica, CA.

Vegas, E., and L. Santibáñez. 2009. *The Promise of Early Childhood Development in Latin America and the Caribbean.* Washington, DC: World Bank.

References

Aboud, F. E. 2006. "Evaluation of an Early Childhood Preschool Program in Rural Bangladesh." *Early Childhood Research Quarterly* 21 (1): 46–60.

Anzalone, S., and A. Bosch. 2005. "Improving Educational Quality through Interactive Radio Instruction: A Toolkit for Policymakers and Planners." Africa Region Human Development Working Paper Series. World Bank, Washington, DC.

Armecin, G., J. R. Behrman, P. Duazo, S. Ghuman, S. Gultiano, E. M. King, and N. Lee. 2006. "Early Childhood Development Through an Integrated Program: Evidence from the Philippines." Policy Research Working Paper 3922. World Bank, Washington DC.

Behrman, J., Y. Cheng, and P. Todd. 2004. "Evaluating Pre-school Programs when Length of Exposure to the Program Varies: A Nonparametric Approach." *Review of Economics and Statistics* 86 (1): 108–32.

Berlinski, S., S. Galiani, and P. Gertler. 2009. "The Effect of Pre-primary Education on Primary School Performance." *Journal of Public Economics* 93 (1–2): 219–34.

Berlinski, S., S. Galiani, and M. Manacorda. 2008. "Giving Children a Better Start: Preschool Attendance and School-Age Profiles." *Journal of Public Economics* 92 (5-6): 1416–40.

Burchinal, M., C. Howes, and S. Kontos. 2002. "Structural Predictors of Child Care Quality in Child Care Homes." *Early Childhood Research Quarterly* 17 (1): 87–105.

Campbell, F. A., C. T. Ramey, E. P. Pungello, S. Miller-Johnson, and J. J. Sparling. 2002. Early childhood education: Young adult outcomes from the Abecedarian Project. *Applied Developmental Science.* 6(1), 42–57.

Department of Woman and Child Development. n.d. "Three Decades of ICDS—An Appraisal." Department of Woman and Child Development, Government of India. Accessed November 13, 2009 from http://www.wcd.nic.in/.

Doherty, G., B. Forer, D. Lero, H. Goelman, and A. LaGrange. 2006. "Predictors of Quality in Family Child Care." *Early Childhood Research Quarterly* 21 (3): 296–312.

Downer, J. T., and R. C. Pianta. 2006. "Academic and Cognitive Functioning in First Grade: Associations with Earlier Home and Child Care Predictors and with Concurrent Home and Classroom Experiences." *School Psychology Review* 35 (1): 11–30.

Early, D. M., K. L. Maxwell, M. Burchinal, S. Alva, R. H. Bender, D. Bryant, K. Cai, R. M. Clifford, C. Ebanks, J. A. Griffin, G. T. Henry, C. Howes, J. Iriondo-Perez, H. Jeon, A. J. Mashburn, E. Peisner-Feinberg, R. C. Pianta, N. Vandergrift, and N. Zill. 2007. "Teachers' Education, Classroom Quality, and Young Children's Academic Skills: Results from Seven Studies of Preschool Programs." *Child Development* 78 (2): 558–80.

Educational Development Center. 2009. "Radio Instruction to Strengthen Education in Zanzibar." Accessed June 7, 2010 from http://idd.edc.org/resources/publications.

Engle P.L., M. M. Black, J. R. Behrman, M. C. de Mello, P. J. Gertler, L. Kapiriri, R. Martorell, and M. E. Young, and the International Child Development Steering Group. 2007. "Strategies to Avoid the Loss of Developmental Potential in More Than 200 Million Children in the Developing World." *The Lancet* 369 (9557): 229–42.

Filmer, D., and N. Schady. 2009. "School Enrollment, Selection and Test Scores." Policy Research Working Paper 4998. World Bank, Washington, DC.

Flood, M., D. Weinstein, T. Halle, L. Martin, K. Tout, L. Wandner, J. Vick, J. Sherman, and E. Hair. 2007. "Quality in Early Childhood Care and Education Settings: A Compendium of Measures." Accessed November 4, 2009, from www.childtrends.org/Files//Child_Trends-2007_12_10_FR_Complete Compendium.pdf.

Garcia, M., A. Pence, and J. Evans (eds.). 2008. *Africa's Future, Africa's Challenge: Early Childhood Care and Development in Sub-Saharan Africa.* Washington, DC: World Bank.

Goelman, H., B. Forer, and P. Kershaw. 2006. "Toward a Predictive Model of Child Care Quality in Canada." *Early Childhood Research Quarterly* 21 (3): 280–329.

Grantham-McGregor, S., Y. Bun Cheung, S. Cueto, P. Glewwe, L. Richer, B. Trupp, and the International Child Development Steering Group. 2007. "Developmental Potential in the First 5 Years for Children in Developing Countries. *The Lancet* 369 (9555): 60–70.

Heckman, J. J. 2008. "Schools, Skills, and Synapses." *Economic Inquiry* 46 (3): 289–324.

HighScope. n.d.. "IEA Preprimary Project." Accessed May 10, 2010 from http://www.iea.nl/ppp.html.

Ho., J., and H. Thukral. 2009. "Tuning in to Student Success: Assessing the Impact of Interactive Radio Instruction for the Hardest-to-Reach." Educational Development Center, Washington, DC.

Hoot, J. L., R. S. Parmar, E. Hujala-Huttunen, Q. Cao, and A. M. Chacon. 1996. "Cross-National Perspectives on Developmentally Appropriate Practices for Early Childhood Programs." *Journal of Research in Childhood Education* 10 (2): 160–69.

Huffman, L. R. and P. W. Speer. 2000. "Academic Performance among At-Risk Children: The Role of Developmentally Appropriate Practices." *Early Childhood Research Quarterly* 15 (2): 167–84.

Issa, S. S., and J. L. Evans. 2008. "Going to Scale with Effective ECD Interventions: What Is Involved? A Costing Model of the Madrasa ECD Programme in East Africa. *Coordinator's Notebook* 30. Consultative Group on Early Childhood Care and Development, Toronto, Canada.

Kagitçibasi, C., D. Sunar, and S. Bekman. 2001. "Long-Term Effects of Early Intervention: Turkish Low-Income Mothers and Children." *Journal of Applied Developmental Psychology* 22 (4): 333–61.

Karoly, L. A., M. R. Kilburn, and J. S. Canon. 2005. "Early Childhood Interventions: Proven Results, Future Promise." RAND Corporation, Santa Monica, CA.

Loeb, S., M. Bridges, D. Bassok, B. Fuller, and R.W. Rumberger. 2007. "How Much Is Too Much? The Influence of Preschool Centres on Children's Social and Cognitive Development." *Economics of Education Review* 26 (1): 52–66.

Malmberg, L. E., P. Mwaura, and K. Sylva. Forthcoming. "Effects of a Preschool Intervention on Cognitive Development among East-African Preschool Children: A Flexibly Time-Coded Growth Model." *Early Childhood Research Quarterly*, in press.

Marcon, R. 2002. "Moving Up the Grades: Relationship between Preschool Model and Later School Success." *Early Childhood Research and Practice* 4 (1). Accessed Sept 22, 2009 from http://ecrp.uiuc.edu/v4n1/marcon.html.

McKay, H., L. Sinisterra, A. McKay, H. Gomez, and P. Lloreda. 1978. "Improving Cognitive Ability in Chronically Deprived Children. *Science* 200 (4339): 270–78.

McMullen, M., J. Elicker, J. Wang, Z. Erdiller, S. Lee, C. Lin, and P. Sun. 2005. "Comparing Beliefs about Appropriate Practice among Early Childhood Education and Care Professionals from the U.S., China, Taiwan, Korea and Turkey." *Early Childhood Research Quarterly* 20 (4): 451–64.

Montie, J. E., Z. Xiang, and L. J. Schweinhart. 2006. "Preschool Experience in 10 Countries: Cognitive and Language Performance at Age 7." *Early Childhood Research Quarterly* 21 (3): 313–31.

Mwaura, P., and B. T. Mohamed. 2008. "Madrasa Early Childhood Development Program: Making a Difference." In Africa's Future, Africa's Challenge: Early Childhood Care and Development in Sub-Saharan Africa." ed. M. Garcia, A. Pence, and J. Evans. Washington, DC: World Bank.

NAEYC. (National Association for the Education of Young Children). 2009. "Developmentally Appropriate Practice in Early Childhood Programs Serving Children from Birth through Age 8." Accessed September 22, 2009 from http://www.naeyc.org/DAP.

———. 2008. "Overview of the NAEYC Early Childhood Program Standards." Accessed May 10, 2010 from http://www.naeyc.org/files/academy/file/OverviewStandards.pdf.

———. 2009. "Position Statement on Developmentally Appropriate Practice." Accessed May 10, 2010 from http://www.naeyc.org/DAP.

———. n.d.. "Accreditation of Programs for Young Children." Accessed June 24, 2010 from http://www.naeyc.org/academy/.

———. n.d.. "The Core of DAP." Accessed May 10, 2010 from http://www.naeyc.org/dap/core.

NAEYC and NAECSSDE. (National Association for the Education of Young Children and National Association of Early Childhood Specialists in State

Departments of Education). 2003. "Early Childhood Curriculum, Assessment and Program Evaluation: Building an Effective, Accountable System in Programs for Children Birth through Age 8." Accessed September 22, 2009 from http://www.naeyc.org/DAP/resources.

NICHD (Early Child Care Research Network). 1996. "Characteristics of Infant Child Care: Factors Contributing to Positive Caregiving." *Early Childhood Research Quarterly* 11 (3): 269–306.

———. 2003. "Does Amount of Time Spent in Child Care Predict Socioemotional Adjustment During the Transition to Kindergarten?" *Child Development* 74 (4): 976–1005.

———. 2002. "Early Child Care and Children's Development Prior to School Entry: Results from the NICHD Study of Early Child Care." *American Educational Research Journal* 39 (1): 133–64.

OECD (Organisation for Economic Co-operation and Development). 2006. *Starting Strong II: Early Childhood Education and Care.* Paris: OECD Publications.

Paxson, C., and N. Schady. 2007. "Cognitive Development among Young Children in Ecuador: The Roles of Wealth, Health, and Parenting." *Journal of Human Resources* 42 (1): 49–84.

Peisner-Feinberg, E. S., M. R. Burchinal, R. M. Clifford, M. L. Culkin, C. Howes, S. L. Kagan, and N. Yazegian. 2001. "The Relation of Preschool Child-Care Quality to Children's Cognitive and Social Development Trajectories through Second Grade." *Child Development* 72 (5):1534–53.

Phillips, D., D. Mekos, S. Scarr, K. McCartney, and M. Abbott-Shim. 2000. "Within and Beyond the Classroom Door: Assessing Quality in Child Care Centers." *Early Childhood Research Quarterly* 15 (4): 475–96.

Phillipsen, L. C., M. R. Burchinal, C. Howes, and D. Cryer 1997. "The Prediction of Process Quality from Structural Features of Child Care." *Early Childhood Research Quarterly* 12 (3): 281–303.

Pianta, R. C., and K. L. Harbers. 1996. "Observing Mother and Child Behavior in a Problem-Solving Situation at School Entry: Relations with Academic Achievement." *Journal of School Psychology* 34 (3): 307–22.

Rolla, A., M. Rivadeneira, D. Leyva, I. Gamboa, M. C. Barata, C. Melo, G. Barra, M. C. Arbour, P. Fernández, and C. Snow. 2009. "Integrated Work with Families in Chile: Parents' Perceptions and Their Interactions with Their Children." Presented at the Annual Meeting of the American Educational Research Association, San Diego, April 13–17.

Schweinhart, L. J., J. Montie, Z. Xiang, W. S. Barnett, C. R. Belfield, and M. Nores. 2005. *Lifetime Effects: The High/Scope Perry Preschool Study through Age 40.* Ypsilanti, MI: High/Scope Educational Research Foundation.

Siraj-Blatchford, I., K. Sylva, B. Taggart, P. Sammons, E. Melhuish, and K. Elliot. 2003. "The Effective Provision of Pre-school Education (EPPE) Project:

Intensive Case Studies of Practice Across the Foundation Stage." Technical Paper 10, Institute of Education, University of London.

Sylva, K., E. C. Melhuish, P. Sammons, I. Siraj-Blatchford, and B. Taggart. 2003. "The Effective Provision of Pre-school Education (EPPE) Project: Findings from the Pre-school Period: Summary of Findings." Institute of Education, University of London. Accessed August 7, 2010 from http://eppe.ioe.ac.uk/eppe/eppepdfs/RB%20summary%20findings%20from%20Preschool.pdf.

Van der Gaag, J., and J.-P. Tan. 1997. "The Benefits of Early Child Development Programs: An Economic Analysis." Human Development Network, World Bank, Washington, DC.

Vazir, S., and K. Kashinath. 1999. "Influence of the ICDS on Psychosocial Development of Rural Children in Southern India." *Journal of the Indian Academy of Applied Psychology* 25 (2): 11–24.

Vegas, E., and L. Santibáñez. 2009. *The Promise of Early Childhood Development in Latin America and the Caribbean*. Washington, DC: World Bank.

Home-Based ECD Programs for Behavior Change in Health, Nutrition, and Parenting

A child's ability to think, form relationships, and live up to his or her full potential is directly related to the synergistic effect of good health, good nutrition, and appropriate stimulation and interaction with others during early childhood. Good health and nutrition are prerequisites for children to survive the first few years of life and to reach their full developmental potential. Maternal and child malnutrition not only increase the mortality and morbidity risks among young children but also jeopardize their long-term development prospects. Indeed, malnutrition can harm children's cognitive development by causing direct structural damage to the brain in utero and during the first five years of life and by impairing motor development and exploratory behavior among infants (Victora et al. 2008). Conversely, evidence shows that appropriate early childhood stimulation (that is, providing the young child with constant opportunities to interact with caring people and to learn about his or her environment from the earliest age) not only promotes socio-emotional and cognitive development, but also enhances the child's health and nutrition (Naudeau 2009).

ECD programs that address the health, nutrition, and early stimulation of young children are typically delivered directly to mothers (as prenatal care, safe delivery, and early postpartum care) and children (as postnatal care, preventive services, and treatment interventions), or indirectly through improving care practices and parenting skills via information and education programs. While these information and education services are sometimes provided outside the home (for example, in a community or health center), they are considered home-based ECD interventions because they focus on promoting behavior change within the home environment where the youngest children typically spend the most time. These interventions are vital to ensuring child survival and enhancing ECD outcomes, because many of the most effective strategies to promote the health, growth, and overall development of the youngest children are home-based, and the evidence points to a large contribution of parenting quality in children's overall development and school readiness.

This note reviews various aspects of household behaviors to ensure the health, growth, and overall development of children; different types of education programs for family behavior change; and potential bottlenecks in program implementation.

Care and Parenting Practices Support the Health, Growth, and Overall Development of Children

Early childhood is both the most vulnerable period of human life and the most opportune period for families to invest in their children through good care and parenting practices. While the terms "care" and "parenting" are used interchangeably in some cases, "care" is often used to describe parental behaviors to meet children's physical and emotional needs, while "parenting" typically refers to parental behaviors that shape children's cognitive and socio-emotional skills and behavior. Engle and Lhotska (1999) define care as "the behaviors and practices of caregivers (mothers, siblings, fathers and child-care providers) to provide the food, health care, stimulation and emotional support necessary for children's healthy growth and development." Parenting involves the home environment that parents provide their children, what they do with their children and in their presence, as well as the ways they communicate and interact with their children.

The life-cycle approach is a useful framework to evaluate the needs of the target population and to make decisions on priority actions. This framework helps one to understand the age-specific vulnerabilities and opportunities during one's life course, and helps to identify necessary inputs in target populations across the different sectors and areas of intervention (see table 3.2.1).

Age group	Vulnerabilities	Desirable parental/family behavior and home environment	Examples of relevant services for health, nutrition, and parent education
Conception to birth	• Exposure to maternal infections, nutritional deficiency resulting in mortality, premature birth, birth defects, and low birth weight	• Balanced diet during pregnancy • Avoidance of alcohol, tobacco, and other teratogens (drugs, pollution, etc.) during pregnancy • Sanitation and hygiene; safe food handling	• Prenatal checkups • Micronutrient supplementation • Immunization • Attended delivery
0–2 years	• Death or permanent disability due to illnesses and accidents • Inadequate nutrition and repeated episodes of illnesses leading to malnutrition and stunting • Stress caused by abuse and neglect could influence the child's later behavior, social-emotional development, and health • Inadequate sensory stimulation (vision, hearing, smell, and touch) could limit developing brain's capability to control language, intellectual, emotional, psychological, and physical responses • Lack of language exposure could result in language delays	• Good infant and child feeding practices (exclusive breastfeeding for 6 months, continued breastfeeding with timely introduction of adequate complementary food after 6 months) • Management of childhood illnesses including continued feeding during illness and increased feeding for catch-up growth after illness • Early stimulation and responsive and warm caregiving • Talking and playing with children • Sanitation and hygiene; safe food handling	• Postnatal care • Neonatal care • Well-baby visits • Growth monitoring and promotion • Micronutrient supplementation • Immunization • Deworming children older than 12 months • Screening for developmental delays and referral • Parenting education and support
3–6 years	• Inadequate early literacy and math skills could limit cognitive development and academic performance • Lack of social interactions with peers could influence children's social-emotional skills and school readiness	• Talking and playing with children • Reading to children and teaching basic concepts such as numbers, shapes, and colors • Taking children to play groups and creating opportunities for peer interaction • Sanitation and hygiene; safe food handling	• Parenting education and support • Immunization and micronutrient supplementation, following national schedule • Screening for developmental delays and referral • Deworming

Source: Authors.

Adequate Nutrition and Early Stimulation Are Essential
Elements of Care Practices That Support Child
Development in the Critical First Two Years after Birth
The first two years are the most critical period for child survival, health, growth, and brain development, and this period is when children are the most vulnerable to lack of adequate care. In particular, a large proportion of infant mortality occurs during the neonatal period, the first 28 days (Black, Morris, and Bryce 2003). Stunting typically occurs in the first 2 years of life and is difficult to reverse after 36 months. There is also growing epidemiological evidence that children who are undernourished for the first two years of life and quickly gain weight during later childhood may experience negative long-term consequences such as gaining fat mass instead of lean body mass, which is associated with a range of long-term health issues (Bhutta et al. 2008).

These first two years are also a crucial period for brain development: severe lack of stimulation and human interaction can have devastating effects on the biology and psychology of the young brain (Nelson 2007).

Infant feeding practices. Infant nutrition and feeding practices are some of the most important care practices for children in this age group. Promotion of exclusive breastfeeding has been identified as the single most promising intervention strategy for improving child survival in the first six months of life.

Exclusive breastfeeding for the first 6 months, followed by continued breastfeeding and the introduction of complementary food at around 6 months and up to 2 years, not only reduces the risk of infection and undernutrition, but also contributes to a child's long-term health and brain development through both rich nutritional inputs and positive socio-emotional interaction between mother and child (Nelson 2007).

Children are particularly at risk of stunting after the recommended period of exclusive breastfeeding (that is, after 6 months of age) as they often do not receive adequate nutrients in suboptimal complementary feeding (Black et al. 2008). There is evidence of the effectiveness of behavioral interventions in preventing stunting and improving developmental outcomes by encouraging mothers to introduce proper complementary foods for children ages 6 months and older. For example, analysis of the Ecuador Demographic and Maternal and Child Health Survey (ENDEMAIN) data suggests that counseling on the appropriate length of exclusive breastfeeding and the optimal timing for introducing complementary food led to less stunting (by about 10 percent) among beneficiaries (World Bank 2007).

A review of evaluations of complementary feeding interventions shows that education programs that highlighted feeding nutrient-rich, animal-source foods seem promising, along with other messages about timing, amounts, hygienic food preparation methods, and so on (Dewey and Abu-Afarwuah 2008). The two interventions with significant gains in both weight and height of children included key messages to regularly feed children locally available and affordable animal-source food; for example, in Peru, chicken liver, egg, or fish, and in China, egg. The review also recommends "a carefully selected, small number of specific key messages about practices that can be feasibly adopted by the target population" and integrating the messages about breastfeeding and hygiene. In Ecuador, a study indicated that families with similar levels of income and food expenditure could have either stunted or normal-size children, depending on the share of animal protein children consumed (which was relatively low for households at such high altitudes) (World Bank 2007).

Responsive (or active) feeding—coupling feeding with stimulation and emotional support—is crucial to meet the nutritional needs of young children. Responsive feeding refers to positive behaviors by caregivers during feeding (for example, encouraging children to eat, offering more servings, smiling and talking to children) and to feeding practices that are attuned to the child's psychomotor abilities (for example, ability to pick up food with fingers or to handle a spoon or a cup). Responsive feeding has been associated with increased food acceptance in Vietnam (Dearden et al. 2009) and greater self-feeding in Bangladesh (Aboud, Shafique, and Akhter 2009). While the effects of responsive feeding on growth and socio-emotional and cognitive development have not been extensively evaluated, this is a potential entry point for introducing early stimulation in existing interventions that focus primarily on nutrition.

Early stimulation. A stimulating and nurturing environment where a child can foster a strong relationship with at least one caregiver is another crucial element for ECD. For instance, a number of studies on orphaned and institutionalized children in Eastern Europe and Russia note that profound deprivation of sensory, cognitive, linguistic, and emotional stimulation in infancy results in a range of developmental problems, including serious medical problems, physical and brain growth deficiencies, cognitive problems, speech and language delays, and social and emotional problems (Nelson 2007). Studies of children from low- and middle-income families in developed countries also consistently show the large effect size of the mother-child relationship and family environment on a child's cognitive outcomes and social adjustment (NICHD 2002). An intervention that focuses on early stimulation can be designed for very young children. For example, an evaluation of a weekly home visitation program for the first 8 weeks of life in Jamaica showed that infants in the program exhibited better problem-solving skills at 7 months than those in the control group (see box 3.2.1). During the home visits, the parents were shown how to communicate with their children, respond to their cues, and show affection (Meeks-Gardner et al. 2003).

Home Environment and Early Learning Enhance School Readiness of Children over Age 2

After age 2, good nutrition continues to play an important role in a child's growth and development. Children from age 2 to school entry also make

---

Box 3.2.1

Early Stimulation Intervention Trials in Jamaica

Children with low birthweight often face multiple risk factors. Studies have identified low birthweight as a risk factor for children's cognitive development (Matte et al. 2001; Richards et al. 2001), particularly when combined with poverty and mothers' lower educational attainment.

A randomized controlled trial in Kingston, Jamaica, of a home-visit program focusing on early stimulation was designed for infants with low birthweight (Meeks-Gardner et al. 2003). One hundred forty infants with low birthweight were randomly assigned to control or treatment groups. The study also followed 94 matched infants with normal birthweight. The intervention aimed at increasing the amount of interaction between mothers and infants through weekly one-hour home visits by community health workers for the first eight weeks of the children's lives. The home visitors also used homemade toys and left them in the homes.

At age 7 months, infants were assessed on their problem-solving skills using the "support" and "cover" tests,[1] and their behavior during the test was rated. Test results showed that infants in the treatment group had significantly higher scores than those in the control group and were more cooperative during the session. Compared to the infants in the matched normal-weight group, infants in the low-birthweight treatment group had significantly lower scores only in the support test and had comparable scores in the cover test, as well as on various behavior ratings, whereas infants in the control group (also low birthweight) had poorer scores on both tests, vocalized less, and were less cooperative, happy, and active than the normal-weight infants.

great strides in cognitive development (understanding concepts), language acquisition (understanding and using larger vocabulary, longer and more complex sentences), and social-emotional development (enjoying playing with peers), as well as pre-academic skills (holding a pencil, recognizing letters and numbers). Parents can encourage this process by providing a stimulating environment.

Home environment should be conducive to learning. Parenting practices that support children's learning are particularly important for children in this 2–6 age group. For example, a large-scale longitudinal study in the United Kingdom found that home activities that clearly provide learning opportunities for children (for example, being read to, playing with numbers, painting and drawing, being taught letters and numbers) had significant positive effects on the level of literacy and numeracy at age 5 (Sylva et al. 2008). Similarly, studies in the United States showed a significant relationship between learning opportunities at home (for example, frequency of being read stories, visiting a library or museum, the number of books at home) and various measures of child development throughout early childhood, including early motor and social development, vocabulary, achievement scores at preschool, and fewer behavior problems (Bradley et al. 2001; National Institute of Child Health and Human Development Early Child Care Research Network 2005).

How parents communicate with children as well as what activities they participate in with their children have positive effects across socioeconomic status. For example, poverty during early childhood is consistently associated with less favorable child development outcomes in the United States, but this association seems to be partially mediated by good parenting practices, such as acting warm and responsive to children and providing literacy stimulation (Mistry et al. forthcoming; NICHD 2002). Home-based early learning may also be a viable program option in some countries. For example, the Turkish Early Enrichment Project trained mothers of children ages 3 to 5, to work with their children with educational materials for two years. Participating children not only exhibited significantly better cognitive skills and social adjustment at the end of the program than children in the control group, but seven years later, they were also more likely to stay in school and have better academic performance and family and social adjustments as teenagers (Kagitçibasi, Sunar, and Bekman 2001).

Opportunities to interact with peers. Studies of children in a preschool setting in developed countries suggest that the strongest cognitive benefits are enjoyed by those children who entered a center-based program between ages 2 and 3 (Loeb et al. 2007). This may indicate that children in this age group learn not only from family members, but also from peers. Although access to preschool may not be widely available in low-income settings, parents may create opportunities for children to play together or participate in group learning activities.

Sensitive and Positive Parenting Behaviors and Two Engaged Parents Increase the Chances of a Child's Academic Success and Support Development of Cognitive and Socio-Emotional Skills

A nurturing home environment is a key factor for development throughout childhood. Family norms and parenting practices vary greatly across cultures; even within the same country, children's experience at home varies widely, depending on their ethnic background, age, and poverty status (Bradley et al. 2001). Thus, it is difficult to determine a set of parental behaviors, or a particular parenting style, that best supports child development. However, studies in developed countries found associations between positive child cognitive and/or socio-emotional outcomes and some aspects of parenting, including warmth and responsiveness, providing age-appropriate learning opportunities (that is, play and experiences), and encouragement of autonomy, exploration, and learning. (Bradley 2002).

Adult-child relationship. Some aspects of the child-parent relationship, in particular, the mother's sensitivity and responsiveness, have been associated with children's cognitive and social-emotional development. For example, a more intimate and affectionate child-mother relationship during play was associated with superior social skills and executive functions (work habits and tolerance to frustration), smoother transition to formal schooling, and lack of behavioral problems reported by kindergarten teachers (Pianta, Nimetz, and Bennett 1997). Moreover, another study found that mothers who are warm and sensitive to children's feelings and who provide encouragement, support, and appropriate instructions when necessary, tend to have children with better academic achievement in grades 2–4 (Pianta and Harbers 1996).

Involvement of fathers. Some studies of parent-child relationships have suggested the importance of father-child relationships in the development of language and early academic skills (Pancsofar, Vernon-Feagans, and the Family Life Project investigators, forthcoming; Martin, Ryan, and Brooks-Gunn 2007). A study in the United States identified the influence of fathers' involvement in children's life on their satisfaction and psychological distress in early adulthood (Amato 1994). Another study in the United Kingdom found that fathers' and mothers' involvement in their children's lives at age 7, independently of each other, predicted children's school attainment at age 20 (Flouri and Buchanan 2004).

Evidence also shows that parent education programs can improve fathers' parenting skills. For example, an evaluation of the U.S. Early Head Start program shows that participating fathers were significantly less likely to report spanking their children than control group fathers. Early Head Start fathers were also observed to be less intrusive and more attentive during play, while participating children were better able to engage their fathers in various activities (Love et al. 2002). Accordingly, several programs are attempting to engage fathers in parenting programs in ways that meet the fathers' specific needs and expectations. In Jordan, for example, the Better Parenting Program started reaching out to fathers by training imams to teach them about positive child-rearing techniques in the mosque, right after the Friday prayers (UNICEF 2009).

Strategies for Family Behavior Change

Counseling and Curriculum-Based Learning Are the Most Common Strategies Used in Parent Education Programs That Aim to Change Family Behavior, and Many Programs Combine Both

Information on child care and parenting can be disseminated using multiple channels at various locations. Program delivery modes can range from regular community meetings in which all eligible parents meet and discuss their needs as a group; to family contacts in the context of health-related activities, such as hospitals at birth (baby-friendly hospitals), immunization days, or growth-monitoring follow-up; to home visits where professionals or paraprofessionals visit each individual household. The most common and promising approaches are reviewed below.

Counseling is one of the most frequently used strategies for parent education. It appears to be effective in promoting breastfeeding and improving complementary feeding (Bhutta et al. 2008; Penny et al. 2005). For example, a meta-analysis of breastfeeding interventions found that both individual and group counseling increased the odds of exclusive breastfeeding in the neonatal period and at 6 months of age (Bhutta et al. 2008). The Cochrane review of 34 breastfeeding studies also identified the effectiveness of face-to-face counseling (as opposed to via telephone) (Britton et al. 2007). The review also found breastfeeding counseling courses offered by the World Health Organization and United Nations Children's Fund (WHO/UNICEF) to be an effective tool for training professionals.

On the other hand, results are mixed for the counseling-based programs that focus on early stimulation/learning. While a number of rigorous studies of the programs that include counseling or case management components have shown positive outcomes for children and parents (Gomby, Culross, and Behman 1999), some evaluations found no significant program effects on child outcomes (Goodson et al. 2000); other studies found that these programs yielded positive outcomes in only two situations: when combined with center-based activities for children (Wasik et al. 1990; Love et al. 2005) or among particular subsets of beneficiaries or geographical locations.

The quality of program staff, that is, the counselors, home visitors, and parent educators, is one of the most important elements of any parent education program. It appears that both professional personnel and trained peer counselors are effective in promoting breastfeeding (Britton et al. 2007). However, when examining counseling-based programs with a focus on early stimulation/learning, there is only limited and mixed evidence as to the staff qualities required for programs to be effective. The results of a meta-analysis of home-visit programs across the United States indicate that professional home visits generated larger effect sizes on children's cognitive development, but that *paraprofessionals* were more effective in reducing child abuse (Sweet and Appelbaum 2004). In turn, the results of a randomized control trial of the Nurse-Family Partnership Program, delivered by different types of home-visit personnel (nurses and paraprofessionals) and targeting low-income families in the United States, indicated that the nurse-visiting model had stronger effects on a wider range of maternal behaviors, and the significant effects were sustained only among children who received professional home visits (Olds et al. 2002; 2004).

Curriculum-based learning has been frequently used in parenting programs to enhance children's cognitive and socio-emotional development and to address behavioral problems. These programs can be delivered in the context of home visits, classrooms, or workshops, or a combination of these. For example, the Turkish Early Enrichment Project mentioned earlier used biweekly home visits and biweekly group meetings on alternate weeks. Using a curriculum based on the HIPPY (Home Instruction Program for Preschool Youngsters) program, the mothers were supplied with learning materials weekly and instruction on how to use the materials with their children. The group meetings consisted of guided discussions on various topics such as nutrition, child health, play activities, discipline, and child-parent communication. Other promising curriculum-based models have been piloted in multiple locations, including Incredible Years (with evidence on child outcomes mostly from studies on high-risk children and children with behavior problems), DARE to be You, and Parents as Teachers; some of these programs have also been implemented in developing countries (see table 3.2.2) (Karoly, Kilburn, and Cannon 2005).

Curriculum-based learning opportunities have also been frequently offered to pregnant women in developed countries, particularly among high-risk populations, such as teenagers and low-socioeconomic-status women, with varying degrees of success, where the focus of the intervention is usually to improve pregnancy outcomes and care practices of infants, including initiation of breastfeeding (Clewell, Brooks-Gunn, and Benasich 1989).

Adapting parent education models in a low-income setting. Adapting these models in a low-income setting poses particular challenges, but these can be mediated by carefully assessing mothers' needs, beliefs, and practices on parenting as well as their preferred method of learning. (See Note 3.3). For example, in Thailand, anecdotal evidence notes that video clips are useful in working with illiterate parents in raising awareness of the child as an individual with early perceptual ability, of the importance of mother-child interaction and play, and of supplementary feeding (Kotchabhakdi 1988).

Combining counseling and curriculum-based learning. Most parent education programs with a focus on child cognitive, social-emotional, and behavioral outcomes involve both counseling, where parent educators/ home visitors address the individual needs of each family and child, and curriculum-based learning, through which parents receive key messages about child care and parenting. In such programs the focus on ECD is associated with family behavior change. For example, the Early Head Start Study in the United States found that more child-focused home

Table 3.2.2   Models of Parent Education

Model	Goals	Entry and exit years of age	Main contents, intensity, and duration
DARE to Be You	Improve parenting skills and child development in ways that contribute to children's resiliency to substance use later in life	Entry and exit: 2–5 years	Parent-child workshops with focus on parenting skills and developmentally appropriate children's activities. Duration: 15–18 hours of parent training workshops and simultaneous children's programs, preferably in a 10–12-week period
HIPPY (Home Instruction Program for Preschool Youngsters)	Help parents with limited education prepare their children for school entry	Entry: 3 to 4 years exit: 5 years	Parenting classes and books given to parents with activities to do with children. Home visits by paraprofessionals biweekly for 45–60 minutes; parents HIPPY materials with children at least 15 minutes daily; parents have group meetings biweekly. Duration: 30 weeks per year for two years
Incredible Years	Promote child social and emotional competence and address children's behavioral and emotional problems	Entry and exit: 2–8 years	Parenting classes and children's programs. Duration: parents 12–14 weeks, 2 hours per week; children 18–20 weeks, 2 hours per week.
Parents as Teachers	Empower parents to give their children a good start in life, prepare children for school entry, and prevent and reduce child abuse	Entry: prenatal or child less than 8 months old Exit: 3–6 years	Home visits by parent educators; group meetings with parents; developmental health, vision, and hearing screening; and building networks to meet family needs. Duration: weekly to monthly home visits/group meetings, 60 to 90 minutes.

Source: Karoly, Kilburn, and Cannon (2005).

visits (that is, visits focused on child development as opposed to addressing family issues) resulted in a greater impact on children's cognitive and language development (Raikes et al. 2006). An in-depth qualitative study of the Parents as Teachers project in the United States identified several challenges to implementing quality programs, including emphasis on parent-educators' role as providers of information and education in addition to providing social support and delivering explicit messages and demonstration about desired behaviors (Hebbeler and Gerlach-Downie 2002).

Community-Based Learning May Also Be Effective in Some Contexts

Community-based learning through women's groups may be a viable and sustainable option in countries with traditions of grassroots action. For instance, a trial of a community-based approach in Nepal facilitated discussions among women in the project villages on various childbirth and child care issues, then these groups formulated and implemented strategies to address the communal issues (such as community-generated funds for maternal or infant care, home visits by a group member to newly pregnant women). In the process, the program participants sought and received information regarding maternal and child health and care. The impact evaluation of the program found lower neonatal death rate, better uptake of prenatal and delivery services, and improved home care practices in the program communities than in the control communities (Manandhar et al. 2004). Similar results were found in the original trial of this approach in the Warmi Project in Bolivia (O'Rourke, Howard-Grabman, and Seoane 1998).

Implementation Challenges to Parent Education Programs

One of the most common problems in implementing parent education programs is a low level of parental participation. In some cases, information alone may not be sufficient to change family behaviors because parents are unable to turn their knowledge into action. In particular, parent education programs are unlikely to have meaningful impacts on child outcomes either when participation is suboptimal or when information alone is not enough.

When Participation Is Suboptimal

In designing a parent education program, it may be found that intended program frequency and duration does not reflect the actual amount of services provided to the family, as the level of parental engagement is often suboptimal. A review of various parent education program models in the United States found that one of the most common implementation problems is the high level of attrition and low level of parental engagement in the program. According to this study, up to 40 percent of families that were invited to enroll in a home-visit program declined to participate, and only 50 percent of those who enrolled actually completed the program (Gomby 2005).

It is also important to consider the quality of parental participation. A close examination by Raikes et al. (2006) of the Early Head Start Research and Evaluation Project Data in the United States showed that the level of parental engagement in the program (as measured by global ratings of engagement by staff and ratings of engagement during each home visit) correlated with better child cognitive and language development, more parental support for children's language acquisition and learning, and a better overall home environment. This program's low intake and high attrition rates, as well as low quality of participation, may be a result of the disconnection that sometimes occurs between program content and the expectations and needs of parents, or of more practical reasons such as inconvenient hours or location.

When Information Alone Is Not Enough

Under some circumstances, parents may not be able to change their parenting practices. In particular, information on nutrition may not be sufficient to prevent or reverse stunting among young children, and the types of most promising interventions may vary depending on the target population. A meta-analysis of 10 programs aimed at improving complementary feeding practices through parenting education found that only three of the programs conducted among food-secure populations (as measured by an average income of more than US$1 per person per day) produced positive effects on children's height-for-age (Bhutta et al. 2008). Further, a pooled analysis of seven evaluations of programs targeting food-insecure populations (as defined above) found that height-for-age increased only among those who were given food supplementation (in addition to or instead of parenting education) (Bhutta et al. 2008). Therefore, a combination of nutrition and health education with food supplementation or income generating programs, including Conditional Cash Transfers (see Note 3.4), may be most relevant for certain populations.

Similarly, information on early stimulation may not be sufficient to promote behavior change among parents if time is a constraint (that is, if they are so involved in income-generating activities that they cannot engage in stimulating activities with their children). Additional strategies, such as training additional family members to play and interact with young children, may be useful in such contexts.

ECD Programs for Behavior Change in Health, Nutrition, and Parenting: Summary and Moving Forward

Key Implementation Considerations
- Promote integrated approaches that include health, nutrition, and stimulation for early learning.
- Identify the key interventions by mapping out vulnerabilities and opportunities for the target population.
- Target children most vulnerable to specific risks (for example, children under 2 for malnutrition, girls, and the poor).
- Hire professional staff when available and provide appropriate training to enhance staff performance and overall quality of service.
- Convey messages in a hands-on and direct fashion during the sessions; demonstrate and explicitly encourage desirable behaviors.
- Make sure that parents (including fathers) participate in as many sessions as possible and are fully engaged during each session.

Areas for Further Research
- Practical ways in which stimulation and early learning messages can be added to health and nutrition services for young children and their families.
- Optimal mix of nutrition, health, and hygiene information with stimulation and early learning information and advice.
- Effectiveness of parent education programs alone (that is, not combined with center-based programs) on child cognitive, academic, and socio-emotional outcomes for various age groups.
- Long-term effects of parenting programs on children's developmental outcomes.
- The extent to which mother's education and other variables at the household and community levels play a mediating role on the impact of health and nutrition or parent education programs, particularly behavioral interventions.
- Optimal ways to scale up small successful programs.
- Interactions between the center-based component and parent education on parenting skills and care practice component of programs using a mixed approach that includes both center-based and parenting services.

- Relationship between program details of parent education programs (including curriculum, staff qualifications, intensity, duration, and location of service delivery) and children's outcomes in developing countries.
- Relative cost-effectiveness of different learning strategies.

Note

1. During the support test, observers tested whether infants could retrieve a toy placed on a cloth by pulling the cloth. In the cover test, infants were required to find a toy covered with a cloth by removing the cloth. The sessions were videotaped for analysis.

Key Readings

Bhutta, Z. A., T. Ahmed, R. E. Black, S. Cousens, K. Dewey, E. Giugliani, B. A. Haider, B. Kirkwood, S. S. Morris, H. P. Sachdev, and M. Shekar, and the Maternal and Child Undernutrition Study Group. 2008. "What Works? Interventions for Maternal and Child Undernutrition and Survival." *The Lancet* 371 (9610): 417–440.

Bradley, R. 2002. "Environment and Parenting." In *Handbook of Parenting*, 2nd ed., ed. M. Bornstein. Hillsdale, NJ: Lawrence Erlbaum.

Evans, J. 2006. "Parenting Programmes: an Important ECD Intervention Strategy." Paper commissioned for the *Education for All Global Monitoring Report 2007: Strong Foundations: Early Childhood Care And Education*. United Nations Educational, Scientific and Cultural Organization, Paris.

References

Aboud, F. E., S. Shafique, and S. Akhter. 2009. "A Responsive Feeding Intervention Increases Children's Self-Feeding and Maternal Responsiveness but Not Weight Gain." *Journal of Nutrition* 139 (9): 1738–43.

Amato, P. R. 1994. "Father-Offspring Relations, Mother-Child Relations, and Offspring Psychological Well-Being in Early Adulthood." *Journal of Marriage and the Family* 56 (4): 1031–42.

Bhutta, Z. A., T. Ahmed, R. E. Black, S. Cousens, K. Dewey, E. Giugliani, B. A. Haider, B. Kirkwood, S. S. Morris, H. P. Sachdev, and M. Shekar, and the Maternal and Child Undernutrition Study Group. 2008. "What Works? Interventions for Maternal and Child Undernutrition and Survival." *The Lancet* 371 (9610): 417–40.

Black, R. E., L. H. Allen, Z. Z. Bhutta, L. E. Caulfield, M. de Onis, M. Ezzati, C. Mathers, and J. Rivera. 2008. "Maternal and Child Undernutrition: Global and Regional Exposures and Health Consequences." *The Lancet* 371 (9376): 243–60.

Black, R. E., S. S. Morris, and J. Bryce. 2003. "Where and Why Are 10 Million Children Dying Every Year?" *The Lancet* 361 (9608): 2226–34.

Bradley, R. 2002. "Environment and Parenting." In *Handbook of Parenting*, 2nd ed., ed. M. Bornstein. Hillsdale, NJ: Lawrence Erlbaum.

Bradley, R. H., R. F. Corwyn, M. Burchinal, H. P. McAdoo, and C. G. Coll. 2001. "The Home Environments of Children in the United States Part II: Relations with Behavioral Development through Age Thirteen." *Child Development* 72 (6): 1868–86.

Britton, C., F. M. McCormick, M. J. Renfrew, A. Wade, and S. E. King. 2007. "Support for Breastfeeding Mothers." *Cochrane Database of Systematic Reviews* Issue 1. Art. No.: CD001141.

Clewell, B. C., J. Brooks-Gunn, and A. Benasich. 1989. "Evaluating Child-Related Outcomes of Teenage Parenting Programs." *Family Relations* 38 (2): 201–09.

Dearden, K. A., S. Hilton, M. E. Bentley, L. E. Caulfield, C. Wilde, P. B. Ha, and D. Marsh. 2009. "Caregiver Verbal Encouragement Increases Food Acceptance among Vietnamese Toddlers." *Journal of Nutrition* 139 (7): 1387–92.

Dewey, K. G., and S. Abu-Afarwuah. 2008. "Systematic Review of the Efficacy and Effectiveness of Complementary Feeding Interventions in Developing Countries." Web appendix in Bhutta et al. 2008.

Engle, P., and L. Lhotska. 1999. "The Role of Care in Programmatic Actions for Nutrition: Designing Programmes Involving Care." *Food and Nutrition Bulletin* 20 (1): 121–35.

Evans, J. 2006. "Parenting Programmes: an Important ECD Intervention Strategy." Paper commissioned for the *Education for All Global Monitoring Report 2007: Strong Foundations: Early Childhood Care And Education.* United Nations Educational, Scientific and Cultural Organization, Paris.

Flouri, E., and A. Buchanan. 2004. "Early Father's and Mother's Involvement and Child's Later Educational Outcomes." *British Journal of Educational Psychology* 74 (June): 141–53.

Gomby, D. 2005. "Home Visitation in 2005: Outcomes for Children and Parents." Committee for Economic Development: Invest in Kids Working Group. Washington, DC.

Gomby, D., P. Culross, and R. Behman. 1999. "Home Visiting: Recent Program Evaluations—Analysis and Recommendations." *The Future of Children* 9 (1) (Spring/Summer).

Goodson, B. D., J. I. Layzer, R. G. St.Pierre, L. S. Bernstein, and M. Lopez. 2000. "Effectiveness of a Comprehensive, Five-Year Family Support

Program For Low-income Children and Their Families: Findings from the Comprehensive Child Development Program." *Early Childhood Research Quarterly* 15 (1): 5–39.

Guldan, G. S., H. C. Fan, X. Ma, Z. Z. Ni, X. Xiang, M. Z. Tang. 2000. "Culturally Appropriate Nutrition Education Improves Infant Feeding and Growth in Rural Sichuan, China." *Journal of Nutrition* 130 (5): 1204–11.

Hebbeler, K. M., and S. G. Gerlach-Downie. 2002. "Inside the Black Box of Home Visiting: A Qualitative Analysis of Why Intended Outcomes Were Not Achieved." *Early Childhood Research Quarterly* 17 (1): 28–51.

Kagitçibasi, C., D. Sunar, and S. Bekman. 2001. "Long-Term Effects of Early Intervention: Turkish Low-Income Mothers and Children." *Journal of Applied Developmental Psychology* 22 (4): 333–61.

Karoly, L. A., M. R. Kilburn, and J. S. Canon. 2005. "Early Childhood Interventions: Proven Results, Future Promise." RAND Corporation, Santa Monica, CA.

Kotchabhakdi, N. 1988. "A Case Study: The Integration of Psychosocial Components of Early Childhood Development into a Nutrition Education Programme of Northeast Thailand." Paper prepared for the Third Inter-Agency Meeting of the Consultative Group on Early Childhood Care and Development, January 12–14, Washington, DC, as quoted in Evans, J. 2006.

Loeb, S., M. Bridges, D. Bassok, B. Fuller, and R. W. Rumberger. 2007. "How Much Is Too Much? The Influence of Preschool Centers on Children's Social and Cognitive Development." *Economics of Education Review* 26 (1): 52–66.

Love, J. M., E. E. Kisker, C. M. Ross, P. Z. Schochet, J. Brooks-Gunn, D. Paulsell, K. Boller, J. Constantine, C. Vogel, A. S. Fuligni, and C. Brady-Smith. 2002. *Making a Difference in the Lives of Infants and Toddlers and Their Families: The Impacts of Early Head Start.* Publication 2002-06-00. Washington, DC.: U.S. Department of Health and Human Services.

———. 2005. "The Effectiveness of Early Head Start for 3-Year-Old Children and Their Parents." *Developmental Psychology* 41 (6): 885–901.

Manandhar, D. S., D. Osrin, B. P. Shrestha, N. Mesko, J. Morrison, K. M. Tumbahangphe, S. Tamang, S. Thapa, D. Shrestha, B. Thapa, J. R. Shrestha, A. Wade, J. Borghi, H. Standing, M. Manandhar, A. M. del Costello and members of the MIRA Makwanpur trial team. 2004. "Effect of a Participatory Intervention with Women's Groups on Birth Outcomes in Nepal: Cluster-Randomised Controlled Trial." *The Lancet* 364 (9438): 970–79.

Martin, A., R. M. Ryan, and J. Brooks-Gunn. 2007. "The Joint Influence of Mother and Father Parenting on Child Cognitive Outcomes at Age 5." *Early Childhood Research Quarterly* 22 (4): 423–39.

Matte T. D., M. Bresnahan, M. D. Begg, and E. Susser. 2001. "Influence of Variation in Birth Weight Within Normal Range and Within Sibships on IQ at Age 7 Years: Cohort Study." *British Medical Journal* 323 (7308): 310–14.

Meeks-Gardner, J., S. P. Walker, C. A. Powell, and S. Grantham-McGregor. 2003. "A Randomized Controlled Trial of a Home-Visiting Intervention on Cognition and Behavior in Term Low Birth Weight Infants." *Journal of Pediatrics* 143 (5): 634–39.

Mistry, R. S., A. D. Benner, J. Biesanz, S. Clark, C. Howes. Forthcoming. "Family and Social Risk, and Parental Investments During the Early Childhood Years as Predictors of Low-Income Children's School Readiness Outcomes." *Early Childhood Research Quarterly.*

National Institute of Child Health and Human Development Early Child Care Research Network. 2005. "Duration and Developmental Timing of Poverty and Children's Cognitive and Social Development from Birth through Third Grade." *Child Development* 76 (4): 795–810.

Naudeau, S. 2009. "Supplementing Nutrition in the Early Years: The Role of Early Childhood Stimulation to Maximize Nutritional Inputs." *Child and Youth Development Notes* 3 (1) (March). World Bank, Washington, DC.

Nelson, C. 2007. "A Neurobiological Perspective on Early Human Deprivation." *Child Development Perspectives* 1 (1): 13–18.

NICHD (Early Child Care Research Network). 2002. "Early Child Care and Children's Development Prior to School Entry: Results from the NICHD Study of Early Child Care." *American Educational Research Journal* 39: 133–164.

Olds, D., H. Kitzman, R. Cole, J. Robinson, K. Sidora, D. W. Luckey, C. R. Henderson, Jr., C. Hanks, J. Bondy, and J. Holmberg. 2004. "Effects of Nurse Home-Visiting on Maternal Life Course and Child Development: Age 6 Follow-Up Results of a Randomized Trial." *Pediatrics* 114: 1550–59.

Olds, D. L., J. Robinson, R. O'Brien, D. W. Luckey, L. M. Pettitt, C. R. Henderson Jr., R. K. Ng, K. L. Sheff, J. Korfmacher, S. Hiatt, and A. Talmi. 2002. "Home Visiting by Paraprofessionals and by Nurses: A Randomized, Controlled Trial." *Pediatrics* 110 (3): 486–96.

O'Rourke, K., L. Howard-Grabman, and G. Seoane. 1998. "Impact of Community Organization of women on Perinatal Outcomes in Rural Bolivia." *Pan American Journal of Public Health* 3 (1): 9–14.

Pancsofar, N., L. Vernon-Feagans, and the Family Life Project investigators. Forthcoming. "Fathers' Early Contributions to Children's Language Development in Families from Low-Income Rural Communities." *Early Childhood Research Quarterly.*

Penny, M. E., H. M. Creed-Kanashiro, R. C. Robert, M. R. Narro, L. E. Caulfield, and R. E. Black. 2005. "Effectiveness of an Educational Intervention Delivered through the Health Services to Improve Nutrition in Young Children: A Cluster-randomised Controlled Trial." *The Lancet* 365 (9474): 1863–72.

Pianta, R. C., and K. L. Harbers. 1996. "Observing Mother and Child Behavior in a Problem-Solving Situation at School Entry: Relations with Academic Achievement." *Journal of School Psychology* 34 (3): 307–22.

Pianta, R. C., S. L. Nimetz, and E. Bennett. 1997. "Mother-Child Relationships, Teacher-Child Relationships, and School Outcomes in Preschool and Kindergarten." *Early Childhood Research Quarterly* 12 (3): 263–80.

Raikes, H., B. Green, J. Atwater, E. Kisker, J. Constantine, and R. Chazan-Cohen. 2006. "Involvement in Early Head Start Home Visiting Services: Demographic Predictors and Relations to Child and Parent Outcomes. *Early Childhood Research Quarterly* 21 (1): 2–24.

Richards, M., R. Hardy, D. Kuh, and M. E. Wadsworth. 2001. "Birth Weight and Cognitive Function in the British 1946 Birth Cohort: Longitudinal Population Based Study." *British Medical Journal* 322 (7280): 199–203.

Sweet, M. A., and M. I. Appelbaum. 2004. "Is Home Visiting an Effective Strategy? A Meta-analytic Review of Home Visiting Programs for Families with Young Children." *Child Development* 75 (5): 1435–56.

Sylva, K., E. C. Melhuish, P. Sammons, I. Siraj-Blatchford, and B. Taggart. 2008. "Effective Pre-school and Primary Education 3–11 Project: Final Report from the Primary Phase: Pre-school School and Family Influence on Children's Development during Key Stage 2 (Age 7–11)." Research Report DCSF-RR061, Institute of Education, University of London.

UNICEF (United Nations Children's Fund). 2009. "Jordan's Early Childhood Development Initiative: Making Jordan Fit for Children." UNICEF MENA-RO Learning Series, vol. 2.

Victora, C. G., L. Adair, C. Fall, P. C. Hallal, R. Martorell, L. Richter, and H. S. Sachdev 2008. "Maternal and Child Undernutrition: Consequences for Adult Health and Human Capital." *The Lancet* 371 (9609): 340–57.

Wasik, B. H., C. T. Ramey, D. M. Bryant, and J. J. Sparling. 1990. "A Longitudinal Study of Two Early Intervention Strategies: Project CARE." *Child Development* 61 (6): 1682–96.

World Bank. 2007. *Nutritional Failure in Ecuador: Causes, Consequences, and Solutions.* World Bank Country Study. Washington, DC: World Bank.

Communication and Media Campaigns Aimed at Families with Young Children

Many case studies and formative evaluations[1] suggest that communication campaigns on child health, nutrition, and overall development are effective. However, only one study was found that used an experimental design to assess the impact of communication campaigns on relevant outcomes at the child and family levels (Alderman 2007). Conducting rigorous impact evaluations of communication campaigns is challenging for two reasons. First, communication campaigns are usually accompanied by other interventions, such as the introduction of new goods or services (for example, distribution of insecticide-treated bed nets), or the strengthening of existing services, thus making it difficult to disentangle the impact of the campaign in and of itself. Second, it is difficult to construct counterfactuals[2] in the evaluation of communication campaigns that use mass media (TV, radio, newspapers) because the entire population is likely to be exposed or because exposure is linked to ownership of or access to the communication channels being used (that is, media ownership), which is not random.

Given the limited evidence on the impact of communication campaigns targeting families with young children, this note focuses on (1) discussing general concepts in communication campaigns and how they apply to ECD, (2) providing examples or case studies of how communication campaigns have been designed for families with young children and implemented in various countries, and (3) summarizing the lessons learned from these experiences.

General Principles of Planning Communication Campaigns

Multiple Types of Communication Campaigns Can Be Implemented to Promote ECD

Communication campaigns use the media and messaging means available, and an organized set of communication activities, to generate specific outcomes among a large number of individuals and in a specified period of time. They are an attempt to change people's behaviors to achieve desirable social outcomes (Coffman 2002). There are two main types of communication campaigns. A *downstream campaign* targets the specific populations whose behaviors and practices are considered suboptimal or even harmful. Communication campaigns for families with young children can include messages about children's health and overall development. They typically aim to improve the attitude, knowledge, and child-care practices of caregivers and other relevant community members in order to enhance the overall development of young children. In practice, these campaigns can be aimed at increasing the length of breastfeeding, improving the family's hygiene (safe cooking practices, hand washing, and so on), alerting parents to the importance and availability of specific services within their community (immunization, vitamin A supplementation, iodine-fortified salt), reducing the incidence of corporal punishment and child abuse and neglect, informing parents about the key developmental milestones that their children should be going through (for example, children should start walking between 8 and 18 months), and providing parents with quick tips for ensuring the safety and stimulating the overall development of their children (for example, "never leave an infant alone on an elevated surface," "talk/sing to your children").

The second type is an *upstream campaign*, usually targeting a larger audience and seeking to generate public and political support for policies and funding and to construct common interests and a community in favor of a specific cause (Coffman 2002). In practice, upstream communication campaigns include activities intended to influence the government and elected officials directly through advocacy or indirectly by changing public will to persuade them to take policy action.

Communication Campaigns for ECD Usually Target Multi-Level Audiences and Rely on Multiple Channels for Delivering Messages

Most communication campaigns are created for multi-level audiences and have comprehensive strategies to cover both upstream and downstream communications. They may use a range of communication media, depending on the technology available and specific living conditions/characteristics of the target populations. Media options include television (public service ads, soap operas, documentaries); radio (thematic programming and talk-shows); printed publications (newspapers, magazines, brochures/flyers, immunization cards); billboards, wall drawings, and posters; special events (fairs, plays, concerts, video shows); and information communication technology (Web-based, short message services [SMS] or cell-phone-based text messages).

Communication programs for ECD usually target parents, grandparents, and other caregivers, but some target children directly. For instance, educational programs like *Sesame Street* (Fisch and Truglio 2000), and messages directed at young children have been broadcast through TV programs, TV spots, cartoon strips, radio jingles and programs, and picture books in many developed countries and increasingly in developing countries. In some cases, communication strategies rely directly on children as agents of change in their community. In the child-to-child model, for instance, children convey messages to other children in the context of school-based activities or cultural events organized at the community level (for example, plays/songs promoting sanitation, health education). These communication strategies seem promising, and evidence is beginning to emerge among projects targeting adolescents (for example, see Sikkema et al. 2005); however, they have not been systematically evaluated for projects targeting young children.

The Private Sector Can Be a Powerful Partner in Promoting Behavioral Change; However, There Is Potential for Conflict of Interest

Communication campaigns by the private sector to sell specific products to families with young children are sometimes referred to as "social marketing." They use marketing concepts and techniques, including advertising and the distribution and selling of goods and services. In some cases, the respective interests of the corporate and social sectors in trying to change specific behaviors among the target population are aligned. For example, handwashing with soap is one of the most critical ways to reduce diarrheal diseases, and there are obvious benefits to both the public and private sectors in promoting this practice. Indeed, increased handwashing would allow the industry to expand its market and sell more soap, and the government can benefit from the private sector's expertise in designing effective communications campaigns to improve public health. Several countries have experimented with public-private partnerships in communication campaigns for families with young children (World Bank 2002). Although the effectiveness and efficiency of such partnerships compared to traditional government-run communication campaigns have not been documented, they appear promising.

In other cases, conflicts of interest can exist between the government and a specific industry when it comes to promoting the use of specific products for families with young children. A classic example is the controversy surrounding the marketing of infant formula in developing countries where access to clean water is limited and women's education level is low, which may expose children to the dangers of using unsafe water or watered-down formula. In 1981, the International Code of Marketing of Breast-milk Substitutes was adopted by the World Health Assembly, and 65 countries have since enacted legislation implementing all or many of its provisions. The code stipulates that there should be absolutely no promotion of breast-milk substitutes or bottles to the general public; that neither health facilities nor health professionals should have a role in promoting breast-milk substitutes; and that free samples should not be provided to pregnant women, new mothers, or families. This example demonstrates that both individual governments and the international community need to be particularly vigilant when specific industries engage in communication campaigns that go against the best interests of young children and to be proactive in taking action against such marketing.

Selected Case Studies

As previously discussed, the impact of communication campaigns is difficult to measure and is rarely evaluated. However, there have been several promising initiatives in communicating messages for promoting ECD. The following three examples illustrate how messages to improve family child-care practices can be developed and communicated through diffusion mechanisms typically available in developing countries.[3]

Uganda Nutrition and Early Child Development Project

Strategic communication was an important part of this 1995–2005 World Bank–financed Uganda Nutrition and Early Child Development Project (Cabañero-Verzosa 2005) whose main components were the following:

- An integrated child-care package that mobilized groups of parents and caregivers at the community level. Child fairs facilitated by "animateurs" (local workers) were held every six months and served as an important service delivery and communication channel through which communities could access integrated health and nutrition services for their children;
- Community support grants and innovation funds that provided financial assistance for child development projects with matching community contributions in cash or in kind; and
- A national support program for child development that focused on supporting national level activities, such as participatory monitoring and evaluation; a micronutrients program; ECD curriculum development; information, education and communication (IEC) and advocacy for children's rights.

These components were implemented using public communication as an integral strategy. Communication activities focused on (1) infant feeding, defined as breastfeeding up to 18 months and introduction of complementary feeding at 6 months and not earlier; (2) deworming of children; and (3) early childhood development for children under 6, with a focus on positive parental interactions and involvement of fathers in the care of children. The program design used a combination of media, and specific messages were crafted for different audiences. For example, new mothers, pregnant women, and grandmothers received messages, targeted specifically to each group, on the ideal timing for starting complementary feeding through counseling, radio, theater, print materials, and posters. Different messages and sometimes different media were used for different audiences such as mothers of children aged 6 month and above. Similarly, messages on the causes and consequences of worms and prevention strategies were communicated to children's parents and guardians through home visits, meetings, rural video showings, a child's day, and the radio. Communication activities were conducted in two phases: the first phase (sensitization) raised awareness of the long-term negative effects of stunting and malnutrition, while the second phase (motivation/adoption) promoted and encouraged the adoption of positive behaviors among families and communities.

Formative research preceding project implementation included (1) a rapid assessment to document local child-rearing practices and to explore the specific reasons for certain behaviors; (2) three qualitative studies on complementary feeding, treatment of worms, and communication research on early childhood development, intended to guide audience segmentation, behavior change objectives, message development, and monitoring and implementation at the project design stage; and (3) an assessment of the existing communication environment and its capacity.

The communication strategy targeted different audiences, and the team produced different communication materials accordingly. These included (1) building a network of parliamentarians supporting the cause, organizing study tours and field visits, and producing audio tapes to advocate and promote awareness among upstream stakeholders (for example, parliamentarians); and conducting a six-week distance learning course on strategic communication to sensitize the media; (2) brochures, inserts in newspapers, local workshops, radio spots, and education-entertainment road-shows to increase grassroots sensitization; and (3) posters, newspaper ads, brochures, radio spots, community events (that is, child's day and education-entertainment road-shows), and interpersonal services such as nutrition counseling and home visits, to promote behavioral change among parents of young children.

A series of impact evaluations found that this project resulted in higher weight-for-age among participating children under the age of 12 months, compared to children in the randomly selected control communities (Alderman 2007), and in improved breastfeeding and complementary feeding practices (Ibid.). In addition, mothers in the project area reported more positive attitudes and behavior to support children's development,[4] as well as a higher level of self-reported fathers' involvement (assessed through four questions to fathers about their activities with their children on the previous day, and two questions on child-rearing attitude), compared to the control group (Britto, Engle, and Alderman 2007).

Cambodia Mother and Child Health Campaign

The Cambodia Mother and Child Health (MCH) Campaign, implemented starting in 2003 by BBC World Service Trust, used multiple media channels to deliver a wide range of messages for families with young children, including information on child and maternal health, HIV/AIDS, and sexual and reproductive health. It consisted of the following interventions: 100 episodes of Cambodia's first television soap opera taking place in a hospital setting ("Taste of Life"); a photo strip magazine on the TV program; three types of radio phone-in programs targeting youth, men, and young couples and parents with small children; and 23 television spots and 22 radio spots. This multimedia campaign was aimed at improving sexual health, increasing condom use, and changing attitudes toward people living with HIV and AIDS. It also addressed the health of young children by encouraging breastfeeding, raising awareness of acute respiratory infections, and promoting handwashing to prevent diarrhea. The programs had wide coverage, with 83 percent of television viewers having watched "Taste of Life" at least once (BBC World Service Trust [c]), 27 percent of radio listeners having tuned in to the radio program for men, 32 percent to the program for youth (BBC World Service Trust [a]), and 19 percent to the program on maternal and child health (BBC World Service Trust [b]).

An evaluation reviewed the difference in knowledge and attitude between viewers/listeners of any TV or radio shows or advertisement spots and non-viewers/listeners, and found that viewers/listeners were better informed about childhood illnesses such as acute respiratory infection and treatment of diarrhea using oral rehydration salt (Power 2005).

First Steps Program in the Maldives

This year-long First Steps Program, initiated by UNICEF in 1999, involved capacity-building to foster print, radio, and television media for and about ECD. Through a baseline survey on knowledge, attitude, and practices and a series of workshops and field visits, the following 12 core messages were formulated:

(1) Babies communicate from the day they are born. They are born with the basic capacity to learn, see, touch, smell, and taste; (2) The most important thing a baby needs is love and attention from key people in her or his family; (3) It is important for both fathers and mothers to nurture their babies and to take part in care-giving practices. There are many simple ways a father who works away from home can show his child how much he loves her or him; (4) Everyday routines can be learning experiences for a child; (5) The habit of looking at and reading books can be beneficial even to the youngest child; (6) Self-esteem usually refers to a child or adult's sense of value and worth as a human being. The best way to help build the self-esteem of children is to make them feel loved, challenged and competent; (7) Both girls and boys are born with the same potential to develop skills in language, music, arts, sports,

science, etc. Girls and boys deserve equal importance, encouragement, and opportunity; (8) Children learn best through play. Forcing children to learn reading or writing before they enter first grade can impede their natural love of learning; (9) Disabled infants and children can learn and be a joy to a family. Children and adults who are disabled have a right to be included in every aspect of family and community life; (10) Older sisters and brothers can help their siblings in many positive ways; (11) Most injuries to babies and young children are preventable; and (12) Children learn best through modeling (UNICEF 2006; the Communication Initiative Network n.d.).

A multimedia campaign included weekly radio and television spots on issues related to early childhood care and development. The program helped train media staff and local educators, including preschool teachers, to communicate these messages to parents (UNICEF 2006; Communication Initiative Network n.d.). No published evaluation is available, but anecdotal evidence points to improvements in child-care practices, in particular increased reading to young children and improved attitudes toward fathers' involvement in child-rearing.

Lessons Learned

As mentioned, evidence-based knowledge is lacking for communication campaigns targeting families with young children. However, keeping in mind the goal of communication strategies, which is behavioral change, several lessons can be drawn from past and ongoing projects.

Develop Messages and Communication Strategy through a Participatory Process to Ensure Local Relevance

Formative research was an integral part of the preparation phase for all the projects described here. Such studies, often conducted through a participatory process, inform the project team about the local cultural, social, and religious contexts, and about parents' beliefs, knowledge, and child-rearing practices. They also help identify the level of linguistic and visual literacy of the target populations, as well as the information channels they are most likely to use—including mass media and social networks. All of this information is key for developing relevant and realistic messages and deciding how the information campaign should be conducted. In addition, draft communication materials should be field-tested among a sample of the targeted population. Feedback from participants can help the project team assess the extent to which draft materials are well received and make adjustments in accordance with their comments.

Reinforce Messages through Interpersonal Communications

Both the Uganda Nutrition and Early Child Development Project and the First Steps Program in the Maldives used a combination of mass media and personal contacts as communication channels. Although the value-added of personal contacts and built-in feedback mechanisms has not been evaluated in either of these two projects, interpersonal communications through child fairs seemed to be more cost-effective than the production and distribution of printed materials and handbooks in Uganda (Cabañero-Verzosa 2005).

Establish Strong Links to Project Outcomes, Operational Activities, and Communication Activities

To demonstrate the project's effectiveness, the project outcomes should be explicit and linked to the messages conveyed by the campaign. The project should be sequenced so that both communication and operational activities address audience-specific needs in a timely manner. For example, in promoting iodized salt, families not only need information about the benefits of consuming iodine but also access to the iodized salt itself. Therefore, operational activities aimed at establishing distribution networks need to precede, or be simultaneous with, the rollout of communication activities.

Engage All Relevant Stakeholders

The three projects discussed earlier successfully used upstream communication to gain support from multiple sectors of the government (such as ministries of health, education, information) as well as from members of the legislative branch (parliamentarians) and the media (journalists and radio broadcasters). This upstream communication took the form of advocacy at the central and local levels from the earliest stages of project design and implementation.

Choose Communication Channels Most Relevant (That Is, Accessible and Popular) to Targeted Populations

Choosing the right communication media and assessing the capacity of existing local channels to produce and distribute communication materials for families with young children are critical to ensuring proper project design, budget, and schedule. In some cases, the media may have experience in communication campaigns, but they may not know much about child development. In other circumstances, local expertise in the production of the communication materials themselves may be very limited. For example, none of the local teams hired to produce the TV soap opera "Taste of

Life" in the Cambodia MCH Campaign had significant television experience before the project started, so the BBC trained the entire team of writers, producers, crew, and cast (BBC World Service Trust n.d.). In the Uganda Nutrition and Early Child Development Project, the government subsidized the media/sponsor of a radio talk show on health issues so that understaffed and underpaid media could spend time researching the issues.

Communication/Media Campaigns for Families with Young Children: Summary and Moving Forward

Key Implementation Considerations

- Study and know the audience, including their beliefs and child-rearing practices, as well as their preferred communication media.
- Craft messages that are locally relevant as well as scientifically sound, and use materials that are tested by the targeted audience.
- Use communication media that are accessible and popular.
- Consider reinforcing mass media messages through interpersonal communication.
- Involve a wide range of stakeholders; include upstream communication as part of the overall strategy.
- Assess the capacity of the medium itself and provide support as relevant.
- Consider the possibility and advantages and disadvantages of involving the private sector in communication campaigns.

Areas for Further Research

- Impact of communication campaigns on parental/child-rearing behavior
- Relative impact of communication campaigns that use different channels
- Cost-benefit analysis of communication campaigns
- Value-added of communication campaigns when implemented in addition to other (more direct) ECD services
- Typology of messages/expected behavioral changes/audiences
- Impact of network-based diffusion models, such as parent-to-parent, child-to-child, and child-to-family communication strategies

Notes

1. Formative (or process) evaluations aim to strengthen or improve the program being evaluated, as opposed to summative evaluations, which evaluate the effects of programs.
2. That is, a group of people who are as similar as possible in both observable and unobservable dimensions to those who participated in the intervention.

3. This selection of case studies is by no means exhaustive. Communication-based projects included here were selected because they focus on several aspects of early childhood development in low-income settings and use multiple channels of communication.

4. Radio spots were broadcast in the control communities as well.

Key Readings

Britto, P. R., P. Engle, and H. Alderman. 2007. "Early Intervention and Caregiving: Evidence from Uganda Nutrition and Early Childhood Development Program." *Child Health and Development* 1 (2): 112–33.

Cabañero-Verzosa, C. 2005. "Counting on Communication: The Uganda Nutrition and Early Childhood Development Project." World Bank, Washington, DC.

UNICEF (United Nations Children's Fund). 2006. "Programme Communication for Early Child Development." UNICEF, New York.

References

Alderman, H. 2007. "Improving Nutrition through Community Growth Promotion: Longitudinal Study of the Nutrition and Early Child Development Program in Uganda." *World Development* 35 (8): 1376–89.

BBC World Service Trust (a). n.d. "Encouraging Cambodians to Talk about Taboo Subjects." http://www.bbc.co.uk/worldservice/trust/whatwedo/where/asia/cambodia/2008/03/080225_cambodia_hivaids_mch_project_real_men.shtml.

BBC World Service Trust (b). n.d. "First Steps: Improving Child and Maternal Health." Accessed December 9, 2008 from http://www.bbc.co.uk/worldservice/trust/whatwedo/where/asia/cambodia/2008/03/080225_cambodia_hivaids_mch_project_first_steps.shtml.

BBC World Service Trust (c). n.d. "Hospital Soap Changes Attitudes and Behaviour around HIV and AIDS." Accessed December 9, 2008 from http://www.bbc.co.uk/worldservice/trust/whatwedo/where/asia/cambodia/2008/03/080225_cambodia_hivaids_mch_project_taste_of_life.shtml.

Britto, P. R., P. Engle, and H. Alderman. 2007. "Early Intervention and Caregiving: Evidence from Uganda Nutrition and Early Childhood Development Program." *Child Health and Development* 1 (2): 112–33.

Cabañero-Verzosa, C. 2005. "Counting on Communication: The Uganda Nutrition and Early Childhood Development Project." World Bank, Washington, DC.

Coffman, J. 2002. "Public Communication Campaign Evaluation: An Environmental Scan of Challenges, Criticisms, Practice, and Opportunities." Harvard Family Research Project, Cambridge, MA.

Communication Initiative Network. n.d. "First Steps—Maldives." Accessed January 22, 2009 from http://www.comminit.com/en/node/119005/303.

Fisch, S. M., and R. T. Truglio, eds. 2000. *G is for Growing: Thirty Years of Research on Children and* Sesame Street. Mahwah, NJ: Lawrence Erlbaum Associates.

Power, G. 2005. "Preliminary Findings from Cambodia Maternal and Child Health Campaign." Presentation at a meeting of The Communication Initiative Partners, Research and Learning Group at the BBC World Service Trust. Dec. 1. Accessed December 9, 2008 from http://www.comminit.com/pdf/Thursday_BBC_MCHFinal.pdf.

Sikkema, K. J., E. S. Anderson, J. A. Kelly, R. A. Winett, C. Gore-Felton, R. A. Roffman, T. G. Heckman, K. Graves, R. G. Hoffmann, and M. J. Brondino. 2005. "Outcomes of a Randomized, Controlled Community-Level HIV Prevention Intervention for Adolescents in Low-Income Housing Developments." *AIDS* 19 (14): 1509–16.

UNICEF (United Nations Children's Fund). 2006. "Programme Communication for Early Child Development." UNICEF, New York.

World Bank. 2002. "Lessons from Building Public-Private Partnerships for Washing Hands with Soap." Water and Sanitation Program, World Bank, Washington, DC.

Conditional Cash Transfers (CCTs) for Families with Young Children

Conditional Cash Transfer (CCT) programs provide money to target households, generally poor families, on the condition that they undertake specific actions, such as sending children to school or making use of preventive health care services. The objective is to foster the human capital accumulation of children as a means to break the intergenerational cycle of poverty. Since Brazil and Mexico started their first CCT programs in the second half of 1990s (*Bolsa Escuela* in 1995 and PROGRESA in 1997, respectively), CCT programs have rapidly been introduced in virtually all countries in Latin America, Africa (South Africa and Malawi), East Asia (Indonesia), South Asia (Bangladesh), the Middle East and North Africa (Republic of Yemen and Morocco), and Europe and Central Asia (Turkey and the former Yugoslav Republic of Macedonia).

While most CCTs targeting families with young children ages 0–6 have focused on improving health outcomes, this note explains that CCTs can be relevant for promoting a broader range of outcomes in this population. The note reviews the thin but promising evidence base available and cautiously indicates that CCTs for families with young children have the potential not only to promote developmental outcomes in young children (including cognitive development) but also to maximize the effect of CCTs targeting older children. Planning for the future, the note identifies a number of specific areas that would benefit from further experimentation and evaluation.

How CCTs Are Relevant for Promoting ECD

In many developing countries, there are steep socioeconomic "gradients" in cognitive and overall development; that is, children from poorer households show significantly worse outcomes early on. In Ecuador, for example, differences in age-adjusted vocabulary among 3-year-old children are generally small. By age 6, however, children in less wealthy households and children born to mothers with low education levels have fallen far behind their counterparts in wealthier or more educated households (see Notes 1.1 and 1.3) (Paxson and Schady 2007). Similar trends are emerging from several World-Bank-supported studies that have measured the same child development outcomes in countries such as Cambodia, Mozambique, and Nicaragua.[1]

These negative developmental trends among poor children early in life are likely to occur for several reasons. First, research increasingly demonstrates that children's development and abilities are as strongly affected by the overall quality of their environment and the amount of nutrition and early stimulation[2] they receive as they are affected by genetics, with genetic influences accounting for only about half of the variance in cognitive abilities, for example (Fernald et al. 2009).[3]

Second, environmental risk factors,[4] such as malnutrition, poor health, unstimulating home environments, and child maltreatment, tend to be more concentrated among poor households with less educated parents (Irwin, Siddiqi, and Hertzman 2007), partly because of demand-side constraints (for example, lack of financial resources to purchase nutritious food for young children; information failures such as lack of parental knowledge about the critical importance of supporting children's growth and development from conception onwards, and so on) and partly because of supply-side constraints (for example, unequal distribution and quality of resources and services for young children).

Given the constraints of this environment, despite the fact that CCT programs are not ECD interventions per se, CCTs typically do two things that can improve ECD outcomes for poor children:

1. **They transfer cash to poor families—in some cases a great deal of cash.** If the cash helps alleviate some of the risks identified above (for example, if parents use the cash to purchase nutritious foods and

learning materials and toys for young children, or if parents spend increased amounts of quality time interacting with their children), then cash transfers can be expected to yield positive developmental outcomes in the children.

2. **The cash transfer is usually conditional upon participation in specific services.** So far, most CCTs targeting families with young children have focused on health conditionalities (for example, attending regular health checkups and growth-monitoring sessions), but in theory cash transfers could also be conditional upon participation in a wider range of services (to the extent that such services are available), including center-based ECD programs (see Note 3.1) and programs that promote behavior change in health, nutrition, and parenting (see Note 3.2). As documented in those two notes, participation in such services often leads to improved developmental outcomes among participating children when the quality, intensity, and targeting strategies are adequate.

Some CCT programs have attempted to expose parents to new child-rearing concepts and practices, particularly in the areas of health and nutrition, by conditioning transfers on participation in information sessions, referred to as *pláticas* in some Latin American countries. In Mexico, for example, evidence suggests that these information sessions have contributed to improved health outcomes through better diets among the children or participating parents (see Hoddinott and Skoufias 2004) and through increased knowledge on a range of health issues (Duarte Gomez 2004). However, much remains to be learned about the optimal content, including how to discuss not only health and nutrition but also early stimulation, and delivery mechanisms for these information sessions.

Evidence on CCT Effects on ECD Outcomes Is Thin but Promising

Generally speaking, CCT programs focused on older children (that is, primary school age and above) have typically had an impact on the utilization of services in both education and health. However, the evidence on the effects of these programs on final learning and health outcomes is more disappointing, which might indicate that the quality of these services may be suboptimal and/or that early developmental delays among children are difficult to reverse later on. Fiszbein and Schady (2009) provide a comprehensive review of CCT program outcomes, which is summarized here.

To some extent, the evidence documenting the effects of CCTs on health among younger children, from birth to age 6, follows a similar pattern. Several evaluations found that CCT programs led to increased use of health services among families with young children. For instance, young children participated more frequently in growth monitoring visits in Colombia and Nicaragua, and attended health checkups more often in Honduras, Jamaica, and Mexico. However, health and nutritional status typically did not improve among these children. If they did, short-term gains were no longer apparent in the medium run.

The available evidence on the impact of CCT programs on immunization coverage among infants and toddlers is also mixed. Significant impacts were found in several countries (for example, full immunization in Turkey, increased DTP coverage among children less than 24 months of age in Colombia and among children less than 3 years in Honduras). In turn, CCT programs did not lead to the expected impact in other settings (for example, DTP coverage for 24- to 48-month-olds did not increase significantly in Colombia; tetanus and measles coverage for children below age 3 did not increase significantly in Honduras, TB vaccination for children below the age of 12 months, and measles vaccinations for 12- to 23-month-old children did not increase significantly in Mexico).

At the same time, a new body of evidence has come to light—mainly from studies in Ecuador, Mexico, and Nicaragua—that indicates that CCTs can have a positive impact on ECD outcomes (other than health) among young children, including effects on their cognitive, linguistic, fine-motor, and socio-emotional development. For example, children ages 0–7 whose families were randomly assigned to participate in Nicaragua's *Atención a Crisis* program for a period of 9 months showed better socio-emotional and language development than children in the control group.[5] There were no program effects on motor development or on the incidence of behavior problems (Macours, Schady, and Vakis 2008). The study also measured intermediate outcomes, including changes in parental behavior and attitude, which can be viewed as positive inputs toward healthy child development, and found that participating children received more nutrient-rich food, more early stimulation at home, and more preventative health care. These results are particularly interesting, given that this CCT program was implemented without the condition that health care be obtained for children in this age group (due to administrative challenges). Macours, Schady, and Vakis (2008) explain that these changes in intermediate outcomes are larger than what can be accounted for by the increase in income among households receiving the CCTs. They also speculate that the information and "social marketing" campaign launched by the program (on the importance of investing in ECD) may have been important. (See Note 3.3 for more information on the role that communication/media campaigns can play in promoting ECD outcomes.)

An evaluation of the BDH (*Bono de Desarrollo Humano*) program (Paxson and Schady 2010) in Ecuador, which was also implemented without the health care condition for young children, did not find any treatment effects for the whole sample, but did find modest effects on fine motor skills and long-term memory among participants in the poorest quartile of the sample (that is, children age 3–7 years who had participated in the program for an average of 17 months). The authors also report positive program effects on health care use (for example, on the likelihood of having received deworming medication), child and maternal hemoglobin status, and the quality of the parenting environment at home. Table 3.4.1 summarizes the findings of the Nicaragua and Ecuador studies.

Finally, a nonexperimental evaluation of Mexico's *Oportunidades* program compared a range of child developmental outcome indicators among various groups of beneficiaries who had received different amounts of cash transfers. The authors found that doubling the size of the transfer resulted in better gross motor skills, long- and short-term memory, visual integration, and language development among children ages 36–68 months (Fernald, Gertler, and Neufeld 2006).

Taken together, these three studies provide promising evidence that CCT programs can help improve ECD outcomes. Further, the results suggest that CCT programs targeting families with young children are also likely to maximize the effects of CCT programs targeting these same children as they get older (that is, when they enter primary and secondary school). Indeed, as mentioned earlier, CCTs that have focused on school-age children have usually resulted in increased school attendance but have not led to improved learning outcomes (for example, in Mexico [Behrman, Parker, and Todd 2005] and Cambodia [Filmer and Schady 2009]). These disappointing results are most likely the result of a combination of factors, including the suboptimal quality of education services these children often receive and the fact that early developmental delays are difficult to reverse later in life (see Note 1.3). Therefore, to the extent that CCTs can prevent or reverse early developmental delays, as documented in the three studies discussed here, they are also likely to foster improved learning and behavioral outcomes among the same children as they get older.

Table 3.4.1   Effect of CCTs on ECD: Data from Ecuador (2004–05) and Nicaragua (2005–06)

Indicator	Ecuador (poorest 40%)	Ecuador (poorest 10%)	Nicaragua
Language (TVIP)	0.005	0.137	0.228***
	(0.098)	(0.129)	(0.084)
Language (Denver)	n.a.	n.a.	0.189***
			(0.065)
Short-term memory	−0.019	0.079	0.070
	(0.100)	(0.143)	(0.058)
Long-term memory	0.141	0.173*	n.a.
	(0.092)	(0.097)	
Visual integration-executive function	0.054	0.256	n.a.
	(0.095)	(0.160)	
Behavioral Problems Index	0.066	0.240	0.037
	(0.091)	(0.147)	(0.064)
Personal-behavioral skills	n.a.	n.a.	0.135**
			(0.066)
Average effect on cognitive outcomes	**0.049**	**0.177***	**0.132***
	(0.066)	**(0.094)**	**(0.040)**

Source: Fiszbein and Schady (2009), who based their calculations on Paxson and Schady (2007) for Ecuador and Macours, Schady, and Vakis (2008) for Nicaragua.
Notes: n.a. = not available; TVIP = Test de Vocabulario en Imágenes Peabody.
Coefficients on the CCT treatment variable and standard errors are in parentheses. Separate regressions were conducted for each of the dependent variables presented in the left column (that is, TVIP, Denver, etc.). All regressions adjust for clustering at the village level. Average effects are calculated by seemingly unrelated regressions. All measures have been standardized so they have mean 0 and a standard deviation of 1. The coefficients therefore can be interpreted as changes in standard deviation units. All regressions include single month-of-age dummy variables and a dummy variable for gender. In both countries, the sample is limited to children aged 36–83 months, for comparability.
* significant at the 10 percent level.
** significant at the 5 percent level.
*** significant at the 1 percent level.

Finally, recent evidence shows that CCTs targeting families with young children can also have a positive effect on school participation among older siblings, particularly for girls. For example, a randomized study looking at the impact of the Mexican CCT program *Oportunidades* on the time that mothers and older sisters spend taking care of children under age 3 found that adolescent girls in treatment households devoted more time to schooling and less time taking care of their younger siblings (Dubois and Rubio-Codina 2010). The study also found that total household time allocated to child care increased, thus indicating that young children in treatment households received more and potentially better (mother provided rather than sibling provided) child care.

Knowledge Gaps and Policy Options for Moving Forward

Although emerging evidence suggests that CCTs have the potential to promote developmental outcomes among young children, knowledge gaps remain in relation to the following questions:

1. **What aspect(s) of the CCT package (that is, the cash, the parenting information received, or a combination of the two) are most critical in explaining positive outcomes?** The Nicaragua study discussed above (Macours, Schady, and Vakis 2008) makes some progress in this area, but further insights would be useful.

2. **Which target groups are likely to benefit most?** Generally speaking, interventions aimed at preventing or reversing stunting are likely to be most effective between conception and the age of 2 years (see Notes 1.2 and 3.2), while interventions aimed at improving the cognitive and socio-emotional development of children can benefit children in the upper range of early childhood as well (see Notes 1.3 and 3.1). Current ECD studies, as documented throughout this guide, also indicate that the largest effects can be expected among the subgroups with the lowest baseline levels, such as the poorest children and girls. However, more research is needed to ascertain whether the effects of CCTs follow similar patterns.

3. **What transfer size is most appropriate for promoting significant ECD outcomes?** Most CCT programs give transfers to women rather than men, in part because women have been found to invest a larger share of the income they control in the welfare of their children (Lundberg, Pollak, and Wales 1997; Thomas 1990). But how much is enough? In theory, the transfer level should reflect both the direct cost of inputs (for example, nutrient-rich food, children's books, other learning materials, transportation to health clinics and other ECD services) and the opportunity costs associated with a given behavior change (for example, the time necessary for parents to take their children to service providers or to engage children in stimulating activities at home). In practice, however, the amount of the transfer that families receive via CCTs varies widely, and little is known about the optimal transfer size for promoting ECD outcomes in a given context.

4. **Does conditionality matter and, if so, to what extent?** In both the Ecuador and Nicaragua studies, the conditionality of health service

attendance was communicated but not enforced. Yet, both programs resulted in positive child development outcomes as well as in positive changes in parental behavior. These results may indicate that the availability of extra cash, along with information on how to promote better child development, may be more important than the enforcement of the conditionality itself. Other studies focusing on the effects of cash transfers among older children also found that outcomes did not vary based on the enforcement of conditionalities (Baird, McIntosh, and Ozler 2010). Given how expensive it can be to track compliance with conditionalities, it would be worthwhile to know whether such investments are indeed warranted.

These questions could be addressed through additional program experimentation and research across a variety of contexts, which would help broaden the scope of the thin evidence base currently available.

In addition, important policy options for moving forward include experimenting with various supply-side interventions, including the following:

1. **Interventions to broaden the *scope* of ECD services available to CCT beneficiaries.** While CCTs targeting families with young children have so far focused on health conditionalities, participation in other types of ECD services (for example, center-based programs (see Note 3.1) or programs that promote behavior change among parents/caregivers (see Note 3.2) could be encouraged when such programs are available locally.

2. **Interventions to improve the *quality* of ECD services available to CCT beneficiaries.** As documented in both the CCT and ECD literatures, quality matters when it comes to whether or not a given service is likely to yield positive effects. Several CCT programs targeting older (school-age) children have attempted to address supply-side quality issues in the education and health sectors through a range of tactics, including by providing grants for better-performing schools, giving cash transfers to teachers or to parent-teacher associations, and establishing health education sessions in response to low health center attendance (Fiszbein and Schady 2009). Similar strategies could be used (and evaluated) in an effort to promote increased participation in a range of quality ECD services among young children and their families.

Conditional Cash Transfers for Families with Young Children: Summary and Moving Forward

Key Implementation Considerations

- Focus on relevant age groups, depending on the program's goals and expected outcomes (for example, programs that aim to improve nutrition outcomes should focus on children younger than 2 years old, while programs that aim to improve broader child development outcomes, including cognitive and social development, can focus on the whole age range of 0–6 years).
- Target the poorest households and ensure that girls participate in and benefit from the program.
- Provide cash transfers to women in the household.
- Clearly communicate information on how transfers are expected to be used.
- Address supply-side constraints by encouraging the provision of quality ECD services (including growth-monitoring services, parenting programs, and daycare/preschools) and by improving the quality of existing ones.

Areas for Further Research

- Impact of CCTs on the developmental outcomes of young children (including physical, cognitive, and socio-emotional), especially outside Latin America and the Caribbean
- Potential value-added of providing parents with child-rearing information (for example, on hygiene, proper nutrition, and early stimulation), in addition to giving them cash
- Optimal targeting strategies
- Optimal transfer size to achieve expected outcomes
- Relationship (or lack thereof) between conditionality and program outcomes
- Creative strategies for alleviating supply-side constraints through CCTs (both in terms of quantity and quality of ECD services)

Notes

1. These data are unpublished as of yet but are expected to become available in December 2010.

2. Early childhood stimulation is defined as providing young children with constant opportunities to interact with caring figures and to learn about their environment from the earliest age. In practice, stimulation is about parents and other caregivers being responsive to the emotional and physical needs of their children from birth onward, playing and talking with them (even before children can respond verbally), and exposing them to words, numbers, and simple concepts while engaging in daily routines.

3. Evidence distinguishing between genetic and environmental factors comes primarily from industrialized nations. For a review, see Plomin (1994).

4. Risk factors are defined as "Personal characteristics or environmental circumstances that increase the probability of negative outcomes for children" (Cole and Cole 2000).

5. The sizes of these impacts were 0.17–0.22 standard deviations in language, and 0.13 standard deviations in socio-emotional skills.

Key Readings

Fiszbein , A., and N. Schady. 2009. "Conditional Cash Transfers: Reducing Present and Future Poverty." World Bank Policy Research Report, World Bank, Washington DC.

Macours, K., N. Schady, and R. Vakis. 2008. "Cash Transfers, Behavioral Changes, and Cognitive Development in Early Childhood: Evidence from a Randomized Experiment." World Bank Policy Research Working Paper 4759. World Bank, Washington, DC.

Paxson, C., and N. Schady. 2010. "Does Money Matter? The Effects of Cash Transfers on Child Health and Development in Rural Ecuador." EDCC (2010), 59 (1): 187–229.

References

Baird, S. C. McIntosh, and B. Ozler. 2010. "Cash or Condition? Evidence from a Randomized Cash Transfer Program in Malawi." World Bank, Washington DC.

Behrman, J., S. Parker, and P. Todd. 2005. "Long-Term Impacts of the Opportunidades Conditional Cash Transfer Program on Rural Youth in Mexico." Discussion Paper 122, Ibero America Institute for Economic Research, Gottingen, Germany.

Cole, M., and S. R. Cole. 2000. *The Development of Children* (4th ed.). New York: Worth.

Duarte Gomez, M. B., Sonia Morales Miranda, Alvaro Javier Ihovó Velandia, Sandra Catalina Ochoa Marin, Siemon Bult van der Wal, Marta Caballero Garcia, and Mauricio Hernandez Avila. 2004. "Impact of Oportunidades on

Knowledge and Practices of Beneficiary Mothers and Young Scholarship Recipients: An Evaluation of the Educational Health Sessions." In *External Evaluation of the Impact of the Human Development Program Oportunidades, 2004 ed.*, ed. Bernardo Hernandez Prado and Mauricio Hernandez Avila. Cuernavaca, Morales, Mexico: National Institute of Public Health.

Dubois, P., and M. Rubio-Codina. 2010. "Child Care Provision: Semiparametric Evidence from a Randomized Experiment in Mexico." IDEI Working Paper Series 542, Institut d'Économie Industrielle (IDEI), Toulouse, France.

Fernald, L. C., P. J. Gertler, and L. M. Neufeld. 2006. "Role of Cash in Conditional Cash Transfer Programmes for Child Health, Growth, and Development: An Analysis of Mexico's Oportunidades." *The Lancet* 371 (9615): 828–37.

Fernald, L., P. Kariger, P. Engle, and A. Raikes. 2009. *Examining Early Child Development in Low-Income Countries: A Toolkit for the Assessment of Children in the First Five Years of Life.* Washington, DC: World Bank.

Filmer, D., and N. Schady. 2009. "In School but Not Learning: The Impact of a Scholarship Program on School Enrollment and Achievement." Unpublished manuscript, World Bank, Washington, DC.

Fiszbein , A., and N. Schady. 2009. "Conditional Cash Transfers: Reducing Present and Future Poverty." World Bank Policy Research Report, World Bank, Washington DC.

Hoddinott, J., and E. Skoufias. 2004. "The Impact of Progressa on Food Consumption. *Economic Development and Cultural Change* 53(1): 37–61.

Irwin, L., A. Siddiqi, and C. Hertzman. 2007. "Early Child Development: A Powerful Equalizer: Final Report for the World Health Organization's Commission on the Social Determinants of Health." WHO, Geneva. http://www.who.int/social_determinants/resources/ecd_kn_report_07_2007.pdf.

Lundberg, S. J., R. A. Pollak, and T. J. Wales. 1997. "Do Husbands and Wives Pool Their Resources? Evidence from the United Kingdom Child Benefit." *The Journal of Human Resources* 32 (3): 463–80.

Macours, K., N. Schady, and R. Vakis. 2008. "Cash Transfers, Behavioral Changes, and Cognitive Development in Early Childhood: Evidence from a Randomized Experiment." World Bank Policy Research Working Paper 4759. World Bank, Washington, DC.

Paxson, C., and N. Schady. 2010. "Does Money Matter? The Effects of Cash Transfers on Child Health and Development in Rural Ecuador." EDCC (2010), 59 (1): 187–229.

Plomin, R. 1994. *Genetics and Experience: The Interplay between Nature and Nurture.* Thousand Oaks, CA: Sage Publications.

Thomas, D. 1990. "Intra-Household Resource Allocation: An Inferential Approach." *The Journal of Human Resources* 25 (4): 635–64.

Costing and Financing

Costing of ECD Projects

This note identifies the challenges in analyzing and comparing cost structures across ECD programs. It also provides information on the financial and economic costs that should be considered in planning and costing an ECD program. An introduction to the objectives of cost-effectiveness and cost-benefit analysis is presented, along with examples of research studies and practical tools that have been developed to cost programs and simulate alternative scenarios of service delivery. Finally, the note provides examples of unit costs for preschool programs in several countries.

The Challenge of Comparing Unit Costs

ECD Programs Are Multifaceted and Have a Broader Definition Than Primary Education Programs

In primary education, there is a set of core program elements and standards for intensity of services, a defined group of beneficiaries, and international protocols for data collection and reporting. However, in ECD programs—which range from health promotion services for infants and toddlers, parenting and caregiver programs to promote early development and stimulation, daycares, and preschools—interventions range widely in content and intensity. Program beneficiaries can include infants, children, or parents/caregivers; and there are few data protocols established to allow program comparability across countries. Table 4.1.1 shows the range of multi-level, multifaceted ECD programs compared to those in primary education, which are fairly straightforward and thus easier to compare.

Direct comparisons of ECD programs, both to each other and to primary education programs, must be calibrated to compensate for differences in program objectives, design, quality, and intensity (Levin and Schwartz 2006). Given the intricacies of ECD programs, it is not uncommon to find cross-country information focused on preschool programs, leaving out equally essential interventions that target infants and children under 2 years of age.

Determinants of Program Costs Are Financial Costs and Economic Costs

Financial costs and economic costs are the two broad cost categories to consider when estimating the cost of an ECD project. Financial costs include the monetary outlays associated with a program, while economic costs include the value of inputs that are provided in-kind, including volunteers' time, donated space, or beneficiary-purchased materials (see table 4.1.2) (Myers 2008b). Both types must be factored in to determine the full cost of ECD programs and to avoid estimation biases that could result in budget shortfalls or incomplete delivery of intervention packages.

Financial Costs for ECD Programs Can Be Subdivided into Two Cost Categories: Investment and Operational Costs

Financial costs include *investment* costs, usually one-time capital investment (for example, new construction or rehabilitation of physical plant), and *operational* costs, which are usually recurrent (that is, weekly, monthly, or annually) for as long as the project is operational. Table 4.1.2 provides examples of the program elements and types of activities typically included in these subcategories.

Staff salaries and benefits are usually the bulk of operational costs. Staffing tends to be the largest cost driver in ECD programs. Staff qualification levels necessary to conduct the program can account for 60 to 90 percent of operational cost, hence the need to factor in the advantages and disadvantages of the skill levels for different types of tasks and

Table 4.1.1   Comparing Domains between Primary Education and ECD Programs

Domain	Early childhood development programs	Primary education
Target	Programs are usually still in expansion mode, many with a focus on vulnerable and disadvantaged children. Different interpretations of "expansion": more children enrolled, more time spent on programs per year, more years, etc.	All primary school-age population attending school
Delivery	A range of modalities from sparsely supported home-based to formal preschool programs	Predominantly formal
Staff required	Professionals, paraprofessionals, parents, siblings, nannies, babysitters. However, untrained caregivers may gradually reach higher levels of professionalism.	Professionals
Focus of the intervention	Children and/or parents (for example, mothers attending literacy programs that address child upbringing)	Children
Entry age	At the earliest, ECD programs can start from before birth (through prenatal programs); at the latest, they start one year before primary school entry.	Officially at age 6 in most countries. In practice, children may enter one or more years later, and occasionally earlier
Frequency and duration	Very diverse: from once a week to 5 days a week, from just a few hours to a full day. The duration also varies widely.	Usually at least 5 days a week, during regular months each year, and usually lasting for 6 years
Number of children served	Different definitions depending on the type of program; most programs do not report using full-time enrollment equivalency, making it difficult to estimate coverage.	Fairly well agreed upon program definition; programs are full-time, with a range of number of instruction hours.
Unit costs	Estimates are scarce.	Rough estimates are available from a broad body of research.

Source: Adapted from van Ravens and Aggio (2008).

Table 4.1.2   Financial and Economic Costs of ECD Programs

	Financial costs
Investment (startup)	• Project development: creating/testing the approach, infrastructure, and materials • Facilities: constructing or upgrading • Equipment: transportation, office, instructional (tables and chairs), storage, and food preparation • Materials: reusable guides, books, and toys • Training: initial training at all levels (trainers, locale, per diems, transport, and supplies) • Consultants: fees, honorariums, and expenses • Micro-enterprise: loans for project-financing schemes
Operational (recurrent)	• Staffing salaries and benefits: ECD administrators, supervisors, directors, ECD workers, health personnel, cooks, support personnel (drivers and maintenance) • Food: purchase cost • Health care: supplies (salaries included above) and facilities (prorated) • Administration: general administration (overhead) costs • Training: in-service training • Communication: telephone, fax, printing, and media • Supplies: non-reusable items • Transportation: gasoline and maintenance of vehicles • Per diems: costs associated with supervision, training, and field visits • Maintenance: facility costs, electricity, telephone, and insurance • Evaluation: periodic monitoring and evaluation activities • Contingency: fund for unexpected costs
	Economic costs
	• In-kind contributions • Donated physical space • Volunteer contributions from parents, caregivers, or community members

Source: Evans, Myers, and Ilfeld (2000).

their financial implications. Staff types that need to be taken into account when designing and budgeting a program include: (1) service staff who interact directly with children, (2) administrative staff who steer the program locally or at the district or national level, (3) supervisory staff who provide oversight and technical training, and (4) support staff located at the site where service is being delivered. The qualifications of each staff type vary significantly depending on the fiscal position of a country or even among local jurisdictions (for example, teacher qualifications); the policy framework on ECD (that is, the priority that preschool programs are given by the government); and the type of beneficiaries targeted (rural, urban, or peri-urban), among others. For example, ECD programs in countries that require a university-equivalent degree for preschool teachers have different cost structure compared to those in countries where preschool services rely on contractual staff (facilitators) or community volunteers. Within a country there can also be great variations between ECD programs in urban areas and those in deep rural communities or isolated places.

Economic costs often reflect the monetized value of in-kind contributions. It is not uncommon for ECD programs to include a variety of in-kind contributions as part of the delivery of services. However, when in-kind contributions are central to the delivery of services, it is important to assign a monetized value to them to ensure that they are also incorporated in the cost structure of the program. Knowing the full cost of a program is important for effective implementation, particularly in situations where the program is to be scaled up or replicated elsewhere at a similar level and standard of services but in a venue in which in kind-services such as donated space or volunteer time may not be available.

Estimating Program Costs

Two common approaches to estimating program costs are (1) inferring costs from official program budgets and expenditure records and (2) constructing cost-simulation models in which all the possible project ingredients (financial and economic costs) are accounted for in a computerized model. Each approach has advantages and disadvantages, and, in practice, it is not uncommon to use both approaches to assign a unit cost to a program and to weigh in the financial implication of scaling up programs under different service delivery parameters. It is important to note that an estimation of unit costs with only official budgets and expenditure information can lead to an underestimation because all too often donated time, supplies, physical space, or other in-kind support are not officially recorded. Simulation models tend to be of greatest use for the design of new programs; their drawback is that they tend to provide aggregate unit cost information that fails to account for the price differences in urban, rural, peri-urban, or other geographic areas within a country, especially for hard-to-reach areas that have higher than average unit costs.

Recent examples of comprehensive simulation models developed to estimate the cost of expanding ECD services include van Ravens and Aggio (2008) and Mingat (2006). Their models estimate the unit costs of ECD programs in terms of per capita GDP in an attempt to estimate the potential cost of expanding services using different parameters of service delivery. Van Ravens and Aggio's findings indicate the expansion of preschool would cost about 20.8 percent of GDP per capita in Sub-Saharan Africa and 12.5 percent in Arab countries. The cost of expansion of home-based programs in Arab countries was estimated at 4.5 percent of GDP per capita. Mingat's simulation analyses in Sub-Saharan Africa point to an estimated cost of 17 percent of GDP per capita for full-time, formal preschool programs and 4.2 percent for community-based programs. These estimates, while aggregate, provide a magnitude of costs of expansion under certain parameters, which are then used in estimating the total level of public and private funds that would be needed to reach a certain level of service delivery.

Other costing simulation models include (1) the ECD Calculator developed by the Amsterdam Institute for International Development (AIID) (Van der Gaag and Tan 1998)[1]; (2) the CARICOM model developed by Charles and Williams (2008) to estimate the costs of setting up quality ECD programs; (3) the Tool for Estimating the Costs of Universal Preschool in the United States developed by the Institute of Women's Policy Studies (Golin, Mitchell, and Gault 2004); (4) the Karoly and Bigelow (2005) paper on how to estimate the costs and benefits of universal preschool in the state of California; and (5) the Brandon (2004) model developed to estimate the cost of financing access to early education for children age 4 years and younger in the United States. These models have wide application because they provide insight into the number and types of cost categories, as well because the parameters to reach different levels of quality and service delivery (van der Gaag and Tan 1998).

A Comprehensive Cost Analysis Framework May Be Useful to Guide Planning and Data Requirements

Any costing study should be clear from the start about the types of information it needs to gather. The following areas are common in most cost analyses: (1) sources of funds to determine who is bearing the cost of the program and where the funds are being generated (see Note 4.2 for more details); (2) a list of investment and operational costs; (3) a breakdown of operating costs to identify the proportion of direct and overhead costs, as well as fixed and variable costs; (4) program setting (rural/urban); (5) costs related to lines of action (materials, supplies, food, training); (6) project stage (pilot, semi-established, or established program); and (7) intensity of services (length of time a service is offered, whether it is full-time or part-time). Once the information is in place, a costing table is then built from which the unit cost of the program can be derived, depending on the total number of beneficiaries expected to be reached.

Unit costs for preschool programs range widely. The annual expenditure on educational institutions offering preschool services (public or private) range widely from a high of US$8,867 in the United States to US$1,315 in Brazil (figure 4.1.1). The average for the Organisation for Economic Co-operation and Development (OECD) is US$5,260. These unit costs should be interpreted with caution; they reflect expenditures for preprimary institutions (mostly formal, center-based) based on full-time enrollment equivalencies. An analysis of non-full-time programs in informal or non-center-based settings would probably yield a lower cost structure, since those programs tend to rely on staffing with different qualification levels and different types of service delivery intensity, particularly for children under 2 years of age.

The van Ravens and Aggio (2008) simulation model estimates the unit cost of preschool programs to range from $58 in Mauritania, $70 in Yemen, $145 in Egypt, $318 in Tunisia—to US$2,739 in the United Arab Emirates. Other nonformal preschool programs, such as the Madrasa

Figure 4.1.1   Annual Expenditure on Preprimary Education per Student (3 Years and Older) (2006)

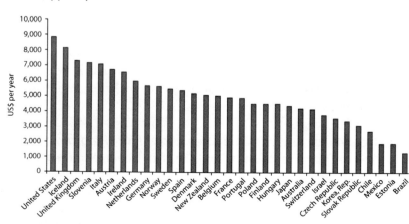

Source: OECD, *Education at a Glance 2009: OECD Indicators.*

ECD program in East Africa (Kenya, Uganda, and Zanzibar), estimated the unit cost to be between $14 and $24 per child per month. Again, these numbers should be interpreted with caution given that the program elements are project-specific (Issa and Evans 2008; Myers 20008a). Similarly, unit cost estimates for programs targeted to the 3–6-year-old age group produced by the *Comisión Económica para América Latina y el Caribe (CEPAL)* and the *Organización de Estados Iberoamericanos para la Educación, Ciencia y la Cultura (OEI)* (CEPAL and OEI 2009) for all countries in the Latin America and Caribbean region, indicate a range from $74 for Nicaragua, $145 in Bolivia, and $161 in Colombia—to $1,078 in Uruguay, $1,170 in Mexico, and $1,966 in Chile.[2]

Information on the unit costs of parenting education programs, including home-visit programs, is even more limited. The Caribbean Child Development Center estimated the cost of a home visiting program at $312 per child per year in Jamaica (Myers 2008a), while unit cost estimates from the van Ravens and Aggio (2008) simulation model for home-based programs yielded a range of annual unit costs: $13 in Mauritania, $23 in Djibouti, $90 in Morocco, $203 in Tunisia, $413 in Lebanon, and $1,252 in United Arab Emirates.[3] Again, these cost estimates should be interpreted with caution given that their technical content and service intensity may vary substantially.

In the absence of information on unit costs for programs targeted to the 0- to 3-year-old age group, CEPAL and OEI (2009) chose to rely on the unit cost information for programs targeted to the 3–6 age group as guiding estimates for the 0–3 age group.[4]

Cost-Effectiveness and Cost-Benefit Analyses

Although there is ample empirical evidence on the importance of ECD programs as an essential step in human capital formation (see Notes 1.1–1.3), public funds tend to have a number of competing demands, which often requires policy makers or program managers to make requests based on cost-effectiveness or cost-benefit analyses.

Cost-Effectiveness Analysis Compares Two or More Programs According to Their Effectiveness and Costs in Accomplishing a Particular Objective

Cost-effectiveness (CE) analysis refers to the evaluation of alternatives according to both their costs and their effects with regard to producing some outcome or set of outcomes. Under CE analysis, both the costs and effects of different alternatives are taken into account in evaluating programs with similar goals. It is assumed that (1) only programs with similar or identical goals can be compared and (2) a common measure of effectiveness can be used to assess them. For example, CE can be used to compare alternative service delivery models to improve school readiness using student test scores as the objective.

The combination of information on effectiveness and costs provides decision makers with information on a given level of effectiveness at a given cost, or the highest level of effectiveness at a given cost. Although CE analysis is useful in selecting between two or more alternatives in terms of effectiveness, it does not provide information on which alternative is worthwhile in an absolute sense. CE analysis is less useful when there are too many objectives under review and there is limited guidance on the decision rule to select among effectiveness alternatives (Levin and McEwan 2002). *The Lancet* 2007 series (Engle et al. 2007) summarized the impact of a range of pilot ECD studies on children's outcomes in cognitive development; however, costing data were not available to compare the effects (outcome) per dollar invested among alternatives.

In Cost-Benefit Analysis, the Outcomes of an Alternative Are Expressed Directly in Monetary Terms

Cost-benefit (CB) analysis provides a framework in which to weigh trade-offs among alternative investments that yield improvements in specific outcomes relative to other investments. CB analysis is based on the "maximum social gain" principle, which assumes that decision makers seek to maximize their own social welfare or well-being, thus the maximum social gain principle would dictate that prospective benefits must exceed anticipated costs, and more importantly, that the excess of benefits over costs must be maximized. Commonly used methods to appraise the value of an investment include the calculation of a ratio that represents the *present value* of the total benefits of the investment or program to the present value of the total cost of undertaking the investment, that is, (1) $\text{Benefits}_0 > \text{Costs}_0$ or $\text{Benefits}_0 - \text{Costs}_0 > 0$; (2) the *Internal Rate of Return* (IRR), which is the rate of discount that makes $\text{Benefits}_0 - \text{Costs}_0 = 0$; (3) and the *benefit-cost ratio* in which projects are selected where the ratio of the present value of benefits to the present value of costs exceeds unity, where projects $\text{Benefits}_0 / \text{Costs}_0 > 1$. All values specified in the benefit-to-cost ratio must be economic benefits and costs measured in monetary terms (Cohn and Geske 1990).

For example, according to findings from Karoly and Bigelow (2005) on the cost of expansion of a preschool program for all children in the state of California, ECD investments have positive CB, generating $2.62 for every dollar invested in the specific programs under their review. A one-year, high-quality universal preschool program in California is estimated to generate about $7,000 in net present value benefits per child for California society (public and private sectors), using a 3 percent discount rate. This equals a return of $2.62 for every dollar invested, or an annual rate of return of about 10 percent over a 60-year horizon. The study also estimated that, using a 70 percent assumption in participation rate in the universal preschool program, each annual cohort of California children served generates $2.7 billion in net present value benefits to California society (using a 3 percent discount rate).

A weakness of CB analysis, however, is that it requires benefits to be measurable and monetized, which is difficult to do in the case of social programs, including ECD interventions. One reason for this is the existence of a number of externalities that are difficult to measure in precise ways, let alone monetize. Estimating the full benefits of ECD programs is a complex undertaking that requires the development of a multi-domain framework for analysis for which time series data are required. Benefits of participating in ECD programs accrue in the short-, medium-, and long-term on domains including school performance, education attainment, employability, earnings from employment, social and emotional competence, health outcomes, social welfare, and quality of life.

When CB analysis is feasible, it can determine whether benefits outweigh costs, which allows for decision making on financial terms alone in an absolute sense. Another advantage of CB analysis is that it provides information about program design and delivery, including which services or combinations of services should begin at what age, how extensive coverage should be, and how programs should be staffed, located, and financially supported. Although CB analysis may provide absolute information on program alternatives, the method is usually data-intensive, requires a longer time for observation, and requires that benefits be monetized, which can be difficult in the social sectors (Wolfe and Zuvekas 1997; Haveman and Wolfe 1984).

In the United States several ECD programs have been analyzed using longitudinal data on the impacts of interventions at different points in time (early school years, adolescence, and adulthood) (Campbell et al. 2002; Schweinhart et al. 2005; Reynolds et al. 2001) (see box 4.1.1). Results from these studies indicate a positive benefit-to-cost ratio, ranging from 3.78 in the case of the Carolina Abecedarian program to 16.24 in the High/Scope Perry Preschool project. The studies show that ECD interventions

Box 4.1.1

ECD Interventions with Long-Term Studies in the United States

In the United States, several longitudinal studies have contributed to our understanding of the long-term impact of high-quality early childhood development programs, where all have recorded remarkable rate of return (as shown in the Table below) to investment in services for low-income children during early years (Committee for Economic Development 2006; Nores et al. 2005; Belfield et al. 2006; Masse and Barnett 2002; Karoly and Bigelow 2005; Aos et al. 2004; Reynolds et al. 2002).

Carolina Abecedarian Early Childhood Intervention: Between 1972 and 1977, 111 infants who were determined to be at high risk for school failure based on a number of parental and family circumstance factors were enrolled in the Carolina Abecedarian program. The infants, who were primarily African American, either received early care and education services from the age of 6 weeks through 5 years or were assigned to the control group. In both the child-care and preschool components, special curricula were developed focusing on language development, and the classrooms had very low child-to-teacher ratios and the teachers had bachelor's degrees. The program participants were followed through adolescence and, most recently, at age 21. The Carolina Abecedarian program enrolled children earlier in the life cycle than other preschool programs, and the longevity of its follow-up provides valuable information on the long-term effects of sustained early education interventions.

Chicago Child-Parent Centers: The Chicago Child-Parent Centers (CPC) are publicly funded preschool centers in high-poverty neighborhoods serving low-income 3–5-year-olds that began operating in 1967 and continues today. The children attend preschool three hours per day during the school year, receiving reading and math instruction by well-qualified public school teachers in small classes. The quasi-experimental Chicago Longitudinal Study follows a cohort of 1,539 students (primarily African American) who attended kindergarten in 1985–86. Of the children in the cohort, 989 attended a CPC center for one or two years prior to kindergarten, while the other 550 did not attend a CPC program (and less than one-quarter of this group attended any preschool). The most recent student follow-up was conducted when the children were age 20 or 21.

High/Scope Perry Preschool Project: The Perry Preschool Project provided high-quality preschooling for a small number of disadvantaged 3- to 4-year-old

(continued)

Box 4.1.1 *(continued)*

African American children in Ypsilanti, Michigan, between 1962 and 1967. The 123 children in the study were born into poverty and at high risk for failing in school. The treatment group received a high-quality preschool education for 2.5 hours each day during the school year, in addition to a 1.5-hour home visit each week, while the control group was not provided any program services. All Perry Preschool teachers had bachelor's degrees and earned 10 percent more than kindergarten teachers in the same school. The program participants were followed throughout their youth and adult years, with the most recent follow-up at age 41.

	US$ per child (discounted at 3%)				Internal
Program	Total benefit	Total cost	Net benefit	Benefit/cost ratio[a]	rate of return (%)
Carolina Abecedarian (2002 dollars)	135,546	35,864	99,682	3.78	7
Chicago CPC (1998 dollars)	47,759	6,692	41,067	7.14	10
Perry Preschool age 40 follow-up (2000 dollars)	244,811	15,166	229,645	16.14	18

Sources: Committee for Economic Development (2006); Nores et al. (2005); Belfield et al. (2006); Masse and Barnett (2002); Karoly and Bigelow (2005); Aos et al. (2004); Reynolds et al. (2002).
a. Ratio differs widely because of differences in the types and measurement of benefits and length of follow-up.

generate lifelong benefits for both direct beneficiaries and society. In the case of the High/Scope Perry Preschool project, the total benefit for each $1 invested (including benefits to individual participants and the public) was estimated at $8.74 (by age 27) (Temple and Reynolds 2007).

A meta-analysis of evaluations of ECD programs in the United States indicates that the favorable effects of early childhood programs can translate into dollar benefits for the government as well as for participants and other members of society. Of the programs reviewed, the study by Karoly, Kilburn, and Cannon (2005) finds seven with information on CB analysis, out of which five were found to generate a range of benefits per child from $1,400 to almost $240,000, or, presented differently, the returns to society for each dollar invested extended from $1.26 to $17.07. Interestingly, the economic returns were found to be positive for programs that focused on home visiting or parenting education, as well as those that combined those services with early childhood education. Impacts were largest for programs that had a longer-term follow-up compared to programs that had a shorter follow-up duration (that is, primary school entry).

A cost-benefit tool developed specifically for early childhood development is the Early Child Development (ECD) Calculator by Van der Gaag and Tan (1998), which calculates the economic benefits of ECD programs by monetizing such things as improvement in the child's ability to take advantage of the schooling system (that is, they are more likely to enroll in school on time and progress to secondary school, and less likely to repeat classes or drop out). The application measures the increase in productivity (that is, net present value of increase in lifetime productivity) that can be expected in an ECD cohort of 1,000 newborns. It has been used in World-Bank-financed projects in Egypt, Indonesia, and Jamaica.[5]

Notes

1. To download the ECD calculator, go to www.worldbank.org/children and click on Costing and Financing. Information from AIID at http://www.aiid.org/index.php?ap=feature.
2. Unit costs may vary given differences in intensity and delivery modality of programs.
3. For specific program parameters see van Ravens and Aggio (2008).
4. Unit costs may vary, given differences in service intensity and delivery modality of programs.
5. See World Bank Project Appraisal Documents for each country listed.

Key Readings

Levin, M., and P. J. McEwan 2002. "Cost-Effectiveness and Educational Policy." *2002 Yearbook.* American Education Finance Association. Eye on Education, Larchmont, NY.

van Ravens, J., and C. Aggio. 2008. "Expanding Early Childhood Care and Education: How Much Does It Cost? A Proposal for a Methodology to Estimate the Costs of Early Childhood Care and Education at Macro-Level, Applied to the Arab States." Working Paper 46. Bernard van Leer Foundation, The Hague.

Wolfe, B., and S. Zuvekas. 1997. "Nonmarket Outcomes of Schooling." *International Journal of Educational Research* 27 (6): 491–501.

References

Aos, S., R. Lieb, J. Mayfield, M. Miller, and A. Pennucci. 2004. *Benefits and Costs of Prevention and Early Intervention Programs for Youth.* Olympia, WA: Washington State Institute for Public Policy.

Belfield, C. R., M. Nores, S. Barnett, and L. Schweinhart. 2006. "The High/Scope Perry Preschool Program: Cost-Benefit Analysis Using Data from the Age-40 Follow-Up." *Journal of Human Resources* 41 (1): 162–90.

Brandon, R. N. 2004. "Financing Access to Early Education for Children Age Four and Below: Concepts and Costs." Paper presented at The Brookings–University of North Carolina Conference on "Creating a National Plan for the Education of 4-Year-Olds." September 9–10, Washington, DC.

Campbell, F. A., C. T. Ramey, E. P. Pungello, S. Miller-Johnson, and J. J. Sparling. 2002. "Early Childhood Education: Young Adult Outcomes from the Abecedarian Project. *Applied Developmental Science* 6 (1): 42–57.

CEPAL and OEI. (*Comisión Económica para América Latina y el Caribe* and *Organización de Estados Iberoamericanos para la Educación, Ciencia y la Cultura*). 2009. *"Metas educativas 2021: Estudio de Costos."* División de Desarrollo Social, Santiago de Chile.

Charles, L., and S. Williams. 2008. A Model to Support ECD Decision-making: Caribbean Regional Experiences with Costs and Simulations. *Coordinators' Notebook* 30: 52. Consultative Group on Early Childhood Care and Development, Toronto, Canada.

Cohn, E., and G. Geske. 1990. *Economics of Education.* Oxford, UK: Pergamon Press.

Committee for Economic Development. 2006. "The Economic Promise of Investing in High Quality Preschool: Using Early Education to Improve Economic Growth and the Fiscal Sustainability of States and the Nation." Committee for Economic Development, Washington, DC.

Engle, P. L., M. M. Black, J. R. Behrman, M. C. de Mello, P. J. Gertler, L. Kapiriri, R. Martorell, and M. E. Young, and the International Child Development Steering Group. 2007. "Strategies to Avoid the Loss of Developmental Potential in More Than 200 Million Children in the Developing World." *The Lancet* 369: 229–42.

Evans, J. L., with R. G. Myers and E. M. Ilfeld. 2000. *Early Childhood Counts: A Programming Guide on Early Childhood Care for Development.* Washington, DC: World Bank, pp. 322–23.

Golin, S. C., A. W. Mitchell, and B. Gault. 2004. "The Price of School Readiness: A Tool for Estimating the Cost of Universal Preschool in the States." Institute for Women's Policy Research, Washington, DC.

Haveman, B., and B. Wolfe. 1984. "Education, Productivity, and Well-Being: On Defining and Measuring the Economic Characteristics of Schooling." In

Education and Economic Productivity, ed. E. Dean, 19–55. Cambridge, MA: Ballinger.

Issa, S. S., and J. L. Evans. 2008. "Going to Scale With Effective ECD Interventions: What Is Involved? A Costing Model of the Madrasa ECD Programme in East Africa." *Coordinators' Notebook* 30: 41–45.

Karoly, L., R. Kilburn, and J. Cannon. 2005. "Early Childhood Interventions: Proven Results, Future Promise." The Rand Corporation, Santa Monica, CA.

Karoly, L. A., and J. H. Bigelow. 2005. *The Economics of Investing in Universal Preschool in California*, p. 82. Santa Monica, CA: The Rand Corporation.

Levin, M., and P. J. McEwan 2002. "Cost-Effectiveness and Educational Policy." American Education Finance Association, Gainesville, FL.

Levin, H., and H. Schwartz. 2006. "Costs of Early Childhood Care and Education Programs." Paper commissioned for the *Education for All Global Monitoring Report 2007: Strong Foundations: Early Childhood Care and Education*. United Nations Educational, Scientific and Cultural Organization, Paris. National Center for the Study of Privatization in Education, Teachers College, Columbia University, New York.

Masse, L., and W. S. Barnett. 2002. "A Benefit-Cost Analysis of the Abecedarian Early Childhood Intervention." National Institute for Early Education Research (NIEER), New Brunswick, NJ.

Mingat, A. 2006. "Early Childhood Care and Education in Africa: Towards Expansion of Coverage and Targeting of Efficient Services." Paper presented at the Association for the Development of Education in Africa (ADEA) Biennale in Gabon, March 2006. ADEA, Paris.

Myers, R. G. 2008a. "Costing Early Childhood Care and Development Programmes." Online Outreach Paper 5. Bernard van Leer Foundation, The Hague.

Myers, R. G. 2008b. "A Note on Costs and Costing of Early Childhood Care and Development Programmes." *Coordinators' Notebook* 30: 29. Consultative Group on Early Childhood Care and Development, Toronto, Canada.

Nores, J. C. R. Belfield, W. S. Barnett, and L. Schweinhart. 2005. "Updating the Economic Impacts of the High/Scope Perry Preschool Program." *Educational Evaluation and Policy Analysis* 27 (3) (Fall): 245–61.

OECD (Organisation for Economic Co-operation and Development). 2009. "Education at a Glance 2009: OECD Indicators." http://www.oecd.org/document/24/0,3343,en_2649_39263238_43586328_1_1_1_1,00.html.

Reynolds, A. J., J. A. Temple, D. L. Robertson, and E. A. Mann. 2001. "Long-Term Effects of an Early Childhood Intervention on Educational Achievement and Juvenile Arrest: A 15-Year Follow-Up of Low-Income Children in Public Schools." *Journal of the American Medical Association* 285: 2339–46.

————. 2002. "Age 21 Cost-Benefit Analysis of the Title I Chicago Child-Parent Centers." *Educational Evaluation and Policy Analysis* 24 (4) (Winter): 267–303.

Schweinhart, L. J., J. Montie, Z. Xiang, W. S. Barnett, C. R Belfield, and M. Nores. 2005. "Lifetime Effects: The High/Scope Perry Preschool Study through Age 40. Ypsilanti, MI: High/Scope Educational Research Foundation.

Temple, Judy A., and Arthur J. Reynolds. 2007. "The Benefits and Costs of Investments in Preschool." *Economics of Education Review* 26(1): 126–44.

van der Gaag, J., and J. P. Tan. 1998. *The Benefits of Early Child Development Programs: An Economic Analysis.* Washington, DC: World Bank.

van Ravens, J., and C. Aggio. 2008. "Expanding Early Childhood Care and Education: How Much Does It Cost? A Proposal for a Methodology to Estimate the Costs of Early Childhood Care and Education at Macro-Level, Applied to the Arab States." Working Paper 46. Bernard van Leer Foundation, The Hague.

Wolfe, B., and S. Zuvekas. 1997. "Nonmarket Outcomes of Schooling." *International Journal of Educational Research* 27 (6): 491–501.

Financing ECD Programs

This note discusses financing mechanisms to fund ECD programs. It identifies the challenges in making cross-country comparisons in ECD investment and offers guidance on dimensions that can be used as variables in a comparative analysis. The note presents a simple framework to organize information on different sources of funding and mechanisms to allocate those funds. A literature search was conducted to compare investments in ECD across countries; country examples are provided to illustrate the variety, intricacies, and complexity of ECD financing schemes across countries. Most countries have a long way to go in raising sufficient revenues to offer quality ECD services. Governments not only need to make a budgetary commitment to ECD services but also need to work with the range of ECD providers and key stakeholders to find innovative, stable, and sustainable sources of revenue.

Investment in Early Childhood Development

Cross-Country Information on ECD Programs and Investments Is Scarce

ECD programs are diverse and heterogeneous in scope, content, and intensity. This sheer diversity of programs, coupled with a lack of universal standards and parameters to guide data collection at the international level, presents a challenge to researchers seeking to analyze ECD programmatic approaches, investments, and outcomes. Comparative information on ECD programs for infants and children under age 3 is particularly difficult to find because of the high degree of fragmentation across sectors, programs, and providers targeting this age group. For children aged 3-6, information is usually more readily available because preschool[1] is an officially recognized education level and a service available in many countries, albeit with various degrees of coverage and a wide variation in program content and intensity.

Accurate Comparisons of ECD Programs and Investments Require a Level of Standardization

Given the heterogeneity of ECD programs, comparative analyses across countries must compensate for differences in program scope, content, and intensity by applying a common set of standards against which individual country programs can be benchmarked. Commonly used features to standardize program information are as follows: [2]

1. *outcomes targeted*: pregnancy, cognitive, socio-emotional, behavioral, health, parenting skills
2. *target person*: child, parent, child-parent, family unit
3. *targeting criteria*: universal, income-based, disability-based, parental risk problems; age of focal child (prenatal to age 6)
4. *location of services*: home, non-home
5. *type of services offered*: educational (preschool, parenting education), family support, health or nutrition-related, job-related, therapeutic
6. *intensity of intervention*: starting age to ending age, hours per week, weeks per year
7. *delivery mode*: individuals, small or large group
8. *program reach*: national, statewide, citywide, single setting
9. *funding sources*: public, private, public-private partnership, international assistance
10. *financing allocation mechanism*: budget line, grants (block or earmarked), vouchers, tax credits, matching funds.

Unless the specificities of different types of programs are standardized using a similar scale for analysis, there is a risk of generating inaccurate or even misleading information, particularly in terms of investment, cost-effectiveness, and outcomes.

International Organizations Have Taken on the Challenge of Gathering Comparable ECD Information

Over the past few years, several international agencies have taken on the challenge of compiling standardized, cross-country data on ECD services to determine the level of service penetration, take-up rates, and investment efforts. Most notable among these efforts are the recent ECD studies from OECD, UNESCO (United Nations Educational, Scientific and Cultural Organization), and the World Bank, which provide comprehensive global and regional information on a range of program dimensions for children age 0–6. Most of these cross-country studies were carried out as a one-time exercise, limiting prospects for conducting longitudinal analyses.

Available Information Indicates That a Public Investment of 1 Percent of GDP Is Required to Offer Quality ECD Services

According to the OECD (2006) report, *Doing Better for Children II*, which provides comprehensive information on ECD investments aimed at children under age 6, countries place a high priority on their youngest cohort. The latest statistics indicate that governments spend an average of 2.36 percent of GDP on a broad range of services for families and young children, including expenditures on preschool programs. The average expenditure on preschool for children aged 3–6 is 0.49 percent of GDP, which includes expenditures from public and private sources. Evidence from OECD research studies (Starting Strong II) suggests a public investment of 1.0 percent of GDP is the minimum required to ensure provision of quality ECD services. Studies from the European Commission Network on Child Care and Other Measures to Reconcile the Employment Responsibilities of Men and Women (1996), and the Consultative Group on Early Childhood Care and Development (2008) suggest similar levels of public investment as a guiding benchmark.

Outside of the OECD, Countries in the Central and Eastern Europe Region Have the Highest Levels of Investment in Preschool

UNESCO's *Education For All (EFA) Global Monitoring Report 2007* (UNESCO 2006), which provides a comprehensive set of statistics on ECD services, ranks countries in Central and Eastern Europe as having the highest level of public expenditure on preschool—on average, 0.5 percent of GNP. Expenditures range from a high of 1.0 percent of GNP in Belarus to 0.3 percent in Estonia and Romania. Latin America and the Caribbean is the second-ranked region, with an average expenditure of 0.2 percent of GNP. Expenditures range from a high of 0.6 percent of GNP in Guyana to a low of 0.02 percent in Nicaragua. Countries in Sub-Saharan Africa have the lowest levels of public expenditure on preschool.

As a Proportion of the Education Budget, Preschool Education Remains a Low-Priority Investment

The *EFA Global Monitoring Report* also shows that public investment in preschool education comprises less than 10 percent of total public spending on education in many countries, and in some, even less than 5 percent. Developing countries with at least 10 percent of public education expenditure devoted to preschool include Belarus, Bulgaria, Costa Rica, Croatia, Czech Republic, Guyana, Hungary, Mexico, Mongolia, Moldova, the Slovak Republic, and Slovenia. Countries in Sub-Saharan Africa had expenditure levels of less than 1 percent of the total public education budget. Gross enrollment rates in preschool follow regional public expenditure patterns; they are highest in the developed world, on average 80 percent, and lowest in the developing world, on average 36 percent. By subregion, gross enrollment rates are highest in the Caribbean (82 percent) and lowest in Sub-Saharan Africa (15 percent) and the Arab states (19 percent).

Financing ECD: Sources of Funds and Allocation Mechanisms

This section presents a financing framework to illustrate the variety of funding and allocation mechanisms shown in table 4.2.1. Although the sources of funds, schemes to generate public revenue, and specific ways to allocate resources are not an exhaustive list, the framework outlines the different financing options for consideration that may resonate with established public financing practices at the country level.

ECD Program Funding Relies on a Combination of Public and Private Funds

Public funds can originate at different levels of government (federal, state, provincial, municipal, or district), and are usually mobilized from taxes (income, sales, payroll, property), lotteries, or fees (toll roads, licensing, admission levies). *Private funds* may be generated from industry enterprises, foundations, community groups and other NGOs, and households

Table 4.2.1   Sources and Modalities for Allocating Funds for ECD Programs

Sources of funds		Modalities for allocating funds	
Public funds	***Funding may originate from different government levels:*** • Federal / central • States / provinces • Municipalities • Districts / localities • Cities ***Funds may be raised through:*** • General revenues from taxes (e.g., sales, income, payroll, property) • Lotteries • Excise taxes on tobacco and alcohol • Fees (e.g. toll roads, licensing, admission levies)	**Direct allocation through:**	• Budget line allocations: recipients can be public or private providers. • Block grants: recipients can be public or private. • Matching or partial matching funds: government "matches" a predetermined level of investment while service providers or households finance the remainder. • Vouchers: recipients can be public or private providers, or program participants. • Direct subsidy for specific program elements (e.g., staffing salaries, physical plant development, curriculum, quality assurance systems, etc.): recipients can be public or private providers. • Conditional cash transfers: recipients are usually program participants.
		Indirect allocation through:	• Need-based sliding scale subsidies • Parental and maternity leave policies • Tax credits and rebates
Private funds	***Funding may be generated from:*** • Private enterprises • Foundations • Community groups/NGOs • Households (user fees, levies, tuition, copayments)	**Direct allocation through:**	• Workplace-based care • Payments to providers • Matching funds
		Indirect allocation through:	• Vouchers • Cash or in-kind donations to faith-based and nonprofit organizations

(continued)

Table 4.2.1   Sources and Modalities for Allocating Funds for ECD Programs
(continued)

Sources of funds		Modalities for allocating funds
Public-private partnerships	*Funding may be generated from:* • Government • Private enterprises • Foundations • Community groups/ NGOs	• Matching funds for capital investment initiatives to expand ECD services
International agencies	*Funding may be generated from:* • International financing agencies (loans and grants) • Bilateral agencies (grants) • International NGOs (grants)	• Funds for government-approved programs: recipients can be public or private providers, or program participants.

Source: Adapted from Belfield (2006).

(through user fees, levies, and tuition)—all of which may be particularly relevant where ECD services are provided to a broad range of ECD beneficiaries, including children from better-off families.

Public-private-partnerships are usually established to raise "matching" funds, especially for large-scale capital improvement initiatives. In countries where revenue generation from public and private sources is constrained, international agencies may finance the design or scaling up of ECD programs, providing loans or grants as a way to extend ECD services.

Modalities for Allocating Public or Private Funds Are Wide Ranging

Funds may be allocated "directly" to ECD service providers by budget allocations, block grants, earmarked grants, matching funds, or to program participants by vouchers, subsidy payments or conditional cash transfers. Funds can also be allocated "indirectly" to providers through tax credits and rebates, or to program participants through the application of generous parental leave policies, need-based sliding-fee scales, or specific tax credits and rebates.

The selection of funding sources or specific modalities to allocate funds depends on a number of factors specific to the country and social context. For example, ECD policies in some countries include a legal entitlement to free services, a public financing mandate, and may even have an earmarked source of revenue. Others countries make decisions on sources and allocation mechanisms on the basis of established state practices on financing social policy programs (strong or limited); desired targeting (universal coverage, income-based, vulnerability-based); and the absorption capacity and sophistication of the "market" for ECD services (this is a particular consideration when making decisions on demand-side financing instruments such as vouchers and conditional cash transfers).

Selecting a Financing Mechanism Requires Balancing Simplicity, Reliability, and Equity

While there is no exact blueprint or optimal balance between public and private financing, the relative weight in the type of funding is likely to have a different effect and may elicit a different response on dimensions such as equity, accountability measures, parental choice, learning standards, and quality assurance. For example, findings from the OECD (Tayler and Bennett 2006) *Starting Strong II* report indicate that direct public funding offers the advantages of a more effective public steering of ECD services, advantages of scale, better national quality, more effective training for educators, and a higher degree of equity in access compared to parent-subsidy models. At the same time, the report highlights the possibility of accommodate private providers effectively when there is a clear institutional quality assurance and financing framework with active monitoring and proper enforcement mechanisms.

Determine the National Principles That Will Guide Options for ECD Financing

Principles to keep in mind when deciding on funding source and allocation mechanisms include (1) simplicity in terms of administration and access, (2) reliability and sustainability of funding streams, (3) likely burden of specific types of taxes on different population segments, (4) enforceability of regulations and standards to ensure a program's quality, and (5) availability of parental choice and opportunities for direct financing across ECD providers, including home provision (particularly important in rural, isolated communities).

Country Examples of Funding Sources and Allocation Mechanisms

Most Countries Rely on a Combination of Public Funds and Household Contributions to Finance ECD Programs

In most countries, public funds are the predominant source of funding for ECD, with households also making a weighty contribution (Vargas-Baron 2008) (see annex table 4.2A-4). The level of household contribution depends on the availability of physical facilities that are publicly provided or sponsored, the eligibility criteria to access these facilities, and the degree to which countries rely on unsubsidized provision in private centers (for child/daycare or preschool). Countries with high levels of provision of publicly provided or sponsored facilities, particularly for children ages 3–6, include Australia, Cuba, Czech Republic, Denmark, Finland, Hungary, and Thailand. Countries with developed markets for child/daycare and preschool provision include the United States and the United Kingdom (child/daycare).

In the United States, parents tend to cover the full cost of daycare and preschool programs, with the exception of federally sponsored programs like Head Start and the Child Care Development Fund, which are available to vulnerable and at-risk children. Preschool programs are usually attached to primary education systems where the proportion of a household's contributions is less than full cost; however, access to such programs vary by state (Tayler and Bennett 2006; Belfield 2006).

Countries such as Brazil, Colombia, and Mexico rely on a mix of public and private funding sources, make the preschool year before the first grade nearly universal, and target various early care and preschool programs to vulnerable groups. Countries that rely almost exclusively on households include Indonesia, Kenya, and Senegal (UNESCO 2006).

Most Countries Rely on Several Mechanisms to Allocate Public Funds

Most countries have several allocation mechanisms in place at any one time to cover specific program objectives and target groups (Belfield 2006; Tayler and Bennett 2006; PEW Center on the States 2009; van Ravens and Aggio 2008; Vegas and Santibáñez 2010). Countries that provide access through publicly provided facilities usually channel resources through direct budget allocations to the institutional authority (central, state, or local) that is responsible for the provision of services (Brazil,

Colombia, Czech Republic, Mexico, and Thailand), or a combination of line budget and block grants (Hungary, the United States, and the United Kingdom). Countries such as Australia, Hungary, United States, and United Kingdom provide subsidies to providers (public or private) or parents to access services, all with varying degrees of targeting and required levels and types of certification from providers.

In most cases, however, households supplement contributions from government sources, whether to cover operational expenses in public centers or as matriculation fees in private centers. Finally, some countries allocate funds "indirectly" to parents through the establishment of generous paid parental and maternal leave policies to care for their young children (for example, Czech Republic, Denmark, Finland, and Hungary) or conditional cash transfers (Ecuador, Mexico, Nicaragua, Panama, and Turkey).

An illustration of the impacts that funding sources and allocation mechanisms have on the access, equity, content and quality of ECD programs is provided by Grun (2008) who compares ECD financing schemes in France, Sweden, United States, England and New Zealand. She found that financing decisions are often driven by factors that, while exogenous to the policy-making process, affect the selection of specific funding sources and allocation mechanisms. These factors, or "drivers," are the locus of capacity, tolerance for variation in services, level of parental voice, participation and knowledge about child-care quality, level of desired budget containment, and degree of heterogeneity in the population. For example, the "French preschool model," which has a central locus of capacity (government finances public provision), a high desire for concrete national standards (low tolerance for variation), and an ability to rely on parental voice (rather than choice), tends to be an effective model in countries where the population is fairly homogeneous and where there is a limited concern over budget containment. From another perspective, the French model would appear to be inappropriate in countries with a strong tradition of decentralization (England or the United States) and private provision (New Zealand or the United States), a strong preference on parental choice (New Zealand, Sweden, the United States), or a high concern over budget containment (England, New Zealand).

How to Increase Funding for ECD Programs

Harmonize Policies and Service-Delivery Mechanisms

Because services for children aged 0–6 are delivered by multiple government ministries at different administration levels (national, state, municipality), and are often delivered in a fragmented manner (health, nutrition, education), there is scope to identify possible overlaps or duplication of efforts to leverage investments across ministries. In an ideal setup, a central-level entity at minimum would be responsible for administrating or coordinating services to guide providers, assure quality of services, provide incentives to increase coverage and quality, and promote research and dissemination. It should be noted, however, that countries have demonstrated success when relying both on the government to be "sole provider" of services and on their own role as active promoter of service provision, irrespective of the type of provider (public, private, or not-for-profit).

Foster the Development of Markets in Child Care Linked with Public-Private Partnerships

Some countries have nurtured the development of new markets, that is, encouraged new providers to enter the market to offer ECD services and programs, by allowing private and not-for-profit providers to access public funds for ECD. More specifically, funds may be allocated when providers meet quality standards (licensing of staff, accreditation of centers, and so on) and institute plans to reach national objectives, targets, or child development outcomes. In such cases, funds can be allocated directly to providers, through earmarked grants, or to parents/caregivers, through vouchers and subsidies (Behrman, Cheng, and Todd 2004).

Explore New and Innovative Funding Sources

Although the bulk of ECD programs are funded by national general budgets, some countries have specialized revenues for financing ECD and other social services. Examples of nontraditional sources of funds include those from France and Colombia, which have a payroll tax dedicated to funding social projects, particularly for children (UNESCO 2006); Brazil, Jamaica, Sweden, the United Kingdom, and the United States, which rely on dedicated income taxes paid by individuals or businesses (Vargas-Baron 2008); South Africa and several U.S. states (Myers 2000), which rely on national or state lotteries; and Mexico, where some revenues from government-run pawn shops are earmarked for early childhood education programs (Vargas-Baron 2008). Although new sources would have to be evaluated on their own merits, as well as on their fiscal neutrality, equity impacts and long-term sustainability, it is important to generate nontraditional options for consideration, especially in a context of multiple and competing demands on traditional sources of public funds.

Annex

Table 4.2A-1   Public Investment in Services for Families and Young Children (Ages 0–6), 2005
percent of GDP

Country	Total cash benefits	Total family services	Public expenditure on ISCED 0* (preschool)	Total public spending (% of GDP)
Australia	2.4	0.5	0.07	2.97
Austria	2.4	0.6	0.42	3.42
Belgium	1.9	0.4	0.58	2.88
Canada	0.9	0	0.2	1.1
Czech Republic	1.5	0.1	0.43	2.03
Denmark	1.5	2.3	0.65	4.14
Finland	1.7	1.4	0.34	3.75
France	1.5	1.3	0.65	3.2
Germany	1.1	0.8	0.40	2.55
Hungary	1.9	0.6	0.73	3.23
Ireland	1.4	0.2	0.39	1.85
Italy	0.6	0.3	0.39	1.29
Korea, Rep. of	0	0.1	0.05	0.15
Mexico	0.1	0.2	0.52	0.82
Netherlands	0.7	0.4	0.37	1.47
Norway	1.9	1.3	0.84	4.04
Portugal	0.7	0.5	0.30	1.55
Sweden	1.8	1.1	0.52	3.42
United Kingdom	1.9	0.3	0.45	2.65
United States	0.1	0.3	0.38	0.78
Average	**1.3**	**0.63**	**0.434**	**2.36**

Source: OECD (2006) *Starting Strong II.* Table 5.2, p. 246.
Note: *ISCED 0—UNESCO defines preschool as level 0 in the ISCED (International Standard Classification of Education). Preschool programs vary in content and duration, thus data may not be entirely comparable.

Table 4.2A-2   Public and Private Expenditure on Preprimary Education (Ages 3–6), 2005
percent of GDP

Country	Public expenditure	Private expenditure	Total expenditure (public and private)
Australia	0.07	0.03	0.1
Austria	0.42	0.13	0.55
Belgium	0.58	0.01	0.59
Canada	0.2	n.a.	0.2
Czech Republic	0.43	0.03	0.46
Denmark	0.65	0.15	0.81
Finland	0.34	0.03	0.38
France	0.65	0.03	0.67
Germany	0.4	0.14	0.53
Hungary	0.73	0.07	0.79
Ireland	0.39	n.a.	0.39
Italy	0.39	0.05	0.44
Korea, Rep. of	0.05	0.11	0.16
Mexico	0.52	0.08	0.61
Netherlands	0.37	0.01	0.38
Norway	0.84	0.18	1.02
Portugal	0.3	n.a.	0.35
Sweden	0.52	0	0.52
United Kingdom	0.45	0.02	0.47
United States	0.38	0.11	0.49
Average	**0.434**	**0.07**	**0.495**

Source: OECD (2006) *Starting Strong II.* Table 5.4, p. 247.
Note: n.a. = not applicable.

Table 4.2A-3   Total Public Expenditure on Education and Preschool Education, 2004
percent of GNP

Country	Total public education expenditure	Public expenditure on preschool education	Preschool % of total public education expenditure
			Spending 10% and more
Moldova	4.2	0.80	19.0
Mongolia	5.7	1.00	17.5
Belarus	5.8	1.00	17.2
Bulgaria	4.4	0.60	13.6
Hungary	6.3	0.80	12.7
Slovak Republic	4.1	0.50	12.2
Guyana	5.8	0.60	10.3
France	6.0	0.60	10.0
			Spending 5%–10%
Slovenia	6.1	0.60	9.8
Chile	4.1	0.40	9.8
Israel	7.5	0.70	9.3
Kuwait	7.6	0.70	9.2
Seychelles	5.7	0.50	8.8
Croatia	4.6	0.40	8.7
Spain	4.6	0.40	8.7
Mexico	5.9	0.50	8.5
Czech Republic	4.8	0.40	8.3
Germany	4.8	0.40	8.3
Argentina	3.6	0.30	8.3
Italy	4.9	0.40	8.2
Romania	3.7	0.30	8.1
Azerbaijan	3.7	0.30	8.1
Costa Rica	5.1	0.40	7.8
Poland	6.6	0.50	7.6
Paraguay	4.3	0.30	7.0
El Salvador	2.9	0.20	6.9
Barbados	7.6	0.50	6.6
Kyrgyz Republic	4.6	0.30	6.5
Peru	3.1	0.20	6.5
Iceland	8.2	0.50	6.1
St. Kitts and Nevis	5.0	0.30	6.0
Jamaica	5.3	0.30	5.7
Netherlands	5.5	0.30	5.5
Estonia	6.0	0.30	5.0
Portugal	6.0	0.30	5.0
			Spending 1%–5%
Greece	4.3	0.20	4.7
Finland	6.6	0.30	4.5

(continued)

Table 4.2A-3   Total Public Expenditure on Education and Preschool Education, 2004
(continued)

Country	Total public education expenditure	Public expenditure on preschool education	Preschool % of total public education expenditure
Norway	7.6	0.30	3.9
Switzerland	5.1	0.20	3.9
Canada	5.4	0.20	3.7
Tajikistan	2.9	0.10	3.4
Bolivia	6.7	0.20	3.0
Nepal	3.4	0.10	2.9
New Zealand	7.3	0.20	2.7
Korea, Rep. of	4.6	0.10	2.2
Mauritius	4.7	0.10	2.1
Australia	4.9	0.10	2.0
Lao PDR	2.5	0.05	2.0
Colombia	5.1	0.10	2.0
Kenya	7.1	0.10	1.4
Benin	3.3	0.04	1.2
Malaysia	8.5	0.10	1.2
			Spending less than 1%
Congo, Rep.	4.4	0.03	0.7
Nicaragua	3.2	0.02	0.6
South Africa	5.5	0.02	0.4
Senegal	4.1	0.01	0.2
Jordan	5.0	0.01	0.2

Source: Adapted from EFA GMR EFA Early Childhood Development (UNESCO 2006).

Table 4.2A-4 Funding Sources and Financing Mechanisms: Country Examples

Country	Source of funds	Allocation mechanism	Coverage
Australia	*Expenditure* *0–3 years* • 0.45% of GDP (67% public) *3–6 years (preschools and kindergartens)* • 0.1% of GDP (0.7% public and 0.3% private) *Funding sources* • Preschool education is the responsibility of state and territory governments. The Department of Education, Science and Training provides supplementary per capita funding to education providers on as-needed basis to accelerate educational outcomes for Indigenous Australians. • Parents cover 22% of the cost.	*0–6 years* • Child Care Benefit (CCB) to parents • Tax rebate for out-of-pocket expenses incurred by families using approved child care	*Family daycare and long-day child care* • 0–1 years: 7% • 1–2 years: 26% • 2–3 years: 40% *Preschools or kindergartens* • 3–4 years: 61% • 4–5 years: 81% • 5–6 years: 28%
Brazil	*Expenditure* *3–6 years* • 0.4% of GDP *Funding sources* • FUNDEB (national basic education fund) includes preschool education as an eligible level. • Privately funded provision is the most common option for 0–3-year-old children.	*0–6 years* • State and municipal revenue from taxes is allocated to public providers.	*Daycare* • 0–3 years: 11.7% *Preschools* • 5–6 years: 57%

(continued)

Table 4.2A-4 Funding Sources and Financing Mechanisms: Country Examples *(continued)*

Country	Source of funds	Allocation mechanism	Coverage
Colombia	*Funding sources* • Payroll tax of 3% on all public and private individuals and enterprises • The central government (Ministry of Education) and municipalities recently launched a joint fund (*Fondo de Fomento a la Atención Integral de la Primera Infancia*) to extend coverage to children under 5 in vulnerable conditions.	*0–6 years* • Taxes are deposited in a central bank account managed by a semi-autonomous institute (*Instituto Colombiano de Bienestar Familiar*). • Budget line provided directly to public providers of preschool services (age 5–6).	*Integrated Services 0–6- Instituto Colombiano de Bienestar Familiar* • 21% of age group *Daycare programs and preschool* • 0- 5-year-olds: 44% • 5- 6-year-olds: 86%
Czech Republic	*Expenditure* *3–6 years* • 0.46% of GDP (0.43% public and 0.03% private) *Funding sources* • Multiple sources including the regional school authority (teacher salaries, books, and equipment); municipalities (operational costs and capital investments); parental fees (capped at 50% of costs for the first 2 years and free for the final year). Funds to improve material conditions or purchase equipment and toys are often generated through sponsoring contracts with private enterprises. Some private and church kindergartens are now in operation, though on a small scale.	*0–2 years* • Parental leave policies, including 28 weeks of paid maternity leave (69% of earnings) followed by a flat-rate parental leave benefit paid until children reach their 4th birthday. *3–6 years—preschools* • Budget line allocations to providers	*Family care/informal arrangements* • 0–3 years: 99.5% *Center-based crèches* • 0–3 years: 0.5% *Mateska skola/kindergartens* • 3–6 years: 76%–95%

Denmark

Expenditure

3–6 years
- 2.1% of GDP
- Parents cover 30%–33% of the cost, with a sliding fee schedule based on need.

Funding sources
- Local authorities are responsible for funding.

0–6 years to kindergarten
- Parental leave policies: 28 weeks paid at full employment and an optional additional 26 weeks paid at 60% of unemployment rate.
- Local authorities finance providers.
- Parents may also be provided with a grant to use the services of a free-choice child minder recognized by the municipality

Family daycare (kommunal dagpleje) and center-based daycare (vuggestuer)
- 0–1 years: 12%
- 1–2 years: 83%

Kindergarten (bornehaver, aldersintegrerede institutioner, and bornenaveklasse)
- 3–5 years: 94%

Finland

Expenditure

0–7 years
- 1.7% of GDP (1.1% family daycare and center-based care, 0.2% preschool class for ages 6–7 years, and 0.4% home care allowance)

Funding sources
- State and local authority taxes
- Parents cover 15% of the costs of daycare, capped at €200 per child per month, while preschool education (6-year-olds) is free.

0–7 years
- Maternity leave policies: 18 weeks paid at full employment, plus 26 weeks paid at 66% of earned income.
- Municipalities allocate funds to public or private providers for daycare services, although parents can also access private child-care allowances. The Ministry of Education receives a budget line for preschool education.

Daycare centers (päiväkoti) and family daycare homes/places
- 1–2 years: 27.5%
- 2–3 years: 43.9%
- 3–4 years: 62.3%
- 4–5 years: 68.5%
- 5–6 years: 73%

Preschool (half-day for the academic year and wrapped around by daycare)
- 6–7 years: nearly universal

(continued)

Table 4.2A-4 Funding Sources and Financing Mechanisms: Country Examples *(continued)*

Country	Source of funds	Allocation mechanism	Coverage
Hungary	*Expenditure* 3–6 years • 0.79% of GDP (0.73% public and 0.07% private) *Funding sources* • 90% of total expenditure is for public provision, while 10% is channeled toward a small nonprofit sector. • Central government provides 25%–30% of costs; municipal local government provides about 60%; and parents provide the remaining 10–15%.	*0–7 years* • Paid maternity leave of 24 weeks for insured (employed) women, covered at 70% of her average salary, and then at a flat rate into the third year. • Universal parental leave child-care allowance for a maximum of 135 weeks (or 53 weeks if the mother has not previously taken maternity leave) at a flat sum equal to the minimum old-age pension. • Block grants from central to local authorities.	*Child-care center / crèche (bölcsde)* • 0–3 years: 8.5% *Kindergarten/preschool/ nursery (óvoda)* • 3–4 years: 85% • 4–5 years: 91% • 5–6 years: 97%
Indonesia	*Funding sources* • The government sponsors an ECD Forum and Consortium to develop policies and protocols. • Households pay as much as 91% of the cost of child/daycare and preschool services.	• There are no parental or maternity leave policies in place.	*Preschool* • 5–6 years: 19% (mostly private)
Kenya	*Funding sources* • Households bear 95% of the cost of child care and preschool. • Most services are private, with households contributing the bulk of expenditures, including caregiver salaries.	• Government finances caregiver training, curriculum support, and information services. Districts finance program officers to train teachers and develop curriculum. • Local districts and communities provide physical space and managerial duties.	*Preschool* 5–6 years: 26%

186

			Educación Inicial
Mexico	*Expenditure*	*0–6 years*	• 0–3 years: 3%
	3–6 years	• 12 weeks paid maternity leave only for women working in the formal sector and enrolled in social security.	*Preschool (general, indigenous, and community-based)*
	• 0.61% of GDP (0.52% public and 0.08% private)	• National government allocates funds to states and municipalities.	• 3-year-olds: 20%
	Funding sources		• 4-year-olds: 63%
	• The federal government covers 80% of the cost of public provision, while parents cover the remaining 20%. Some states and municipalities also raise revenues to supplement funding.		• 5-year-olds: 81%
Senegal	*Funding sources*	• Most preschool services are financed by households or NGOs. The Ministry of Education allocates some funds for central-level staff to regulate, train, build capacity, and inspect preschool centers.	*Public nursery schools and private preschool*
	• Most services are private (formal preschool and religious schooling) with households contributing the bulk of expenditures. The church subsidizes religious preschools.		• 5- 6-year-olds: 3%
	• Government funds are mainly for staffing central services to regulate, train, build capacity, and inspect preschool centers.		
Thailand		*0–6 years*	*Kindergarten, preschool, and child development centers*
	• The government is the major funding source, although funds are also raised from private sectors, NGOs, communities, parents, and external sources.	• Budget allocations to central entities responsible for infrastructure, equipment, teacher and staff salaries, foods, utilities, and basic operational expenses. Many child development centers require monthly fees (varies by center) from parents to cover excess expenses such as meals, materials, and sometimes partial salaries for caregivers).	• 4–6 years: 85%

(continued)

Table 4.2A-4 Funding Sources and Financing Mechanisms: Country Examples *(continued)*

Country	Source of funds	Allocation mechanism	Coverage
United Kingdom (England)	*Expenditure* 3–6 years • 0.47% of GDP (0.45% public and 0.02% private) *Funding sources* • Main contributors to funding are families 45%, nursery education 38% (public), Sure Start general grant 10% (public), child-care tax credit 5% (public), and employers 2%. • Public provision is provided to families both in the form of free services and indirectly through tax credits and grants that parents may use in any area of the marketplace. Fees in the child-care sector are largely set by the market. • Costs to parents vary greatly according to service provider, service type, and income category. The average contribution of parents to child care is estimated to be 45% of full costs. Costs for low-income and some middle-income parents may be covered to 80%, but parents using private child-care and preschool services (the majority) often pay full costs.	*0–6 years* • 26 weeks paid maternity leave paid at 90% of earnings for 6 weeks, followed by a fixed rate for the remaining period. 26 additional weeks unpaid leave are available plus 26 weeks unpaid leave if a mother has worked for an employer for more than 26 weeks. • Public subsidy at provider and user levels. Providers receive start-up costs while families (based on need) receive tax credits through the Working Tax Credit Child Care Element. • Public subsidies through grants/fees are paid to profit-making or nonprofit providers, the latter being predominant in provision for children up to compulsory schooling. • Tax and national insurance contribution exemptions for employer-supported child care have been introduced; however, few employers provide assistance, financial or otherwise, to child care. • A large part of the public sector subsidy (the Sure Start Grant) is channeled to Children's Trusts in Local Authorities, which commission and plan local services.	*Child minders / day nurseries/ playgroups / children centers* • 0–3 years: 20% *Nursery education* • 3–4 years: 96% • 4–5 years: full enrollment

United States

Expenditure
3–6 years
- 0.4% of GDP

Funding sources
- Eligible population is limited to economically disadvantaged children and families.
- For child care, on average the contribution is as follows: federal government 25%, state and local government 15% and parents the remaining 60%. Low-income parents pay on average 18% of family income per child enrolled in child care.
- For preschool (3–6 years), approximately 34% comes from public sources and 66% from private sources, half of this being from household expenditure.
- Federal funding is largely targeted to children with disabilities and children from low-income families.

0–6 years
- For the Head Start program, the federal government provides block grants to local agencies ("Head Start Grantees") to offer services.
- The federal government provides Child Care Development Fund grants to states to subsidize child-care costs for eligible families or improve the quality/availability of child-care services. Some funds require matching contributions. In turn, states: provide subsidies (certificates or in cash) to parents to purchase services.
- Disadvantaged/special needs children can also benefit from federal funds under Title 1 of the Elementary and Secondary Education Act of 1965.

Daycare / child care
0–3 years: 38%

Pre-kindergarten and kindergarten
3–5 years: 56.4%
4-year-old: 80%
5–6 years: 90%

(continued)

189

Table 4.2A-4 Funding Sources and Financing Mechanisms: Country Examples *(continued)*

Country	Source of funds	Allocation mechanism	Coverage
United States	• States raise revenues using different schemes, including state lotteries (Georgia, North Carolina, and Tennessee); "sin" taxes on tobacco (Kentucky, California); community partnerships (Massachusetts); special car license plates, marriage licenses, and donations (Missouri). Only 10 states have no state-funded pre-kindergarten program (Hawaii, Idaho, Indiana, Mississippi, Montana, New Hampshire, North Dakota, South Dakota, Utah, and Wyoming). • Some local districts raise revenue through property taxes and include them as part of their school finance formula (Texas Early Childhood and Pre-Kindergarten Initiative)		

Sources: OECD (2006); UNESCO (2006); Vegas and Santibáñez (2010); Belfield (2006); Pew Center on the States (2009); U.S. Department of Health and Human Services, Administration for Children and Families; Stone (2008).

Notes

1. UNESCO defines preschool as level 0 in the ISCED (International Standard Classification of Education). Preschool programs vary in content and duration, thus data may not be entirely comparable

2. See "Key Dimensions of Early Childhood Intervention Programs" in Karoly, Kilburn, and Cannon (2005). "Early Childhood Interventions: Proven Results, Future Promise". The Rand Corporation. Santa Monica, CA.

Key Readings

Tayler, C., and J. Bennett. 2006. *Starting Strong II: Early Childhood Education and Care*. Paris: Education Directorate of the Organisation for Economic Co-operation and Development.

UNESCO (United Nations Educational, Scientific and Cultural Organization). 2006. *Education for All Global Monitoring Report 2007: Strong Foundations: Early Childhood Care And Education*. UNESCO, Paris.

Vargas-Baron, E. 2008. "Observations on the Financing of Early Childhood Development at the National Level." *Coordinators Notebook* 30. Toronto: The Consultative Group on Early Childhood Care and Development.

References

Behrman, J., Y. Cheng, and P. Todd. 2004. "Evaluating Preschool Programs When Length of Exposure to the Program Varies: A Nonparametric Approach." *Review of Economics and Statistics* 86 (1):108–32.

Belfield, C. 2006. "Financing Early Childhood Care and Education: An International Review." Paper commissioned for the *Education for All Global Monitoring Report 2007: Strong Foundations: Early Childhood Care And Education*. United Nations Educational, Scientific and Cultural Organization, Paris.

Consultative Group on Early Childhood Care and Development. 2008. "Funding the Future: Strategies for Early Childhood Investment, Costing and Financing." *Coordinators' Notebook, An International Resource for Early Childhood*, No. 30.

European Commission Network on Childcare and Other Measures to Reconcile the Employment Responsibilities of Men and Women. 1996. "Quality Targets in Services for Young Children: Proposals for a Ten-Year Action Programme."

Grun, R. 2008. "Financing Early Childhood Development." Note for the Department of Education of Khanty-Mansiysk, Russian Federation. World Bank, Washington, DC.

Karoly, L., R. Kilburn, and J. Cannon. 2005. "Early Childhood Interventions: Proven Results, Future Promise." The Rand Corporation, Santa Monica, CA.

Myers, R. 2000. "Financing Early Childhood Education and Care Services." *International Journal of Educational Research* 33 (1):75–94.

Pew Center on the States. 2009. *Votes Count: Legislative Action on Pre-K Fiscal Year 2010*. Pew Center on the States, Washington, DC.

Stone, D. 2008. "Funding the Future: States' Approaches to Pre-K Finance: 2008 Update." Pre-K Now, Pew Center on the States, Washington, DC.

Tayler, C., and J. Bennett. 2006. *Starting Strong II: Early Childhood Education and Care*. Paris: Education Directorate of the Organisation for Economic Co-operation and Development.

UNESCO (United Nations Educational, Scientific and Cultural Organization). 2006. *Education for All Global Monitoring Report 2007: Strong Foundations: Early Childhood Care and Education*. UNESCO, Paris.

Van Ravens, J., and C. Aggio. 2008. "Expanding Early Childhood Care and Education: How Much Does It Cost? A Proposal for a Methodology to Estimate the Costs of Early Childhood Care and Education at Macro-Level, Applied to the Arab States." Working Paper 46, Bernard van Leer Foundation, The Hague.

Vargas-Baron, E. 2008. "Observations on the Financing of Early Childhood Development at the National Level." *Coordinators Notebook* 30. Toronto: The Consultative Group on Early Childhood Care and Development.

Vegas, E., and L. Santibáñez. 2010. "The Promise of Early Childhood Development in Latin America and the Caribbean." World Bank, Washington DC.

Descriptions of Projects and Studies Included in *Investing in Young Children*

1. IEA Preprimary Project

Location: 10 economies (some analysis includes only 7): Finland; Greece; Hong Kong SAR, China; Indonesia; Ireland; Italy; Poland; Spain; Thailand; United States.

Study: A longitudinal, cross-national study of preprimary care and education to identify how process and structural characteristics of the settings children attended at age 4 are related to their age-7 language and cognitive performance.

Design: Phase 1, a household survey to identify child-care options; phase 2, an observational study to document the structural and process characteristics of settings and age 4 assessment; phase 3, follow-up at age 7. Analysis employed a 3-level, hierarchical linear model.

Sample: Phase 2, n = 2904 children and 838 settings; phase 3, n = 2247 children.

Outcome measures: Language and cognitive skills at ages 4 and 7.

Ages at baseline and follow-up: 4 and 7 years.

Main findings: The findings consistent across countries include: children's language skills improved as teacher's number of years of full-time schooling increased and when the predominant type of activity was free choice. Children's cognitive performance improved as children spent less time in whole group activities and the variety of equipment and materials available increased. Also, a number of findings varied across countries, depending on particular country characteristics. The findings support child-initiated activities and small group activities and were consistent with developmentally appropriate practices promoting active learning.

Reference: Montie, Xiang, and Schweinhart (2006).

Note: 3.1.

2. Madrasa Resource Center Study 1

Location: 3 countries: Kenya, Uganda, and Tanzania's Zanzibar region.

Impact Evaluation: Madrasa Early Childhood Development is a community-based preschool program in which women in the community serve as teachers. It targets Muslim children from poor socioeconomic backgrounds.

Madrasa preschools use culturally appropriate curricula that encourage active learning while providing children with learning skills to succeed in secular primary schools.

Design: Comparison of the quality of Madrasa preschools and other types of preschools, using standard quality scale. The study also included assessment of child outcomes.

Sample: 53 preschools (Kenya: 9 program and 8 comparison schools; Uganda: 13 program and 5 comparison schools; Zanzibar: 10 program and 8 comparison schools). The sample selection methodology was not clearly noted. The study sampled 464 children (program, n = 174; control, n = 157).

Outcome measures: The quality of classrooms measured by the Early Childhood Environment Rating Scale and the curriculum-related extension, revised (ECERS-RE). Children's cognitive development (measures adapted from the British Ability Scales and the African Child Intelligence Test.

Ages at baseline and follow-up: Ages varied and were included in the analysis; 3 tests were conducted for child assessments (1 pretest and 2 posttests).

Main findings: Compared to other typical preschools in Africa, including government schools in Kenya, Madrasa preschools scored higher on all the environmental dimensions assessed using ECERS-RE. Regarding child outcomes, those who were in preschools performed better than children who stayed at home. In addition, the Madrasa preschool provided better value-added than the other types of preschools.

Reference: Mwaura and Mohamed (2008).

Note: 3.1.

3. Madrasa Resource Center Study 2

Location: 3 countries: Kenya, Uganda, and Tanzania's Zanzibar region.

Impact Evaluation: See Madrasa Resource Center Study 1.

Design: A cross-sequential study over three time-points during preschool to evaluate the effectiveness of Madrasa preschools compared to other types of local preschools.

Sample: 46 Madrasa schools at the first data collection, dropping to 35 by the third data collection point. 321 (program = 168, comparison = 153) children were originally selected, dropping to 179 (program = 92, comparison = 87) by the third data collection round. Comparison schools were matched with the Madrasa preschool in each geographical area for the proportion of trained teachers, location within 3 km, and having been operational for at least 2 years.

Outcome measures: Children's cognitive ability measured through an adapted version of the British Ability Scale II and the African Child Intelligence Test, and adjusted for child age. Preschool quality was assessed using the ECERS-R.

Ages at baseline and follow-up: Mean ages of children at the three rounds of data collection were 4.3, 6.0, and 7.1 years.

Main findings: Madrasa preschoolers and other children did not differ in cognitive performance at beginning of preschool, while children in Madrasa programs increased cognitive scores by .40 SD per year more than children in the comparison group. When included in the analysis, school quality was a significant predictor of cognitive abilities for Madrasa children but did not have a significant effect on the comparison group.

Reference: Malmberg, Mwaura, and Sylva (forthcoming).

Note: 3.1.

4. School Construction Program Study 1

Location: Argentina

Impact Evaluation: The public school system in Argentina provides 3-year preprimary education to 3–5-year-olds. The curriculum is focused on developing (1) communication skills, (2) personal autonomy and behavioral skills, (3) social skills, (4) logical and mathematical skills, and (5) emotional skills. Children typically attend preprimary classes for 3.5 hours a day, 5 days a week, during 9-month school year. The average class size is 25.

Following introduction of a new law in 1993 to expand compulsory education to include the last year of preprimary education, the government invested in construction of more than 3,500 new preprimary classrooms.

Design: The study evaluated the impact of a large construction program of preprimary school facilities on enrollment and maternal labor market behavior using pooled household survey data.

Sample: The data from the Argentine household survey *Encuesta Permanente de Hogares* (EPH) that is representative of the urban population of Argentina, pooling repeated cross-sections of individual-level data from the May waves of the survey covering the 1992–2000 period. The pooled data had 29,817 households with at least one child between 3 and 5.

Outcome measures: Maternal employment, preschool attendance among children aged 3–5.

Ages at baseline and follow-up: Not applicable.

Main findings: The construction program had a sizeable impact on preprimary school enrollment among children aged 3–5. The program explains about half of the 15 percentage-point increase in gross enrollment experienced from 1991 to 2001. The results are similar for households with and without spouses present, and with and without children younger than 3.

For women with young children, maternal labor force participation and child care are jointly determined. If stock of rooms is increased from 0 to 1 and there is full take-up of the newly constructed places, the likelihood of maternal employment would increase between 7 and 14 percentage points.

Reference: Berlinski and Galiani (2007).

Note: 1.1.

5. School Construction Program Study 2

Location: Argentina

Impact Evaluation: See School Construction Program Study 1.

Design: Non-experimental. Analysis of data from the national standardized test. The data do not contain systematic information on preprimary school attendance, thus the study only estimated intent-to-treat effect— the net effect of the supply of preprimary school on subsequent child outcomes. Exposure to the program was estimated using information on the number of classrooms constructed by year and municipality.

Sample: The impact on 3rd-grade performance was estimated based on 126,106 (math) and 117,515 (Spanish) observations.

Outcome measures: Student performance from the administrative records of the standardized achievement tests in math and Spanish. Teachers' rating of students' attitude and behavior.

Ages at baseline and follow-up: The study is not longitudinal; it used outcome data at 3rd grade.

Main findings: The enrollment rate for preprimary education increased from 49% in 1991 to 64% in 2001. Analysis of nationally administered standardized test scores and teacher surveys estimated that one year of preprimary education increased the standardized 3rd-grade test scores in Spanish and mathematics by 8% of the mean or by 23% of the standard deviation. It also found positive effects of preprimary education in areas of attention, effort, and discipline as well as class participation among 3rd graders.

Reference: Berlinski, Galiani, and Gertler (2009).

Note: 3.1.

6. Community-Based Preschool Program (No Project Name)

Location: Bangladesh

Impact Evaluation: A half-day, 6-day-a-week preschool program for 3–6-year-olds includes free play, stories, and instruction in reading and math. The program was initiated by the Plan Bangladesh and was in operation for 5 years at the time of evaluation. The objectives are to develop skills related to the learning process, a positive attitude toward learning through a child-friendly approach, individual learning styles through play, and reading and math preparation for primary school. Curriculum includes skills related to language, cognition, and an awareness of the environment. Started with more child-initiated free play and structured group games and rhymes; later, more teacher-directed instruction was introduced to meet parents' demands. Communities provide the space, recruit candidates for teachers, and create play materials, while the NGO provides training and supervising of teachers and instructional materials. Parents pay a nominal monthly fee if they can.

Design: Impact evaluation, but the assignment to treatment was not random. A cross-sectional comparison of preschool children and comparison group from nearby villages where preschools were not yet available.

Sample: Cluster sampling of program and control villages, 22 villages each. Children were randomly selected from each group; program = 213 and comparison = 188.

Outcome measures: Cognitive development (WPPSI-III subtests on vocabulary, visual concepts, analytic reasoning, similarities); a school readiness test (colors, shapes, letters, numbers, math concepts and operations, adapted from Wechsler Preschool and Primary Scale of Intelligence (WPPSI)); social skills (Play Observation Scale); weight and height are measured as control variables. The study also collected data on quality using modified version of ECERS.

Ages at baseline and follow-up: 4.5–6.5 years old. Not longitudinal.

Main findings: After the analysis controlled for child's age, nutritional status, mother's education, and household assets, preschool children performed better than control children on measures of vocabulary, verbal reasoning, nonverbal reasoning, and school readiness. Effect sizes for WPPSI tests were modest, while it was large for school readiness. Also, during play, preschool group showed more interactive play, more conversations than control group (although the level of interaction was less than the program aimed for). Cognitive level of play was not significantly different.

Reference: Aboud (2006).

Notes: 1.3, 3.1.

7. Responsive Feeding Intervention

Location: Bangladesh

Impact Evaluation: Both the intervention group and the control group received 12 sessions on child development that discussed how parents could help children learn, provide stimulation through toys and talk, and use gentle discipline, as well as 12 monthly sessions on health and nutrition, including complementary feeding. The intervention group additionally received 5 weekly sessions on responsive feeding and one follow-up session 4 months later.

Design: Cluster-randomized controlled trial of the impact of education on responsive feeding.

Sample: A total of 108 mother-toddler pairs randomly selected from 19 communities were randomly assigned to the intervention group; 95 mother-toddler pairs from 18 communities were assigned to the control group.

Outcome measures: Child weight, mouthfuls eaten, self-fed mouthfuls, and mother's responsive verbal acts.

Ages at baseline and follow-up: Not applicable. Children were 8–20 months at recruitment, data collected at recruitment (pretest), 2 weeks after the sessions ended, and 5 months after the sessions ended as well as 6 weeks after the follow-up session.

Main findings: The intervention was successful in increasing self-feeding by children and verbal responsiveness by mothers. However, the number of mouthfuls eaten by children did not differ, nor did the low levels of weight gain. Weight gain may require more nutritional inputs, especially in areas of high food insecurity.

Reference: Aboud, Shafique, and Akhter (2009).

Note: 3.2.

8. PIDI *(Proyecto Integral de Desarrollo Infantil)*

Location: Bolivia

Impact Evaluation: Project provided home-based, integrated services (full-time child care, nutrition, and educational activities) to children aged 6 months to 6 years from poor families in urban areas. The goals of PIDI are to improve health and early cognitive/social development by providing children with better nutrition, adequate supervision, and stimulating environments. The children in the program are cared for in groups of 15 by two or three caregivers in the home of a local woman selected by the community. Under the program, the children receive two meals a day and a snack, approximately 70% of their caloric requirements, and participate in stimulating, structured, and age-appropriate play. They also receive basic health services including routine immunization and growth monitoring. The project provides daycare providers with training in child development and loans or grants to upgrade their homes.

Design: Analysis of a nonexperimental data set. Program impacts are estimated nonparametrically as a function of age and duration. A generalized version of the method of matching is developed and used to control for nonrandom selectivity into the program or into alternative program durations.

Sample: Program, n = 364 (randomly selected from program participants); control A, n = 745 (randomly selected children in communities where program has not started yet); control B, n = 392 (randomly selected children in the same neighborhood).

Outcome measures: (1) bulk motor skills, (2) fine motor skills, (3) language-auditory skills, (4) psychosocial skills, (5) height-for-age percentile, (6) weight-for-age percentile.

Ages at baseline and follow-up: Age is part of independent variable. No description of mean age at baseline. Two rounds of data collection, about 1 year apart.

Main findings: Program increased cognitive and psycho-social test scores, but only for children who participated in the program for at least 7 months. There were increasing marginal impacts with greater program exposure. The benefit/cost ratio is estimated at 1.7 to 3.7.

Reference: Behrman, Cheng, and Todd (2004).

Notes: 3.1, 4.1.

9. Warmi Project

Location: Bolivia

Evaluation without a control group: Project aimed to improve maternal and child health through community-based intervention in a remote province with limited access to medical facilities. A project team (2 auxiliary nurses) made monthly (or more frequent) visits to all women's organizations focused on initiating and strengthening the women's organizations, developing women's skills in problem identification and prioritization, and training community members in safe birthing techniques.

Design: Comparison of outcome indicators pre- and post-intervention.

Sample: 50 communities in Inquivisi Province. The total population in the project area is 15,000 (no random assignment of treatment, no control group).

Outcome measures: Perinatal and neonatal mortality rate.

Ages at baseline and follow-up: Not applicable.

Main findings: Perinatal mortality decreased from 117 to 43.8 per 1,000 births, a change large enough to suggest attribution of the program. The number of women who received prenatal care was greater after the intervention, and there was an increase in the number of women who breastfed on the first day of life.

Reference: O'Rourke, Howard-Grabman, and Seoane (1998).

Note: 3.2.

10. Mother and Child Health (MCH) Campaign

Location: Cambodia

Evaluation without a control group: 100 episodes of Cambodia's first television soap opera taking place in a hospital ("Taste of Life"); a photo strip magazine on the TV program; three types of radio phone-in programs targeting youth, men, young couples, and parents with small children; 23 television spots and 22 radio spots. Programming focused on improving sexual health, increasing condom use, and changing attitudes toward people living with HIV and AIDS. It also addressed the health of young children by encouraging breastfeeding, raising awareness of acute respiratory infections, and promoting handwashing to prevent diarrhea. The programs had a good coverage, with 83% of television viewers having watched "Taste of Life" at least once, 27% of radio listeners tuned in to the radio program for men, 32% to the program for youth, and 19% to the program on maternal and child health.

Design: Comparison of viewers and listeners vs. unexposed; assignment is not random.

Sample: 2,274 respondents at baseline and 2,280 at end line.

Outcome measures: Knowledge of childhood illnesses (acute respiratory infection [ARI] and diarrhea).

Ages at baseline and follow-up: Not applicable; data collection was implemented one year apart.

Main findings: Exposed groups compared to unexposed or the baseline are more likely to have knowledge on specific childhood illnesses.

Reference: Power (2005).

Note: 3.3.

11. Predictors of Quality in Family Child Care (No Project Name)

Location: Canada

Study: The study tested the influence of the structural variables in family child-care centers on process quality using data from seven jurisdictions in Canada.

Design: Analysis of center-level data using hierarchical regression models.

Sample: Randomly selected family child-care centers, n = 231 centers.

Outcome measures: The quality of care measured using FDCRS. Data on caregiver background information (age, family, education, training on ECE, income from child care, experience, etc.) was collected through self-report questionnaires and interviews.

Ages at baseline and follow-up: Not applicable.

Main findings: The findings indicated that physically and emotionally safe child care was the norm in the sample, but almost two-thirds of the centers failed to provide children with adequate opportunities to develop language and cognitive skills. The study found that intentionality (caregiver's commitment to child-care work), training on ECE, and use of support services (such as provider networking, use of toy library/library) were the important predictors of quality. The caregiver's level of general education was associated with the quality, but once the variable for ECE training was included in the model, it did not emerge as a predictor. (The sample included many caregivers who majored in ECE, thus intercorrelation was high.) The results suggest that the 60–150 hours of training received was not long enough to have an impact; college ECE programs provide a greater depth and breadth of knowledge and skills.

Reference: Doherty et al. (2006).

Note: 3.1.

12. Second Phase of the Canadian "You Bet I Care" Project (YBIC)

Location: Canada

Study: The study focused on identifying the predictors of quality in child-care center programs in seven provinces/jurisdictions in Canada.

Design: Analysis of center-level data. The study used path analysis to identify direct and indirect predictors of quality.

Sample: Randomly selected child-care centers, n = 326 classrooms in 239 centers.

Outcome measures: The quality of centers measured by the Caregiver Interaction Scale (CIS), the Infant/Toddler Environment Rating Scale (ITERS), and the Early Childhood Environment Rating Scale–Revised

(ECERS-R). Questionnaires for centers and staffs were administered to collect information on structural quality of the centers (wages, working conditions, satisfaction levels of staff, center operations, and finances).

Ages at baseline and follow-up: Not applicable.

Main findings: As observed in the Cost, Quality, and Outcomes (CQO) U.S. study, staff education levels were significant predictors of quality in Canada, as were adult-child ratios, staff wages, and auspice (nonprofit vs. for-profit). This study found that the education level of caregivers and their wages represent direct predictors of quality, while adult-child ratios and auspice influence quality indirectly. The number of staff or adults was a significant direct predictor of quality, just as the presence of a student-teacher was a significant indirect predictor. In cases of preschool classes, staff satisfaction with work environment, colleagues, and parent fees were significant predictors of quality. The overall levels of child-care quality were disturbingly low, with most ITERS and ECERS scores in the minimal range.

Reference: Goelman, Forer, and Kershaw (2006).

Note: 3.1.

13. Nutrition Education Project (No Project Name)

Location: China

Impact Evaluation: A pilot nutrition program was a 1-year intervention for all pregnant women and women with infants up to 1 year old in the study in villages in Sichuan province. The messages were delivered through monthly home visits by trained nutrition educators. During the visits, the educators provided advice and counseling on feeding and nutrition, and they weighed the children. The main messages were on breastfeeding for up to 6 months, improving quantity and quality of complementary foods, and continued breastfeeding.

Design: Impact evaluation of a home visit/nutrition counseling pilot program.

Sample: Randomization at the township level (one level above the villages); the study included 495 children (control, n = 245; program, n = 250) from 4 townships.

Outcome measures: Child growth (weight-for-age, weight-for-height, and height-for-age Z scores), child hemoglobin levels, mother's breastfeeding practice and awareness, and complementary feeding practices and awareness.

Ages at baseline and follow-up: Participants were recruited while pregnant or infant, and the assessment of outcomes was done one year later.

Main findings: After 1 year of intervention, children in the program were longer and heavier than those in the control group at 12 months and had higher breastfeeding rates. The mothers in the program group also showed significantly higher nutrition knowledge and better reported infant feeding practices than the mothers in the control group.

Reference: Guldan et al. (2000).

Note: 3.2.

14. China Famine Study (No Project Name)

Location: China

Study: Epidemiological investigations of the effect of famine on prevalence of adult schizophrenia in Wuhu area of Anhui Province, China.

Design: Using the records of all psychiatric referrals in the only psychiatric hospital in the region and records of birth and deaths, the risk of schizophrenia for each year of birth was calculated, then the affected cohorts (1959–62) were compared with births occurred outside of famine period (1956–58 and 1963–65).

Sample: Not a sample survey.

Outcome measures: Prevalence of schizophrenia.

Ages at baseline and follow-up: Not applicable; the birth cohorts described above and the records at the psychiatric hospital were followed 1971–2001.

Main findings: The birth rates in Anhui decreased approximately 80% during the famine years. Among the births that did occur, the adjusted risk of developing schizophrenia in later life increased significantly from 0.84% in 1959 to 2.12% in 1960 and 1.81% in 1962. Prenatal exposure to famine increases risk of schizophrenia in later life.

Reference: St. Clair et al. (2005).

Note: 1.2.

15. Cali Study

Location: Colombia

Impact Evaluation: 5-day-a-week, 6 hours of daily integrated health, nutrition, and educational activities (4 hours for education and 2 hours for health and nutrition). Nutrition program provided a minimum of 75% of recommended daily caloric and protein intake, supplemented with vitamins and minerals. Daily observation of all children and referral service were provided under the health activity. The education program used an integrated curriculum model focused on cognitive processes, language, social abilities, and psychomotor skills.

Design: A randomized controlled trial to evaluate if length of treatment has additional effects. The treatment group was assigned to 5 groups— 4 different treatment periods (one period = 180 days/9months) and one group receiving one treatment period plus prior nutritional supplementation and health care. They also observed children with high SES during the same period.

Sample: Random selection of low-income children. Sample size at baseline (end line): treatment, n = 301 (248); control, n = 116 (72); sample with high SES = 38 (30).

Outcome measures: Cognitive/language measures including language usage, short-term memory, fine motor control, information, vocabulary, quantitative concepts, spatial relations, and logical thinking.

Ages at baseline and follow-up: Baseline, 43 months, the follow-up was conducted at 19, 63, 77, and 87 months.

Main findings: Combined nutrition, health, and educational treatments between 3.5 and 7 years of age can prevent large losses of potential cognitive ability, with significantly greater effects when starting earlier. As little as 9 months of treatment prior to primary school entry appears to produce gains. And the effects persisted through age 8.

Reference: McKay et al. (1978).

Note: 3.2.

16. Baseline for an Evaluation of the *Bono de Desarrollo Humano*

Location: Ecuador

Study: Data were collected as a baseline for an evaluation of a CCT program. The authors examined the relationship between early cognitive development, SES, child health, and parenting in Ecuador.

Design: Analysis of a single cross-section of observational data using multivariate regressions to understand the relationship between SES factors and performance on the language test. The authors also compared the results with evidence from the United States.

Sample: 3,153 children in 158 parishes in 6 provinces. As the data collection was a part of the evaluation of the cash transfer project, the sample consisted primarily of children from young, poor families.

Outcome measures: Receptive language (TVIP). Background variables used in analysis include SES (wealth, parental education, etc.); health (height, weight, hemoglobin level); parenting measures (number of siblings, home environment).

Ages at baseline and follow-up: There was no follow-up; at the time of survey, children were ages 36–71 months.

Main findings: Strong associations were found between socioeconomic status and children's vocabulary. These gradients were larger for older children, especially in relation to household wealth.

Child health (hemoglobin level and height) and the quality of parenting are associated with a child's cognitive development. Parenting quality accounts for a substantial share of the association between parental education and cognitive development.

Reference: Paxson and Schady (2007).

Notes: 1.1, 1.3, 3.1, 3.4.

17. *Bono de Desarrollo Humano*

Location: Ecuador

Impact Evaluation: CCT program targeted families in rural and poor urban areas living below poverty level (first quintiles of the poverty index). Transfer of US$15/month was given directly to women. The average monthly transfer was $10.51. Initially, the conditionality included taking children younger than 6 years of age for bimonthly visits to public health clinics and sending school-aged children to school, but the conditionality was never implemented.

Design: A randomized controlled trial to evaluate the impact of a CCT program on ECD outcomes and family practices.

Sample: 1,124 households (1,124 children 3–7 at follow-up).

Outcome measures: *Children's* physical well-being and growth (hemoglobin level, height-for-age, and fine motor skills); cognitive development, (vocabulary [PPVT] cognitive, long-term memory, short-term memory, visual integration [Woodcock-Muñoz battery]); and behavior (mother's report on behavioral problems). *Mothers:* Physical and mental health— hemoglobin level, maternal depression, maternal punitiveness and lack of warmth, stress, number of hours worked, self-rated social status.

Ages at baseline and follow-up: Not applicable; exposure to CCT program was 17 months on average.

Main findings: For the entire sample, the study found modest treatment effects of the program on fine motor skill (0.16 SD) and long-term memory (0.19 SD). There were positive but not significant effects on other outcome indicators. Effects were larger for the bottom quartile, including significant effects on hemoglobin (0.39 SD), fine motor control (0.29 SD), long-term memory (0.23 SD), and behavior problems scale (0.39 SD).

No difference in effects by children's age was found. Program effects were consistently larger among girls than boys. Significant effects among the poorest quartile include the mean of cognitive and behavioral measures (0.39 SD for girls and 0.11 SD for boys). Girls in poorest quartile were more disadvantaged than boys outside the BDH program. Effects were larger for children with more highly educated mothers. Intermediate outcomes included the following: (1) Treatment group mothers saw themselves as better-off than control mothers; and (2) mothers' hemoglobin levels improved (the gains were larger for the poorest). Survey results show that nearly half the households spent all or most of transfers on food. No significant effect was found on parental mental health and stress level. There was no significant effect on the use of growth-control visits, but those visited were more likely to receive deworming.

Reference: Paxson and Schady (2010).

18. Helsinki Cohort

Location: Finland

Study: Epidemiological study of the associations between low birth-weight and rapid weight gain in childhood (ages 3–11) and incidence of type 2 diabetes and coronary heart disease (CHD).

Design: Using a large longitudinal dataset, the study calculated odds ratios for type 2 diabetes and hypertension, as well as CHD.

Sample: The Helsinki cohort comprised 15,846 individuals born 1924–33 and 1934–44. This study looked at the data for 13,517 men and women whose measurements at birth and BMI at age 11 were available. The data were matched with the data from national registers of hospital discharges by cause, registers of people receiving medication for chronic illness, and registers of death by cause. Analysis of cumulative effects of childhood weight gain was limited to the people who were born 1934–44 for whom growth data were available from birth through infancy and early childhood and into school years.

Outcome measures: Odds of developing type 2 diabetes, hypertension, and CHD.

Ages at baseline and follow-up: Birth, age 11, and later in life.

Main findings: The risks for type 2 diabetes and hypertension fell with increasing birthweight and rose with increasing BMI at age 11. When comparing different groups of people (by birthweight and changes in BMI), those with the highest birthweight and a subsequent decrease in BMI score had less than half the incidence of type 2 diabetes than all other groups combined. For CHD too the risks of disease fell with increasing birthweight and rose with increasing BMI at 11. Based on 279 (men) and 66 (women), hospital admissions and death, among men, ponderal index (birthweight/birth length 3) was more strongly related to disease, and, among women, length at birth was stronger.

Reference: Barker et al. (2002).

Note: 1.2.

19. Preschool Study in Guinea and Cape Verde

Study: The purpose was to develop a preliminary picture of the impacts and effectiveness of an ECD program. A survey was conducted to identify different programs and preschool models and to detail their characteristics.

A sample of preschools was selected to identify the impact that preschool attendance, different preschool programs/models, and various preschool characteristics had on cognitive and physical development of the children who attended them. The range of existing programs in each of the countries was examined to determine the programs and characteristics that appeared to be most effective and least costly in supporting children's development.

Design: Multivariate analysis of nonexperimental data using preschool attendance as the independent variable, along with family and child characteristics.

Sample: Guinea, p = 529, c = 348. The majority (64%) attended *ecole maternelle* (traditional French preschool model); 22%, community-based (CEC) preschool, *Jardin d'enfants;* CV, p = 490, c = 313. There was no description of types of schools, only of those entities that manage the program (i.e., public, private, NGO, communal, religious).

Outcome measures: Cognitive development (a simplified version of the Boehm Basic Concept Test); height-for-weight ratio.

Ages at baseline and follow-up: Not longitudinal, cognitive development measured only for 5-year-olds.

Main findings: Preschool attendance increased child cognitive development by 4.41 points in Guinea and 7.27 points in Cape Verde. Preschool attendance did not have a significant impact on height-for-weight ratio. Although family background is the most influential determinant, preschool attendance increases the explanatory power to approximately 16–20%. Effect is disproportionate on children at risk (i.e., the poor in Guinea, children from large families and with mothers who work, and girls in both countries). Religious school in Cape Verde and community education centers are most effective in raising cognitive development scores. Language of instruction also affects learning; in Guinea, schools with a single language scored better than bilingual schools, while in Cape Verde, bilingual schools scored better. School curriculum did not seem to matter. High-cost schools did not necessarily perform better, but parent fees had a positive effect.

Reference: Jaramillo and Tietjen (2001).

Note: 3.1.

20. Guatemala Nutrition Supplementation Trial Study 1

Impact Evaluation: Impact evaluation of nutrition supplementation from gestation to early childhood. In the 2 treatment villages, a high-protein energy drink (Atole) was provided, and in the 2 control villages, a non-protein, low-calorie drink (Fresco) was made available at food supplementation centers and was available daily on a voluntary basis to all members of the community. The subjects of the study were all village children aged 7 years or younger and all pregnant and lactating women. Individual intake was recorded carefully.

Design: Quasi-experimental, randomization occurred at the village level. The evaluation assessed the long-term impact of inputs in nutrition during early childhood on physical work capacity.

Sample: This follow-up sample included 1,574 persons, or about 73% of all original participants (2,392, all children less than 7 in the randomly selected 4 villages). The assessment of physical performance was conducted for 364 subjects (randomly selected, then when selected person declined, filled in with volunteers).

Outcome measures: (1) Physical work capacity (oxygen consumption at maximum physical exertion) other measurements were made as confounding factors; (2) anthropometry and body composition (fat-free mass); (3) skeletal maturity.

Ages at baseline and follow-up: At baseline all children were less than 7 (data collection on early nutrition ended at age 7); the youngest children included in the study were about 6 months. Follow-up was conducted when children were 11–26 years old. The sample was grouped in 3 cohorts: cohort 1, 11–14 years old who received supplementation from gestation to varying age; cohort 2, 14–18 years old who received the intervention throughout gestation and the first three years of life; and cohort 3, 18-26 years who were born before the intervention started and had complete exposure from 4 to 7 years of age.

Main findings: Among cohort 2 (full exposure to the intervention from gestation to 3 years), men who had taken Atole had significantly higher physical work capacity than those consuming Fresco, after controlling for body weight and fat-free mass; also there was a significant positive relationship between the amount of supplement consumption and the physical work capacity. The supplementation effect in women of similar age was not statistically significant.

Reference: Haas et al. (1995).

21. Guatemala Nutrition Supplementation Trial Study 2

Impact Evaluation: See Guatemala Nutrition Supplementation Trial Study 1. This follow-up study examined the impact of early childhood nutrition supplementation on economic productivity as adults.

Design: See study 1. This study looked at economic productivity as adults.

Sample: Of 2,392 individuals included in the original study, 1,855 were eligible for the follow-up; 1,571 at least partially participated and 1,424 completed the interview.

Outcome measures: Annual earned income, hours worked in the last year, average wage rate.

Ages at baseline and follow-up: See study 1 for the baseline. At this follow-up, participants were aged 25–42 years.

Main findings: Exposure to Atole before, but not after, age 3 was associated with higher hourly wages, but only for men. For exposure from 0 to 2 years, the increase was US$0.67 per hour, which meant a 46% increase in average wages. There was a nonsignificant tendency for hours worked to be reduced and for annual incomes to be greater for those exposed to Atole from ages 0 to 2.

Reference: Hoddinott et al. (2008).

22. Jamaican Supplementation Study 1

Impact Evaluation: The study participants (stunted children aged 9–24 months) were assigned randomly to four groups: (1) control, (2) nutrition supplementation only, (3) stimulation only, and (4) both nutrition and stimulation intervention. Nutrition supplementation consisted of supplying 1 kg/week milk-based formula, and stimulation consisted of weekly 1-hour home visits by community health workers with the objective of improving mother-child interactions through play. Both types of intervention lasted for 2 years.

Design: A randomized controlled trial to evaluate the effects of nutrition supplementation and stimulation, as well as combined effects of both supplementation and stimulation.

Sample: 129 stunted children aged 9–24 months were identified through a house-to-house survey of poor Kingston neighborhoods; these children were randomly assigned to 4 groups. 32 nonstunted children matched for age, sex, and neighborhood were also identified for the study. 127 stunted children and all 32 nonstunted children were located at the end of the intervention.

Outcome measures: (1) anthropometric measurements (2) child development (gross motor, hand and eye coordination, hearing and speech, cognition [shape recognition, block construction, block patterns]); using an adapted version of the Griffiths Mental Development Scales.

Ages at baseline and follow-up: At the baseline, children were 9–24 months old; the first follow-up was conducted after 2 years.

Main findings: Supplementation benefited the children's growth, whereas stimulation did not. Supplementation and stimulation benefited the children's development (7 and 8 developmental quotient points, respectively). The effects of combined treatments were additive and the group receiving both was the only one to catch up to the nonstunted group.

Reference: Grantham-McGregor et al. (1991).

Note: 1.2.

23. Jamaican Supplementation Study 2

Study: See study 1. This follow-up study was conducted 4 years after the 2-year intervention (age 7 or 8).

Design: See study 1.

Sample: See study 1. 122 stunted children and 32 nonstunted children were located at this follow-up. 52 additional nonstunted children (who were also identified in the original survey) were added.

Outcome measures: This follow-up included (1) academic achievement (test scores on reading, spelling, arithmetic); (2) IQ (Stanford Binet

Test); (3) vocabulary (PPVT); (4) visual reasoning (Raven's Progressive Matrices); (5) categorical fluency; (6) verbal analogies; (7) long-term semantic memory; (8) learning ability; (9) auditory working memory; (10) visual-spatial working memory (Corsi blocks); (11) fine-motor coordination.

Ages at baseline and follow-up: This follow-up study was conducted at ages 7–8.

Main findings: There was an extremely small (not significant) but wide range of positive trends among children in the treatment group. The only significant effects were found in the perceptual-motor factor (the stimulation group), and only in supplemented children whose mothers had higher PPVT scores. The size of the benefits remaining after 4 years was less than anticipated, and no suggestion remained of the additive effect.

Reference: Grantham-McGregor et al. (1997).

Note: 1.2.

24. Jamaican Supplementation Study 3

Study: See study 1. This follow-up study was conducted at ages 17–18.

Design: See study 1.

Sample: See study 1. 103 stunted children and 64 nonstunted children were identified.

Outcome measures: This follow-up included (1) IQ (WAIS), (2) non-verbal reasoning (Raven's Matrices), (3) visual-spatial working memory (Corsi blocks), (4) auditory working memory, (5) verbal analogies, (6) vocabulary (PPVT), (7) reading, (8) mathematics, (9) school dropout.

Ages at baseline and follow-up: This follow-up study was conducted at ages 17–18.

Main findings: Stunting in early childhood is associated with cognitive and educational deficits in late adolescence, which are reduced by stimulation at a young age. There were no significant effects of nutritional supplementation. Compared to the control group, stimulation resulted in higher scores for IQ, vocabulary, verbal analogy, and reading tests. Overall, children in the stunted control group had significantly poorer scores for 11 of 12 cognitive and educational tests and were more likely to have dropped out of school. Stunted children who received stimulation intervention compared to the control group sustained cognitive and educational benefits with effect sizes of 0.4–0.6 SD. Although stimulation showed substantial benefits to stunted children, their performance was consistently lower than the nonstunted (and no intervention) group, with two of these measures significantly lower.

Reference: Walker et al. (2005).

25. Home Visitation Program

Location: Jamaica

Impact Evaluation: The program was delivered to the families through a weekly 1-hour visit by a paraprofessional (community health worker) for the first 8 weeks of life. The home visitors showed parents how to communicate with infants, respond to their cues, and show them affection.

Design: A randomized controlled trial to evaluate the impact of a home visitation program to enhance psychosocial development of low birthweight infants.

Sample: Pregnant women were randomly selected. Low birthweight infants were randomly assigned in two groups: control (n = 69), treatment (n = 66); in addition, matched normal birthweight infants (n = 87) were identified.

Outcome measures: Infant's intentional problem-solving skills at 7 months. Infant's behavior rated by the examiners.

Ages at baseline and follow-up: Birth and 7 months.

Main findings: The infants in the program scored higher than the control group in problem-solving skills, and they were happier and more cooperative during the test session.

Reference: Meeks-Gardner et al. (2003).

Note: 3.2.

26. *Oportunidades*

Location: Mexico

Impact Evaluation: Distribution of monthly stipend conditional on family members obtaining preventive medical care. Children's health check-ups; pregnant women and children 2–5 years old with low weight received a fortified food supplement. Education scholarships awarded to children with 85% attendance at school and who did not repeat a grade more than twice; size of education stipend is higher for higher grades and for girls. Conditionality is verified before each transfer.

Design: Estimating the effect size for each outcome that is associated with a doubling of cash transfers while controlling for a wide range of background characteristics.

Sample: At follow-up early intervention group: 1,681 children aged 24–68 months and 5 years of exposure; 768 children aged 24–50 months and 3–5 years of exposure.

Outcome measures: Children 24–68 months. Physical (height-for-age, BMI, gross motor skills); children 36–68 months. Cognitive— long-term memory, short-term memory, visual integration (Woodcock-Muñoz battery). Language (PPVT).

Ages at baseline and follow-up: All children were in the program during their entire lives.

Main findings: Cumulative income transfers were associated with positive outcomes in most domains. Doubling of CT was associated with height-for-age, lower prevalence of stunting, improvements in endurance, long-term memory, short-term memory, visual integration, and language development. (Impact on cognitive development is modest at 0.08–0.18 SD.)

No association was found for motor development or hemoglobin level.

Reference: Fernald, Gertler, and Neufeld (2006).

Note: 3.4.

27. Community-Based Participatory Intervention (No Project Name)

Location: Nepal

Impact Evaluation: Project villages received visits by a facilitator who was briefly trained in perinatal health issues. The women's group met monthly to discuss childbirth and care behaviors in the community, identification of priority issues and strategies, and implementation and assessment of their strategies. During this process, women sought more information about perinatal health.

Design: A cluster-randomized controlled trial of community-based participatory learning.

Sample: Out of 43 communities, 24 were matched and randomly assigned as control and program communities, including data on 2,945 deliveries in program communities and 3,270 deliveries in control communities.

Outcome measures: Neonatal mortality rate identified by surveillance. Care behaviors and health-care seeking behavior.

Ages at baseline and follow-up: Not applicable.

Main findings: The estimated mortality baseline rates were comparable in both program and control communities. The post-intervention neonatal mortality rate was 26.2 in program communities and 36.9 per 1,000 in control communities. Maternal mortality rate was 69 per 100,000 in program and 341 per 100,000 in control communities. Women in program communities were more likely to have prenatal care, institutional delivery, trained birth attendance, and hygienic care than controls.

Reference: Manandhar et al., (2004).

Note: 3.2.

28. Atención a Crisis

Location: Nicaragua

Impact Evaluation: Women in beneficiary households received sizable cash transfers every 2 months, averaging about 15% of per capita expenditures; $145 for families with no children. Households with children between 7 and 15 enrolled in primary school received in addition $90, and an additional $25 per child. Conditionality was children's primary school and health service attendance.

Design: a randomized controlled trial of (1) a CCT conditional on children's primary school and health service attendance; (2) the CCT plus a scholarship that allowed one of the household members to choose and take a vocational training course; (3) the CCT plus a productive investment grant, to encourage starting a small non-agricultural activity for households that devised a business development plan.

Sample: treatment, 3,002 households; control, 1,019 households.

Outcome measures: (1) For all children: socio-personal, language, and fine and gross motor skills using subtest of the Denver Developmental Screening test. (2) For children ages 36–83 months: Receptive Vocabulary (PPVT) short-term memory test and a leg motor test from McCarthy test battery; caregiver's report on behavior using Behavior Problem Index. *Intermediate outcomes:* expenditure patterns, child food intake, stimulation, birthweight, child's weight and height, preventative health care, caregiver's mental health; caregivers observed parenting behavior using the HOME Inventory score.

Ages at baseline and follow-up: Not applicable; exposure to CCT program was 9 months.

Main findings: Treatment effects of 3 types of interventions were similar. Significant effects were found for socio-personal (0.13 SD), language (0.17 SD), vocabulary (0.22 SD) domains. There were positive but not significant effects on other outcome indicators. There were also significant effects on food consumption and child food intake of nutrient-rich food; early stimulation (reading to child and story-telling, availability of books, paper, and pencil); preventative health care (growth checkups, received vitamins, iron, and de-worming drugs). There were also marginally significant improvements on early enrollment to primary school and caregivers' mental health. However no effects were found on child anthropometric measures or on birthweight. Observed changes in intermediate outcomes and child development outcomes were larger for older children.

Reference: Macours, Schady, and Vakis (2008).

Note: 3.4.

29. Nutrition Education Project (No Project Name)

Location: Peru

Impact Evaluation: The intervention aimed to raise the profile of nutrition in the health facilities and to integrate nutrition services into existing child-oriented national programs (such as immunization, monitoring of growth and development, and management of acute respiratory infections and diarrhea) by enhancing the quality of nutrition counseling through training and provision of simple, standardized, age-appropriate messages to be used at all points of contact with young children in the facility. Three key messages were: (1) a thick puree satisfies and nourishes your baby, equivalent to three portions of soup: at each meal, give puree or thick-food preparation first; (2) add a special food to your baby's serving: (chicken) liver, egg, or fish; and (3) teach your child to eat with love, patience, and good humor. Facilities were assisted in developing their own messages. The project also provided communication materials and clinical history forms designed to prompt physicians to include brief questions and advice on nutrition. The intervention included demonstrations of preparation of complementary foods and group sessions for caregivers of children of similar ages. The intervention also provided training to improve anthropometry skills in health-care workers.

Design: A cluster-randomized control trial of a nutrition education program.

Sample: Among 21 health facilities identified in the study area, 6 were randomly assigned to the control and 6 to program groups. Data on 187 babies in the program group and 190 in the control group were used in the analysis.

Outcome measures: Child growth (weight, length, and weight-for-age and length-for-age Z scores at 18 months).

Ages at baseline and follow-up: Birth, and 3, 4, 6, 8, 9, 12, 15, and 18 months.

Main findings: At 18 months, children in the intervention group were 1 cm taller and three times less likely ($p = 0.018$) to be stunted than children in the control group, even after controlling for the effect of birthweight. Their nutritional intake was better than children in the control group (higher energy intake at 18 months, higher intakes of energy from animal sources at 15 and 18 months, higher iron and zinc intake). The mothers in the program also had better health-care-seeking behavior and knowledge about breastfeeding and complementary feeding.

Reference: Penny et al. (2005).

Note: 3.2.

30. ECD Program

Location: Philippines

Impact Evaluation: Integrated ECD services that offered options of family daycare for 3–5-year-olds, community-based parent education programs, 8-week school-readiness program for children entering formal education, growth monitoring, improved service of health and nutrition. A new service provider, the "child development worker" was placed in all program areas; this worker had the task of complementing the roles of midwives and health workers in providing food and nutritional supplements, monitoring children's health status, and conducting community-based parent education on ECD.

Design: IE analyzing three rounds of surveys. No random assignment of treatment. Sample communities were randomly selected for treatment/control groups. Estimates were "intent to treat" effects, as the program was quite complex. IE estimated the project impact using "intent-to-treat" difference-in-difference propensity score-matching estimators.

Sample: Stratified cluster sampling of communities. Children in communities where pilot was implemented, n = 4,140; children in target communities in phase 1 of the project, n = 194; non-program areas, n = 2,359.

Outcome measures: Gross motor skills, fine motor skills, receptive language, expressive language, cognitive development, socio-emotional development, self-help.

Ages at baseline and follow-up: Three rounds of surveys. Children were 0–4 years old at baseline (Apr.–Aug. 2001). The first follow-up was conducted in Sept.–Nov. 2002, and the 2nd follow-up in Sept.–Nov. 2003.

Main findings: There has been a significant improvement in the cognitive, social, motor, and language development and in short-term nutritional status of children who reside in ECD program areas compared to those in non-program areas, particularly for those under age 4 at the end of the evaluation period. The proportions of children below age 4 with worms and diarrhea also have been lowered significantly in program compared to non-program areas; however, there were effects in the opposite direction for older children, thus the overall impact on these two indicators is mixed.

Reference: Armecin et al. (2006).

Note: 3.1.

31. Cebu Longitudinal Health and Nutrition Survey Study 1

Location: Philippines

Study: The Cebu Longitudinal Health and Nutrition Survey is part of an ongoing study of a cohort of Filipino women who gave birth between May 1, 1983 and April 30, 1984. Using the data from the survey, the author assessed the long-term impacts of early childhood nutrition on school outcomes. Originally conceptualized as a study of infant feeding patterns, the research is now focused on the long-term effects of prenatal and early childhood nutrition and health on later adult outcomes, including education and work outcomes, and development of chronic disease risk factors. The current study assesses the long-term impacts of early childhood nutrition on school outcomes.

Design: Analysis of a large cohort survey using a sibling differences procedure. The survey included data on younger siblings of the selected sample (index child).

Sample: Randomized cluster sample. Original sample consisted of 3,289 children from 33 randomly selected districts in Cebu. For this study, a sample of 1,016 siblings pairs were included.

Outcome measures: School attainment and academic achievement (English and math tests) when the index child was 11. Other information collected in the survey included (1) anthropometric measurements, health and nutrition data (including during pregnancy 7–8 months) every 2 months in the first 2 years; (2) anthropometric data on the index children and younger siblings when the index child was 8 years old.

Ages at baseline and follow-up: Birth to ages 8 and 11.

Main findings: After controlling for parental inputs and family environment, children better nourished in early childhood perform significantly better in school, partly because they enter school earlier, but mostly because they learn more per year of schooling. The cost-benefit analysis identified that a dollar invested in early childhood nutrition programs could potentially return at least 3 dollars worth of gains in academic achievement.

Reference: Glewwe, Jacoby, and King (2001).

Notes: Introduction, 2.1.

32. Cebu Longitudinal Health and Nutrition Survey Study 2

Location: Philippines

Study: Using data from the Cebu Longitudinal Health and Nutrition Survey, authors evaluated whether nutrition during particular months (e.g., the first 6 months) of the first 24 months is more important than during other periods in a child's cognitive development.

Design: Analysis of the longitudinal data using two multiple regression models (the reduced form and conditional demand estimates).

Sample: See study 1. At age 8 years, 2,264 children of the original 3,080 in the set time frame for this study were evaluated.

Outcome measures: Outcome indicator was the score of the Philippines Nonverbal Intelligence Test at age 8. Change in height in the first 2 years was used as a proxy for nutritional intake; other variables included rainy season and the prices of staple foods.

Ages at baseline and follow-up: Baseline at birth; follow-up at 8 years old.

Main findings: Neither of the models supports the hypothesis that nutrition in the first 6 months of life or during the prenatal period is more critical than at other time periods for cognitive development. On the contrary, the estimates suggest that the period from 18 to 24 months may be critical. Imprecise evidence indicated that price subsidies for corn and infant formula could improve children's nutritional status.

Reference: Glewwe and King (2001).

33. Turkish Early Enrichment Project Study 1 and Study 2

Location: Turkey

Impact Evaluation: The project included two studies: (1) original 4-year study, designed to investigate the separate and combined effects on children of an educational preschool environment and a mother training program and (2) a follow-up conducted 6 years after the end of the original study. Children in three categories of early child-care environment were recruited for the study (i.e., children in educational nursery school, custodial care, and home care.) The 2-year parent education program consisted of biweekly paraprofessional home visits where mothers learned to use materials based on the HIPPY program during the school year (Home Intervention Program for Preschool Youngsters), focusing on children's language, problem-solving, and sensory and perceptual discrimination skills. In addition, the project organized biweekly group meetings to share information about children's overall development and the well-being of the mother and health of the family relationship. The mothers received educational materials every week and were supposed to work with their children on a daily basis for 15–20 minutes.

Design: A cluster-randomized control trial. Study 1 followed up with children in 5 poor towns for 4 years, comparing the impacts of educational daycare, custodial daycare, and parent education programs in early childhood. The impact of the combination of 3 types of child-care environment (educational center, custodial center, and home care) and intervention were studied.

Sample: For Study 1, a total of 280 children aged 3 and 5 living in a lower-income area of Istanbul. Daycare/nursery school participants were selected from among the preselected three educational and three custodial centers. In some centers, all children in the age group were included; if there were too many children, participants were randomly selected. Home-care children were randomly selected from the same shantytown neighborhoods as the other two groups. Study 2 included 217 child and mother pairs from Study 1.

Outcome measures: In Study 1 all outcomes were measured and reported for the 4th year. Cognitive skills (Stanford-Binet Intelligence Test, Analytical Skills, Children's Embedded Figures Test, Academic Achievement in Turkish, math and general ability, grades at primary school); personality and social development (by mother's report on autonomous/ dependent behavior/aggression/self-concept/school adjustment, emotional problems); home environments (by observation); and mother's interviews (understanding and perception of child's development, family relationship, etc.). For Study 2: child's attitudes toward school and education; relationship with parents; expectations for education and occupation; self-concept; social adjustment; vocabulary (from the WISC-R); Embedded Figures Test, school grades; mother's attitudes and practices on child-rearing, family relations, expectations for her child, etc. Fathers were also interviewed.

Ages at baseline and follow-up: In Study 1, children were either 3 or 5 at the baseline and followed up for 4 years. Study 2 was conducted 7 years after Study 1.

Main findings, Study 1: At the end of the intervention, educational-center-based care and mothers' training approaches improved the children's cognitive skills, social relationships, and school adjustment.

Main findings, Study 2: A significantly larger proportion of children from the mother training group (86%) were still in school compared to the control group (67%). More of the effects of the mother training program were sustained compared to educational-center-based care (for example, school attainment, school achievement, academic orientation, socio-emotional development, and social adjustment). Despite the earlier lead in cognitive development in children in educational-center care, there were no differences among the three types of environments in terms of grades or school attainment by the end of the 5th year of primary school.

Reference: Kagitçibasi, Sunar, and Bekman (2001).

Notes: 1.1, 1.3, 3.1, 3.2.

34. Turkish Early Enrichment Project Study 3

Location: Turkey

Impact Evaluation: A follow-up at 19 years after the intervention (see Studies 1 and 2).

Design: See Studies 1 and 2.

Sample: 131 of the original participants were included in the study.

Outcome measures: (1) achievement and cognitive skills (school attainment, college attendance, vocabulary test scores); (2) socioeconomic success (age entering workforce, occupational status, expenditure as proxy for income, integration to modern urban society); (3) life satisfaction, family relationships, and childrearing values.

Ages at baseline and follow-up: 19 years after Study 1 (around age 25).

Main findings: Parent-education participation or educational preschool attendance had significantly positive associations with higher school attainment, entering into workforce later, and higher occupational status. Other findings included: (1) pre-intervention cognitive skills had consistent effects over the entire developmental trajectory; (2) children who were in the bottom 25% of the distribution of the cognitive skills at entry did not show any effects of the intervention, while the other 75% did in various domains, and (3) the impact of the intervention was greater for males than for females in the achievement/cognitive domains.

Reference: Kagitçibasi et al. (2009).

35. National Child Development Survey Study 1

Location: United Kingdom

Study: A continuing longitudinal study of some 17,000 children born in England, Scotland, and Wales in 1958, intended to better understand the factor affecting human development over the whole life span. Authors examined the long-term effects of test scores at age 7.

Design: Analysis of a longitudinal cohort survey, using multivariate models (including various background factors such as parental SES, parental education) to predict multiple long-term outcomes.

Sample: The data from the National Child Development Survey were used. The survey is a longitudinal study of all of the approximately 17,000 children born in Great Britain between March 3 and 9, 1958. At the last wave (5th) of the survey, the response rate was 72%.

Outcome measures: Reading and math test scores at 16; school attainment (O level); employment at 23 and 33; wages at 23 and 33. At age 7, reading and math skills were measured.

Ages at baseline and follow-up: The same respondents were followed starting at infancy: ages 7, 11, 16, 23, 33, and 42.

Main findings: The test scores measured at age 7 had significant effects on future educational and labor market outcomes. For example, respondents in the lowest quartile of the reading test score distribution at age 33 had wages 20% lower than those who scored in the higher quartiles.

The analysis of interactions between SES and test scores at age 7 found that educational attainments and employment at age 33 were influenced as follows: low-SES children reap both larger gains from having high age-7 test scores and smaller losses from having low test scores at age 7. The opposite is true among high-SES children, who suffer larger losses from low scores and smaller gains from high scores. There was little evidence of comparable interactive effects for wages.

Reference: Currie and Thomas (1999).

Note: 1.3.

36. National Child Development Survey Study 2

Location: United Kingdom

Study: See Study 1. This particular analysis looked at the individual contributions that mothers' and fathers' involvement makes to their children's schooling.

Design: Analysis of longitudinal data using hierarchical regression analysis to explore early predictors of educational attainment, in particular, contribution of father's and mother's involvement at age 7, measured by self-report of frequency of activities (reading, outings) and level of interest/involvement.

Sample: Of the 7,259 observations with valid data on parental involvement at age 7 and education attainment at age 20, 3,303 were included in the final analysis.

Outcome measures: Educational attainment at age 20. The variables included in the model, other than parental involvement, are: behavior problems at age 7, general ability at age 11 and academic motivation at age at age 16.

Ages at baseline and follow-up: See Study 1.

Main findings: Father and mother involvement at age 7 independently predicted educational attainment at age 20. The association between parents and learning was not stronger for sons than daughters. Father involvement was not more important for educational attainment when mother involvement was low rather than high.

Reference: Flouri and Buchanan (2004).

Note: 3.2.

37. 1970 British Cohort Study

Location: United Kingdom

Study: The data from the 1970 British Cohort Survey, which used a nationally representative sample (17,196 at birth) out of which 10% was randomly selected for measuring cognitive outcomes at early years along with those who were considered to be most at risk from fetal malnutrition (2,457 at 22 months, and 2,315 at 42 months). The same cohort was followed through 26 years; at 26, there were 9003 respondents. Analysis of a large cohort study in the United Kingdom investigating the associations between early childhood development (22 and 42 months) and long-term outcomes.

Design: The study examines the associations between early skills and later performance, as well as between test rank at different ages and SES, as well as the ranking of previous tests.

Sample: Out of randomly selected cohort, 9,003 participants were followed at age 26.

Outcome measures: Educational qualifications at 26. As a predictor of the final outcome, development in early years (e.g., completing a range of tasks, including pointing to body parts, putting on their shoes, stacking cubes, and drawing lines at 22 months, and counting, speaking, copying and drawing simple geometric shapes at 42 months).

Ages at baseline and follow-up: Starting at birth, 22 months (subsample); 42 months (subsample); ages 5, 10, and 26.

Main findings: The score at 22 months is related to family background, and the difference expands as children grow. The performance at 22 months predicts educational qualifications at age 26, although the 42-month score is a better predictor of the final outcome.

Family background (SES) plays a large role in influencing the mobility of children within the distributions of ability at different ages. Most low-SES children in the bottom quartile stay there at age 10, while high-SES children show considerably more upward mobility, and are more likely to be in the top quartile than the lowest by age 10.

Reference: Feinstein (2003).

Note: 1.3.

38. Effective Provision of Pre-School Education (EPPE) Project, Phase 1

Location: United Kingdom

Study: EPPE is a large-scale, longitudinal study of the progress and development of 3,000 children in various types of preschool education. This study is intended to explore the characteristics of different kinds of preschools and how preschool education influences children's later adjustment.

Design: A longitudinal cohort study to investigate the progress and development of individual children (including the impact of personal, socioeconomic, and family characteristics), and the effect of individual preschool centers on children's outcomes at both entry to school (aged 4+) and through and at the end of primary school (age 7+).

Sample: The sample was stratified by type of center and geographical location to maximize the likelihood of identifying the effects of individual centers and also the effects of various types of provision. Within each geographical area, centers of each type were selected by stratified random sampling, bringing the sample total to 141 centers, n = 3,171, including 300 children who did not attend preschool.

Outcome measures: (1) Age 3 cognitive skills: verbal comprehension, naming vocabulary, knowledge of similarities seen in pictures (nonverbal comprehension), and block building (spatial awareness). A profile of each child's social and emotional adjustment was completed by the preschool educator. (2) Cognitive skills at school entry, a similar cognitive battery was administered along with knowledge of the alphabet, rhyme/alliteration, and early number concepts; the social/behavioral profile completed by the teacher. (3) Grades 1 and 2 standardized math and reading, information on National Assessments were collected along with attendance data and information on a child's special needs status.

Ages at baseline and follow-up: 3, school entry, grades 1–2, and 5–6.

Main findings: *At preschool:* Preschool experience enhances all-round development in children. Duration of attendance is important; an earlier start (under age 3 years) is related to better intellectual development. Full-time attendance led to no better gains for children than part-time provision. Disadvantaged children benefited significantly from good quality preschool experiences, especially where they are with a mixture of children from different social backgrounds. High-quality preschooling is related to better intellectual and social/behavioral development. Settings that have staff with higher qualifications have higher quality scores and children in such settings make more progress.

Quality indicators include warm interactive relationships with children, having a trained teacher as manager, and a good proportion of trained teachers on the staff. Where preschools view educational and social development as complementary and equal in importance, children make better all-round progress. Effective pedagogy includes interaction traditionally associated with the term "teaching," the provision of instructive learning environments, and "sustained shared thinking" to extend children's learning. For all children, the quality of the home learning environment is more important for intellectual and social development than parental occupation, education, or income. What parents do is more important than who parents are.

Follow-up study at year 2 (age 7): The study shows that the benefits are sustained throughout that period, in particular children who received quality preschooling scored better on English and math. By grade 6 (age 11), in general attending a preschool compared with not attending has a positive effect on children's outcomes in English and math. Attainment in both English and math was enhanced by preschool quality. In both cases, the higher the level of quality, the greater the level of attainment. Those children who attended low-quality preschools no longer show a significant cognitive benefit in attainment after six years in primary school. There are clear longer-term advantages to attending a preschool, irrespective of parental qualification level, although children who have parents with higher SES do better.

References: Sylva et al. (2003) and Sammons et al. (2008).

Notes: 3.1, 3.2.

39. Effective Pedagogy in the Early Years (EPEY) Study (Part of the EPPE Project)

Location: United Kingdom

Study: The study was developed to identify the most effective pedagogical strategies to support the development of young children's skills, knowledge, and attitudes, and to ensure they make a good start at school, using quantitative techniques.

Design: Case studies of 14 centers. For the qualitative study, careful, detailed case studies were conducted in each setting which included detailed documentation of naturalistic observations of staff pedagogy and systematic structured observations of children's learning. Information was also gathered and analyzed using interviews with parents, staff, and managers, and through intensive and wide-ranging documentary analysis and a literature review of pedagogy in the early years.

Sample: n = 14 centers; 12 of the settings were chosen on the basis of child social/behavioral and cognitive outcomes from the EPPE project as "good practice" settings; 2 settings were added later for in-depth case studies.

Outcome measures: Not applicable.

Ages at baseline and follow-up: Not applicable.

Main findings: The findings show that good outcomes for children are linked to early years settings and that they have the following characteristics:

- View cognitive and social development of children as complementary and do not prioritize one over the other.
- Have strong leadership and long-serving staff (3 years plus).
- Provide a strong educational focus with trained teachers working alongside and supporting less qualified staff.
- Provide children with a mixture of practitioner-initiated group work and learning through freely chosen play.
- Provide adult-child interactions that involve "sustained shared thinking" and open-ended questioning to extend children's thinking.
- Have practitioners with good curriculum knowledge combined with knowledge and understanding of how young children learn.
- Have strong parental involvement, especially in terms of shared educational aims.
- Provide formative feedback to children during activities and provide regular reporting and discussion with parents about their child's progress.
- Ensure behavior policies in which staff support children in rationalizing and talking through their conflicts.
- Provide differentiated learning opportunities that meet the needs of particular individuals and groups of children (e.g., bilingual, special needs, girls/boys, etc.).

Reference: Siraj-Blatchford et al. (2003).

40. EPPE Phase 2 (Ages 7–11)

Location: United Kingdom

Study: See EPPE phase 1. A follow-up study of the EPPE cohort up to age 11.

Design: The second phase report looks at some of the reasons for different developmental trajectories among high- and low-performing children. Individual, family, and home learning environment (HLE) influences on pupils' developmental outcomes at age 11 are explored as well as the educational influences of the primary school, showing how the academic effectiveness of each primary school is related to pupils' outcomes.

Sample: See EPPE phase 1.

Outcome measures: Children's cognitive (reading/English and mathematics) and social/behavioral outcomes ("self-regulation", "pro-social" behavior, "hyperactivity" and "anti-social" behavior) at ages 10 and 11 in years 5 and 6 of primary school.

Ages at baseline and follow-up: See EPPE phase 1.

Main findings: Only the findings related to home environment and early childhood education are listed here.

- Mother's highest qualification level and early years home learning environment (HLE) are still among the strongest predictors of better academic and social-behavioral outcomes at age 10 and 11, in line with findings at younger ages.
- There were strong reciprocal relationships between pupils' self-perceptions and their academic and social/behavioral outcomes and progress/development, particularly between "academic self-image" and attainment and progress in math and reading, and between "behavioral self-image" and social/behavioral outcomes and development.
- Additional child case study evidence showed that having a high early years HLE, family attitudes that valued education as a means of improving life chances, support for learning from family members, and high parental expectations helped disadvantaged pupils "succeed against the odds."
- The positive benefits of both medium- and high-quality preschool education have persisted for attainment in reading/English and mathematics and all social/behavioral outcomes. Also attending a more effective preschool showed long term benefits for mathematics.
- Moreover, having attended a high-quality preschool was especially beneficial for boys, pupils with special educational needs, and those from disadvantaged backgrounds for most social/behavioral outcomes.
- High-quality preschool was especially beneficial for the most disadvantaged pupils and for those of low-qualified parents in promoting better mathematics outcomes at age 11.
- Children who had attended poor-quality/less effective preschools generally showed no significant benefits at age 11 in improved outcomes

compared to those who did not attend any preschool. However, they did show better pro-social behavior but poorer ratings for hyperactivity.

Reference: Sylva et al. (2008).

41. National Longitudinal Survey of Youth (NLSY) Study 1

Location: United States

Study: The NLSY is a nationally representative sample of 12,686 young men and women who were 14–22 years of age when first surveyed in 1979. Various data, particularly those related to employment and schooling, were collected. Since 1986, detailed information on the development of children born to women in the NLSY 79 cohort has supplemented the data on mothers and children collected during the main NLSY 79, referred to as the "Children of the NLSY 79."

Design: Using the "Children of the NLSY 79" dataset, the study examined the childhood experience and how these exposures are related to participants' well-being.

Sample: Among the female participants who were followed up in 1994, 5,715 with children younger than 15 received assessment of home environment; then those with missing values and questionable ethnic group membership and those with children older than 13 were dropped from this study. The sample size is not clearly stated in the article.

Outcome measures: Children's physical development and social skills up to 48 months (mothers' reports on motor and social development); cognitive/academic performance (Peabody Individual Achievement Test on math and reading for those older than 5); vocabulary (PPVT for those older than 3); problem behavior. The home environment was measured with the Home Observation for Measurement of the Environment-Short Form.

Ages at baseline and follow-up: Not applicable. The biennial survey started following up with the cohort in 1986.

Main findings: Learning stimulation at home was consistently associated with early motor and social development, language competence, and academic achievement in all ethnic groups and at almost every age for both poor and nonpoor children. However, the relationships of parental responsiveness and spanking varied as a function of outcome, age, ethnicity, and poverty status. The evidence indicated slightly stronger relations for younger compared to older children.

Reference: Bradley et al. (2001).

Note: 3.2.

42. Family Child Care and Relative Care Study (FCC Study); California Licensing Study (CLS)

Location: United States

Study: Under the FCC study, family child-care settings in California, North Carolina, and Texas were observed. (The article does not elaborate on this data set.) The CLS was originally designed to examine the impact of adding two school-age children to existing child-care homes. The authors studied these two datasets to identify the structural characteristics that predict quality.

Design: Secondary analysis of two datasets to identify the structural characteristics that predict quality.

Sample: *FCC:* random sampling of families that use child care in three sites; then recruiting their providers for the study. *CLS:* random sampling of the providers from registered providers. The sample used for this analysis was n = 100 for CLS; n = 108 for FCC licensed caregiver; n = 46 for FCC relative; and n = 53 for FCC unlicensed caregiver).

Examples of collected data: information on structural indicators of quality, such as group size and ratio, weighted (by ages) points of child-adult ratio, caregiver background, etc. The global quality of the care was measured by FDCRS and CIS.

Ages at baseline and follow-up: Not applicable.

Main findings: Caregiver characteristics, such as training, are a better predictor of quality than group size or child-adult ratios. Neither observed ratios nor weighted points (that represent child-adult ratio and the mix of children with different ages) were significantly related to quality of teacher sensitivity when other caregiver characteristics were also considered. (Group size in the licensed child-care homes averaged around 6 children with a range of 1–13). Caregivers with training acted less detached in relation to children, and their homes provided higher-quality practices and interactions. The study found inconsistent evidence that more experienced caregivers tended to be slightly more detached and provided lower quality care. Child-care home providers with more education and training tended to have more children per adult, though fewer children than in a typical child-care center. Lower-quality child-care homes tended to have a higher proportion of babies than higher quality homes.

Reference: Burchinal, Howes, and Kontos (2002).

Note: 3.1.

43. Abecedarian Program

Location: United States

Impact Evaluation: Full-time (8 hr/day, 5 days/wk, 50 wk/ yr), high-quality educational intervention in a child-care setting from infancy through age 5, where each child had an individualized prescription of educational activities. Educational activities consisted of "games" incorporated into the child's day, and activities focused on social, emotional, and cognitive areas of development but gave particular emphasis to language. The program provided half of each group with additional academic support from first through third grade in a "school-age intervention" to determine the impact of intervention timing.

Design: A randomized controlled trial of effect of high-quality ECD from infancy to age 5 and beyond on at-risk children. Longitudinal study followed children from birth to age 21.

Sample: Selected at the outset of the longitudinal study were 111 healthy infants (average age 4.4 mo.) who were found to be at "high risk" because of family income and maternal education level. Of that original sample, 57 were randomly assigned to enroll in the Abecedarian program, and the remaining 54 were assigned to the control group. Of those, 104 were followed up at age 21.

Outcome measures: Cognitive development at ages 3–8 years: the Stanford-Binet Intelligence Scale and the Wechsler Preschool and Primary Scale of Intelligence; math and reading ability of 8–21-year-olds (WJ); monitoring of children's progression in education system. Outcomes at age 21 included intellectual level and academic skill (Wechsler Adult Intelligence Scale-Revised, WJ-R in reading and math); educational attainment; skilled employment; self-sufficiency; social adjustment (self-reports of lawbreaking).

Ages at baseline and follow-up: Ages 3, 4, 5, 6.5, 8, 12, 15, and 21.

Main findings: The strongest effects of the Abecedarian preschool program occurred while the children and their families were participating in the project. But the academic achievement effects endured through the teen years and early twenties, more than a decade after participants had left the program.

The program participants had a lower rate of grade retention in grades KG–9 (31.2% vs. 54.5%); were less likely to need special education in grades KG–9 (24.5% vs. 47.7%); had higher adjusted mean reading and math scores. Relative to their peers in the control group at the age of 21, the program participants: had completed more years of school (12.2 vs. 11.6); were more likely to have attended a 4-year college (35.9% vs. 13.7%); were more likely to be in school (42% vs. 20%); were more likely to be engaged in skilled jobs (47% vs. 27%). In terms of gender, women who had been in the preschool program earned 1.2 more years of education than their peers in the control group (12.6 vs. 11.3), but the difference for men was not significant.

At age 21, the treatment group scored significantly higher on intellectual and academic measures, attained significantly longer years or education, were more likely to attend a 4-year college, and were less likely to have had teenage pregnancy. School-age intervention served to maintain the preschool advantage in reading, but the effects were generally less than the preschool intervention.

References: Project website: http://www.fpg.unc.edu/~abc/assets/pdf/1974_abc_brochure.pdf and Campbell et al. (2002).

Notes: 1.1, 3.1, 4.1.

44. Comprehensive Child Development Program (CCDP)

Location: United States

Impact Evaluation: A combination of case management and parenting education delivered through home visits. Case managers conducted biweekly 30–90-minute home visits to each family. During the home visits, they assessed family needs; prepared a family service plan; counseled parents; made referrals for services. Delivery of ECD for 0–3-year-olds depended on the project (location), but in most programs, an early childhood specialist visited the same family biweekly on alternating weeks. This visit focused on parent education rather than providing direct services to children. On average, families were enrolled in the program for 3.3 years. The program was intended to last 5 years, starting while the mother is pregnant or child is younger than 1 year.

Design: A randomized control trial of 21 of the 24 CCDP projects.

Sample: Randomly selected, eligible 4,410 families (below the poverty line, child age, willingness to participate), half assigned to the program and the other half assigned to the control group.

Outcome measures: Child's cognitive functioning using various standardized scales/measures. (MDI of the Bayley scales, PPVT, etc.); parent ratings of child' social and emotional development and health status; parent attitudes and beliefs about child-rearing; incidents of child abuse and neglect; family's level of economic self-sufficiency, employment status, education/training by self-report. Home environment and the quality of the parents' interaction with children were assessed through observation.

Ages at baseline and follow-up: 18 months, 1, 2, 3, 4, and 5 years.

Main findings: The evaluation found no statistically significant impact on program families compared to the control families on child outcomes (cognitive and social/emotional development and health) or on parent outcomes (parenting, family economic sufficiency, and maternal life course).

Reference: Goodson et al. (2000).

Note: 3.2.

45. Early Childhood Longitudinal Study (ECLS) Study 1

Location: United States

Study: ECLS collects national data on children's status at birth and at various points thereafter; children's transitions to nonparental care, early education programs, and school; and children's experiences and growth through 8th grade. The program includes three longitudinal studies that examine child development, school readiness, and early school experiences. The birth cohort of the ECLS-B is a sample of children born in 2001 and followed from birth through KG entry. The KG class of 1998–99 cohort is a sample of children followed from KG through 8th grade. The KG class of 2010–11 cohort will follow a sample of children from KG through 5th grade.

Design: Analysis of a longitudinal cohort study. Effects estimated using OLS, matching, and instrumental variables estimates. Only the KG dataset was used for analysis.

Sample: Nationally representative sample of children; study analyzed data for 14,162 children. (No explanation of sampling methods, etc.)

Examples of collected data: Information on child-care arrangements; child outcomes, including reading and math test at KG; teacher rating on social-behavioral skills and problems; family characteristics.

Ages at surveys: Information was collected in fall and spring of KG (1998–99), fall and spring of 1st grade (1999–2000), spring of 3rd grade (2002), spring of 5th grade (2004), and spring of 8th grade (2007).

Main findings: Overall, center-based care raises reading and math scores, but has a negative effect for socio-behavioral measures. However, for English-proficient Hispanic children, the academic gains are considerably higher and the socio-behavioral effects are neutral. The duration of center-based care matters: the greatest academic benefit is found for children who start at ages 2–3 rather than at younger or older ages; negative behavioral effects are greater the younger the start age. These patterns are found across the distributions of family income. The intensity of center-based care also matters: more hours per day leads to greater academic benefits, but increased behavioral consequences. However, these intensity effects depend on family income and race.

Reference: Loeb et al. (2007).

Notes: 1.3, 3.1, 3.2.

46. Early Childhood Longitudinal Study (ECLS) Study 2

Location: United States

Study: See Study 1.

Design: Consisted of two types of analyses. The first was analysis of a cohort study with a nationally representative sample. The first study examined the patterns of children's school readiness, using cluster analysis to examine how different dimensions of development at school entry (at KG/last year of preprimary) present themselves in terms of strengths and risks within children. The authors' hypothesis was that there would be distinct patterns of school readiness in the sample. The second study used the school readiness profiles from the first study in regression models to predict the first-grade outcomes, controlling for background characteristics and characteristics of the KG classrooms.

Sample: The ECLS followed approximately 22,000 children; the first study included all the first-time KG (n = 17,219), and the second study included only those children with a school readiness profile and with valid longitudinal weights (n = 13,397).

Outcome measures: *Study 1* measured 5 dimensions of school readiness: (1) physical health, (2) social-emotional development, (3) approaches to learning, (4) language development, and (5) cognitive development The category "approaches to learning" was later dropped as there was very little variability. *Study 2* measured child outcomes in 1st grade via teacher and/or parent interview on the dimensions of physical/motor, social/emotional, approaches to learning, and direct assessment of math and reading.

Ages at baseline and follow-up: See Study 1. Assessment was conducted at KG entry and spring of grade 1.

Main findings: The analysis found four cluster groups at KG entry had the best statistical and conceptual fit: (1) comprehensive positive development—children who scored the mean on all four dimensions of school readiness (30.37% of the sample); (2) social/emotional and health strengths—children who scored above average in the dimensions of health and physical well-being and social/emotional well-being, but scored below average in language and cognition (33.95%); (3) social/emotional risk—children who scored below average on all four dimensions of readiness, but were distinguished by being significantly below the mean on social/emotional scores (13.24%); (4) health risk—children who were more than 1 SD below the mean in health and physical well-being, as well as below the mean on both language and cognition (22.5%).

The study found that children with comprehensive positive development have more advantageous backgrounds (higher-income families, not low birthweight, English spoken at home, having two parents, older parents, etc.). Children with other profiles also tended to have certain demographic backgrounds. Even after controlling for background characteristics and KG experiences, the comprehensive positive development profile performed the best across most of the outcomes. Children with health risk and social/emotional risk profiles performed worse than those with the social/emotional and health strengths profile on all measures.

Reference: Hair et al. (2006).

47. Early Head Start (EHS) Research and Evaluation Study: Study 1

Location: United States

Impact Evaluation: The EHS program targets low-income families and children with disabilities from the prenatal period to age 3. The 17 research programs included four center-based programs (which provided child development services mainly in center-based child care along with parenting education and a minimum of 2 home visits a year to each family); 7 home-based programs (which provided child development services to families mainly through weekly home visits and at least 2 parent-child group socialization activities a month for each family); and 6 mixed-approach programs (which provided home-based and/or center-based services, either to different families or in combination to families either simultaneously or at different times). Overall service receipt was comparable across the three program approaches.

Design: A randomized control trial of EHS, the program type (either mixed approach, center-based, or home-based only) varied by the programs.

Sample: Applicants to the EHS program in the study areas were randomly assigned by family to the program (n = 1,513) or the control (n = 1,488) group.

Outcome measures: Child's cognitive and language development (MDI of the Bayley Scales of Infant Development, PPVT-III); social-emotional development; child health; and parent behavior.

Ages at baseline and follow-up: Children under 12 months were enrolled in the program, and child assessments were planned when children were 14, 24, and 36 months old.

Main findings: Overall, EHS programs had significant impacts on a range of child and parent outcomes when the children were 3 years old. There were no significant impacts on cognitive and language development in programs that were solely home-based, but impacts of center-based and mixed-approach programs yielded effect sizes greater than expected. However, significant impacts were found on social-emotional development in home-based and mixed-approach programs (although more were found in mixed-approach programs). There were significant impacts on several parenting variables in mixed-approach and home-based programs. The fact that there were more and larger impacts in the mixed-approach programs suggests that offering a combination of center-based and home-based services may be a particularly effective way to provide two-generation services. Furthermore, in assessing the effect of implementation within the most effective program approach, the impacts for mixed-approach programs that were fully implemented early were considerably larger than the overall impacts.

Reference: Love et al. (2005).

Note: 3.2.

48. Early Head Start Research and Evaluation Study: Study 2

Location: United States

Study: Using the data from 11 sites that participated in the EHS Research and Evaluation Study, this study examined more closely the role of parent involvement in home visiting.

Design: Secondary analysis of data, a close look at different aspects of parent involvement: quantity of home-based service, quality of engagement, and content of visit; how it may be related to family characteristics; and whether different parent involvement relates to child and family outcomes.

Sample: See Study 1. The sample was selected from the treatment group only (n = 372–579, depending on the item).

Outcome measures: The same as above, plus parent supportiveness, home environment.

Ages at baseline and follow-up: Same as Study 1.

Main findings: Three components of home visits represented distinguishable aspects of home visit services: (1) quantity of involvement, including number of home visits, duration in the program, length of visits and intensity of service; (2) quality of engagement, including global ratings of engagement by staff and ratings of engagement during each home visit; and (3) the extent to which home visits were child focused.

Demographic variables predicted components of involvement, and home visit involvement components were differentially related to outcomes at

36 months, after controlling for demographic/family factors and earlier functioning on the same measure.

Only one quantity of involvement variable (duration) predicted improvements in home language and literacy environments at 36 months. Quality of involvement variables were negative predictors of maternal depressive symptoms at 36 months. Finally, the proportion of time during the visit devoted to child-focused activities predicted children's cognitive and language development scores, parent HOME scores, and parental support for language and learning when children were 36 months.

Reference: Raikes et al. (2006).

Note: 3.2.

49. Early Head Start Research and Evaluation Study: Study 3

Location: United States

Study: From the Early Head Start Research and Evaluation Study data, observations were used that had both father/mother interviews and videotaped observations of father-child and mother-child interaction at 24 months as well as child assessment outcomes at 5 years. The study identified the separate associations between father's and mother's parenting styles and child performance; configurations of mother-father characteristics in terms of parenting style; associations between father-mother parenting combinations and children's cognitive outcomes; and, among children with one supportive parent, whether it makes difference if it is the mother or the father.

Design: Data were unique because it included father-child interaction, which enabled the authors to identify separate impact of father's parenting and combined effect of mother's and father's parenting on child outcomes.

Sample: From the dataset, only the observations including all components (mother, father, and child) were included in the study (n = 200). All samples are EHS applicants with low-income background.

Outcome measures: Children's cognitive outcomes (math = WJ-R applied problems subtest; language = PPVT-III).

Ages at baseline and follow-up: Interviews and observation of mother-child and father-child interaction were conducted at 24 months; child cognitive achievement was assessed at 5 years.

Main findings: Parenting patterns were classified as Highly Supportive (41% of mothers and 34% of fathers); Somewhat Supportive (35% and 42%); Unsupportive-Negative (15% and 9%); and Unsupportive-Detached (10% and 15%). Children of Highly Supportive mothers scored highest and children of Unsupportive-Detached mothers scored lowest (0.65 SD in math and .57 SD in language). Children of Highly Supportive mothers tended to do better than other groups as well, but with no statistical significance. Children of Highly Supportive fathers also had the highest scores, and those of Unsupportive-Negative had the lowest scores. The differences between the two groups are .71 SD for math and .49 SD for language.

Overall, Highly Supportive parents and Unsupportive-Negative parents were disproportionately likely to be coupled together. However, Somewhat Supportive and Unsupportive-Detached parents were also disproportionately likely to be coupled together. Children with two Highly Supportive parents scored the highest; compared to children with no supportive parents the difference was 1.07 SD on math and .59 on language. They also scored significantly higher than children with one supportive parent. Among children with only one supportive parent, there were no significant differences in math and language according to the sex of the parent.

Reference: Martin, Ryan, and Brooks-Gunn (2007).

Note: 3.2.

50. Early Head Start Research and Evaluation Study: Study 4

Location: United States

Study: Using the Early Head Start Research and Evaluation Study data, this study examined the relationships among cumulative family and social risk during infancy and the preschool years, and children's achievement, self-regulatory skills, and social behavior.

Design: The study focused on the timing of family and social risk and investigated how cumulative risk influenced children's school readiness, and if this relationship is mediated by family processes (responsive parenting practices and the provision of language and literacy stimulation using structural equation modeling [SEM]).

Sample: Analyses were based on a subset of 1,851 children.

Outcome measures: School readiness measures included cognitive/academic achievement (reading and math competency, symbolic-learning, problem-solving (subscales of the WJ III); vocabulary (PPVT); and book knowledge and reading (the CAP Early Childhood Diagnostic Instrument). Attention/behavioral regulation measures included: sustained attention; child behavior during parent-child structured play activity; quality of play; problematic social behavior (Behavior Problems Scale). Other variables in the analyses included: family and social risk (composite index of risk factors, e.g., single parenthood, income, maternal depression, receiving benefits); maternal warmth/responsiveness (Home Inventory Scale); and other child and family characteristics.

Ages at baseline and follow-up: Data concerning family risk factors were collected for children 0–12 months, 12–24 months, and 24–36 months. Child outcomes were assessed at 36 months.

Main findings: Risk exposure during infancy was observed to be the most detrimental for children's school readiness. It appears this is in part because of its influence on parents' ability to provide a responsive, supportive, and stimulating home environment for the child. It was partially mediated by risk exposure and family processes, as changes in parental warmth/responsiveness and linguistic stimulation across toddlerhood and preschool years were associated with better school readiness.

Reference: Mistry et al. (forthcoming).

Note: 3.2.

51. Early Head Start Research and Evaluation Study: Study 5 (the Early Head Start Father Studies)

Location: United States

Impact Evaluation: Quoting only topic (fatherhood) relevant to the text. The description of the research project is noted in Study 1.

Design: The same as Study 1.

Sample: A subset of 12 of the 17 sites participated in father studies. Sample size (727 at 24 months and 698 at 36 months); around 300 father-child pairs were observed to assess father-child interaction.

Outcome measures: Father Activities with Child measures the frequency with which the father or father figure reported engaging in different activities with the child over the past month. Father well-being (Parenting Stress Index), Family Environment Scale, Severity of Discipline Strategies, father-child interaction.

Ages at baseline and follow-up: Interviews with fathers were conducted when children were 24 and 36 months.

Main findings: EHS had significant favorable impacts in several areas of fathering and father-child interactions, although the programs had less experience in providing services to fathers (compared with mothers). A subset of 12 of the 17 sites participated in father studies. EHS fathers were significantly less likely to report spanking their children during the previous week (25.4%) than control group fathers (35.6%). In sites completing observations, EHS fathers were also observed to be less intrusive; and program children were observed to be more able to engage their fathers and to be more attentive during play. Fathers and father figures from the program group families were significantly more likely to participate in program-related child development activities, such as home visits, parenting classes, and meetings for fathers.

Reference: Love et al. (2002).

Note: 3.2.

52. Head Start/Public School Early Childhood Transition Project

Location: United States

Impact Evaluation: The evaluation studied the impact of enhanced social and educational services in addition to Head Start, KG, and 1st grade. This included 3-day teacher training on developmentally appropriate practice (DAP).

Design: Quasi-experimental study to assess the value of additional social and educational services.

Sample: Randomly selected two cohorts of children in 13 schools; treatment and control groups were determined by two groups matched for ethnicity and income. 140 children and 28 observed classrooms were in the sample.

Outcome measures: Classroom assessment of developmental appropriateness using the Assessment Profile for Early Childhood Programs (Research Version); assessment of cognitive skills using WJ-R.

Ages at baseline and follow-up: Not longitudinal, one cohort in KG and the other in 1st grade.

Main findings: There were no apparent effects of the DAP training in the control and treatment groups. The achievement was significantly higher in the more developmentally appropriate classrooms for letter-word identification and applied problems over time. The finding suggests that DAPs can improve children's performance in urban settings.

Reference: Huffman and Speer (2000).

Note: 3.1.

53. Article: "Moving Up the Grades: Relationship between Preschool Model and Later School Success" (No Project Name)

Location: United States

Impact Evaluation: Full-time, center-based program for low-income urban children (84% pre-KG, 16% Head Start). Quasi-experimental study of three approaches (child-initiated, academically directed, combination).

Design: Quasi-experimental study comparing three different approaches for their effect on children's development. All children in the sample attended free, full-school-day preschool in the same urban district for 2 years. All teachers held a BA degree or higher. 33% of children attended classrooms with a child-initiated approach, 35% attended academically directed preschool, and 32% attended middle of the road preschool.

Sample: Initial sample at year 1 had been randomly selected (stratified sample to represent socioeconomic, administrative, and local variations within the school system). Sample for year 5, n = 160; year 6, n = 183.

Outcome measures: Data on report cards (grade point average) based on competency-based curriculum that are supposed to show children's mastery of academic skills, combined score of arithmetic, reading, language, spelling, handwriting, social studies, science, art, music, physical education, and citizenship. Special education placement.

Ages at baseline and follow-up: Year 1 (age 4), year 5, and year 6.

Main findings: At year 5 there were no differences in children's performance or special education placement among those who had experienced the three different preschool models. By year 6, children from academically directed preschools received significantly lower grades compared to children who had attended child-initiated preschools.

Reference: Marcon (2002).

Note: 3.1.

54. National Institute for Child Health and Development (NICHD) Study of Early Child Care (SECC)

Location: United States

Study: The NICHD Study of Early Child Care (SECC) is a comprehensive longitudinal study characterized by a complex and detailed study design that takes into account many variables, including characteristics of child-care and family environments.

Design: A longitudinal cohort study that assessed children's development using multiple methods (trained observers, interviewers, questionnaires, and testing) and measuring many facets of children's development (social, emotional, intellectual, language development, behavioral problems and adjustment, and physical health), following the children, and measuring their development at frequent intervals from birth through adolescence.

Sample: Original participants in the study in phase 1 were recruited from designated hospitals at 10 data collection sites. A total of 1,364 families with full-term healthy newborns were enrolled. Participants were selected in accordance with a conditionally random sampling plan, which was designed to ensure that the recruited families (1) included mothers who planned to work or to go to school full-time (60%) or part-time (20%) in the child's first year, as well as some who planned to say at home with the child (20%); and (2) reflected the demographic diversity (economic, educational, and ethnic) of the sites.

Examples of collected data: Various measures were used for different age groups. (See the project website.)

Ages at baseline and follow-up: Phase 1 (birth through 36 mo), phase 2 (54 mo through grade 1), phase 3 (grades 2–6), phase 4 (ages 14 and 15).

Main findings: See the findings for each study described below.

Reference: RTI International (n.d.).

Notes: 3.1, 3.2.

55. NICHD Study of Early Child Care, Study 1

Location: United States

Study: Using the data of the NICHD Study of Early Child Care, this study examined (1) the quality of interactions between (nonmaternal) caregivers and infants, and (2) the structural (group size, child-to-adult ratio, physical environment) and caregiver (education, specialized training, child-care experience, and beliefs about child rearing) characteristics of the environment.

Design: At 6 months of age, infants were observed in nonmaternal child-care environments. The analyses were conducted to identify whether structural/caregiver characteristics have significant associations with the better caregiver-child interactions, in each of different settings (centers, family/in-home child care, babysitters, grandparents, and fathers).

Sample: See NICHD Study above. 576 infants were included in this study.

Outcome measures: Ratings and frequency of positive caregiving, measured by the Observational Record of the Caregiving Environment (ORCE), an instrument that focuses on caregiver's behavior with a specific child versus overall ratings of a setting (such as ECERS).

Ages at baseline and follow-up: Not applicable. Data collected when infants were 6 months old.

Main findings: Higher positive caregiving ratings and frequencies were observed in child-care arrangements with fewer children and lower child-to-adult ratios, in settings rated safer and physically more stimulating, and in programs where caregivers had more formal education and held more nonauthoritarian beliefs about child rearing. In backward elimination regression analysis, it was found that group size, child-to-adult ratio, and non-authoritarian child-rearing beliefs all accounted for significant variation in the positive caregiving frequencies and ratings.

Reference: NICHD Early Child Care Research Network (1996).

56. NICHD Study of Early Child Care, Study 2

Location: United States

Study: See Study 1. The data were used to explore the associations between child outcomes at age 4.5 years and child-care arrangements.

Design: Hierarchical linear model analyses were used to describe longitudinal patterns of change in caregiving arrangements and caregiving environment. Multivariate regression models tested if child functioning at 4.5 yrs varied as function of child-care quantity, quality, and type.

Sample: See Study 1; n = 1,083.

Outcome measures: Pre-academic skills, short-term memory, language competence, social competence, problem behaviors rated by caregivers and mothers.

Ages at baseline and follow-up: The study used the data up to age 4.5.

Main findings: Even after controlling for multiple child and family characteristics, children's development was predicted by early child-care experience. Higher-quality child care, improvements in the quality of child care, and experience in center-type arrangements predicted better pre-academic skills and language performance at 4.5 years. More hours of care predicted higher levels of behavior problems according to caregivers.

Reference: NICHD Early Child Care Research Network (2002).

57. NICHD Study of Early Child Care, Study 3

Location: United States

Study: See Study 1. The objective of this analysis was to identify the effect of center-based care on socio-emotional adjustment at 4.5 years.

Design: NICHD data were analyzed through a series of nested regression models.

Sample: See Study 1; n = 982.

Outcome measures: Child adjustment at 4.5 years; social competence; behavior problems rated by mothers, KG teachers, and caregivers; teacher-student relationship rated by teachers and caregivers; dyadic peer interaction–qualitative analysis of video; behavior in child care rated in observation periods.

Ages at baseline and follow-up: The study used the data up to age 4.5.

Main findings: The more time children spent in any of a variety of nonmaternal care arrangements across the first 4.5 years of life, the more externalizing problems and conflict with adults they manifested at 54 months of age and in KG, as reported by mothers, caregivers, and teachers. These effects remained, for the most part, even when quality, type, and instability of child care were controlled, and when maternal sensitivity and other family background factors were taken into account. The quantity-of-care effects were modest and smaller than those of maternal sensitivity and indicators of family socioeconomic status, though typically greater than those of other features of child care, maternal depression, and infant temperament. There was no apparent threshold for quantity effects. More time in care not only predicted problem behavior measured on a continuous scale in a dose-response pattern, but also predicted at-risk (though not clinical) levels of problem behavior, as well as assertiveness, disobedience, and aggression.

Reference: NICHD Early Child Care Research Network (2003)

58. NICHD Study of Early Child Care, Study 4

Location: United States

Study: See Study 1. This study explored the relationship of duration and timing of poverty to children's development from birth to age 9.

Design: The impact of timing of poverty was assessed using hierarchical linear models, comparing children from families who were never poor, poor only during the child's infancy (0–3), poor only after infancy (4–9), and chronically poor.

Sample: See Study 1. Missing data (300 families) were imputed using multiple imputation.

Outcome measures: Child cognitive and social development, and child externalizing problems at 24, 36, 54 months and in first and third grade.

Ages at baseline and follow-up: This study used the data up to 3rd grade.

Main findings: Chronically poor families provided lower-quality child-rearing environments, and children in these families showed lower cognitive performance and more behavior problems than did other children. Any experience of poverty was associated with less favorable family situations and child outcomes than never being poor. Being poor later tended to be more detrimental than early poverty. Mediational analyses indicated that poverty was linked to child outcomes in part through less positive parenting.

Reference: NICHD Early Child Care Research Network (2005).

59. NICHD Study of Early Child Care, Study 5

Location: United States

Study: See Study 1. This study focused on investigating determinants of academic achievement and cognitive development at grade 1.

Design: NICHD data were analyzed using hierarchical regression analysis.

Sample: Study 1; n = 832 children.

Outcome measures: Relative change in cognitive ability from 54 months to grade 1.

Ages at baseline and follow-up: The study used the data up to age 4.5.

Main findings: Gender and race, family income-to-needs ratio, maternal education and sensitivity, and home learning environment were significant predictors of child outcomes in children's learning from 54 months to grade 1. Preschool academic cognitive functioning served as a significant mediator between child characteristics, early family factors, childcare quality, and grade 1 child outcomes. The most potent predictor of grade 1 functioning was a child's own cognitive skills at 54 months. Academic readiness appears to be already well established toward the end of a child's preschool years. Social competence played a secondary yet significant role in determining relative change within the academic and cognitive domains across the preschool to grade 1 transition.

Early in the study, cumulative maternal sensitivity and home learning environment were consistently among the strongest predictors of academic and cognitive performance at grade 1. Mother's education was a significant and robust predictor of both academic and cognitive outcomes. Cumulative child-care hours and quality from birth to 54 months were unrelated to grade 1 academic and cognitive functioning, whereas quality of child care was only a significant predictor of short-term memory skills. In terms of children's experience in school, the amount of content-specific instruction makes a significant contribution to the relative change in reading, phoneme, and long-term retrieval ability, but not to math skills or other cognitive abilities.

Reference: Downer and Pianta (2006).

60. Nurse-Family Partnership (NFP) Denver Study 1

Location: United States

Impact Evaluation: The treatment group received home visits by either professionals (nurses) or paraprofessionals from pregnancy through the first 2 years of child's life, with the broad goals of improving maternal and fetal health, health and development of children by better parenting/caregiving, and parents' life course (education, employment, family planning). Nurses were required to have nursing degrees and experience in community or maternal and child health nursing. Paraprofessionals had a high-school education but were excluded if they had college preparation in the helping professions or a bachelor's degree in any discipline. On average, women visited by paraprofessionals received 6.3 home visits during pregnancy and 16 visits during infancy. Nurses completed an average of 6.5 visits during pregnancy and 21 visits during infancy. The control group received developmental screening and referral services for their children at 6,12,15, 21, and 24 months.

Design: A randomized control trial of home visits program by professionals and paraprofessionals.

Sample: Stratified random sampling. control, n = 255; paraprofessional visits, n = 245; nurse visits, n = 235.

Outcome measures: Women's substance use, use of preventive and emergency services during pregnancy; maternal life course (educational achievement, employment and use of welfare); mother-infant interaction rated using videotapes; infant's home environment; child's emotional development (emotional reactivity, vulnerability, and vitality assessed at the lab at 6, 21, and 24 months); child's language development at 21 months; child's mental development at 24 months.

Ages at baseline and follow-up: Pregnancy through children at age 24 months.

Main findings: Paraprofessional-visited mother-child pairs in which the mother had low psychological resources interacted with one another more responsively than their control-group counterparts (99.45 vs. 97.54 standard score points). There were no other statistically significant paraprofessional effects. In contrast to their control-group counterparts, nurse-visited smokers had greater reductions in cotinine levels from intake to the end of pregnancy (259.0 vs. 12.32 ng/mL); by the study child's 2nd birthday, women visited by nurses had fewer subsequent pregnancies (29% vs. 41%) and births (12% vs. 19%); they delayed subsequent pregnancies for longer intervals; and during the 2nd year after the birth of their first child, they worked more than women in the control group (6.83 vs. 5.65 months). Nurse-visited mother-child pairs interacted with one another more responsively than those in the control group (100.31 vs. 98.99 standard score points).

At 6 months of age, nurse-visited infants, in contrast to their control group counterparts, were less likely to exhibit emotional vulnerability in response to fear stimuli (16% vs. 25%), and nurse-visited infants born to women with low psychological resources were less likely to exhibit low emotional vitality in response to joy and anger stimuli (24% vs. 40% and 13% vs. 33%). At 21 months, nurse-visited children born to women with low psychological resources were less likely to exhibit language delays (7% vs. 18%); and at 24 months, they exhibited superior mental development (90.18 vs. 86.20 Mental Development Index scores) than their control-group counterparts. There were no statistically significant program effects for the nurse visits on women's use of ancillary prenatal services, educational achievement, use of welfare, or their children's temperamental or behavioral problems. For most outcomes on which either visitor produced significant effects, the paraprofessionals typically had effects that were about half the size of those produced by nurses.

Reference: Olds et al. (2002).

Note: 3.2.

61. NFP Denver Study 2

Location: United States

Impact Evaluation: Follow-up of NFP Denver Study after 2 years.

Design: See Study 1.

Sample: See Study 1.

Outcome measures: Maternal life course (subsequent pregnancies, education, employment, use of welfare); children's behavior problems reported by mothers; sensitiveness and responsiveness of mother-child interaction; home environment; children's language, cognitive, fine motor, and gross motor skills; children's executive functioning and behavioral adaptation rated by the examiners.

Ages at baseline and follow-up: Pregnancy through children at age 48 months.

Main findings: Two years after the program ended, women who were visited by paraprofessionals, compared with control subjects, were less likely to be married (32.2% vs. 44.0%) and to live with the biological father of the child (32.7% vs. 43.1%), but worked more (15.13 months vs. 13.38 months) and reported a greater sense of mastery and better mental health. Paraprofessional-visited women had fewer subsequent miscarriages (6.6% vs. 12.3%) and fewer low-birthweight newborns (2.8% vs. 7.7%). Mothers and children who were visited by paraprofessionals, compared with control subjects, displayed greater sensitivity and responsiveness toward one another and, in cases in which the mothers had low levels of psychological resources at registration, had home environments that were more supportive of children's early learning.

Nurse-visited women reported greater intervals between the births of their first and second children (24.51 months vs. 20.39 months) and less domestic violence (6.9% vs. 13.6%), and they enrolled their children less frequently in preschool, Head Start, or licensed daycare than did control subjects. Nurse-visited children whose mothers had low levels of psychological resources at registration, compared with control group counterparts, demonstrated home environments that were more supportive of children's early learning, more advanced language, superior executive functioning (score of 100.16 vs. 95.48), and better behavioral adaptation during testing. There were no statistically significant effects of either nurse or paraprofessional visits on the number of subsequent pregnancies, women's educational achievement, substance use, use of welfare, or children's externalization of behavior problems.

Reference: Olds et al. (2004).

Note: 3.2.

62. Family Life Project

Location: United States

Study: The Family Life Project was designed to study families in two geographical regions with the highest child poverty rate (around 50%): eastern North Carolina and central Pennsylvania. The sample included 1,292 children recruited as infants. The study followed up with children through 36 months. This article looked at fathers' contribution to language development.

Design: The study examined the associations between a father's characteristics and child language development, after controlling for key demographic, child, and maternal characteristics using unique data-language transcript data (videotaped) of both mother's and father's interactions with their infants while reading picturebooks in the home environment at 6 months.

Sample: The sample was 555 (baseline); 514 (at 15 months); 500 (observation of mother-child book activity at 6 months); 477 (observation of father-child book activity at 6 months); and 486 (at 36 months).

Outcome measures: Language skills: communication skills at 15 months and preschool language scale at 36 months.

Ages at baseline and follow-up: Children were recruited as infants, parent-child interaction was observed at 6 months, and child language skills were assessed at 15 month and 36 months.

Main findings: Father's education was positively associated with child's expressive language development at 36 months. Father's vocabulary (using diverse vocabulary with child) at 6 months independently predicted child's language development at 36 months, and communication skills at 15 months, after controlling for maternal education and vocabulary.

Reference: Pancsofar, Vernon-Feagans, and the Family Life Project Investigators (forthcoming).

Note: 3.2.

63. Cost, Quality, and Outcomes (CQO) Study

Location: United States (California, Connecticut, Colorado, and North Carolina)

Study: A study of center-based community child care and children's longitudinal outcomes in four states over 5 years.

Design: A longitudinal cohort study. Descriptive analysis and inferential analysis using hierarchical longitudinal analysis.

Sample: Subsample of 183 preschools of 401 child-care centers randomly selected from the 4 states, n = 826 in year 1; n = 345 in second grade.

Outcome measures: Child outcomes: vocabulary (PPVT-R), pre-academic skills (WJ-R), reading and math skills; teacher's rating on social and cognitive skills; and teacher's rating on the relationship with the child. Other data included information on child-care centers such as the quality of the classroom environment (ECERS), teacher sensitivity (CIS), teaching style (ECOF), teacher responsiveness to children (AIS); information on the school in KG and grade 2 such as quality of classroom environment and instructional environment; demographic and household characteristics of children.

Ages at surveys: 4–8 years; 1-year-old before KG through grade 2; survey conducted every year.

Main findings: Child-care quality has a modest long-term effect on children's patterns of cognitive and socio-emotional development, at least through KG, and in some cases, through 2nd grade. Observed classroom practices were related to children's language and academic skills, whereas the closeness of the teacher-child relationship was related to both cognitive and social skills, with the strongest effects for the latter. Moderating influences of family characteristics were observed for some outcomes, indicating stronger positive effects of child-care quality for children from more at-risk backgrounds.

Reference: Peisner-Feinberg et al. (2001).

Note: 3.1.

64. Article: "Within and Beyond the Classroom Door: Assessing Quality in Child Care Centers" (No Project Name)

Location: United States

Study: The objectives of the study were to identify (1) associations among quality of care defined by structural features, process indicators, and compliance with state regulations; (2) variation in quality based on the stringency of state child-care regulations and center compliance; and (3) specific quality indicators that show especially strong links to children's experiences in child care.

Design: Analysis of data collected through interviews and classroom observations.

Sample: Randomly sampled licensed centers and classrooms (98 infant rooms, 112 toddler rooms, and 106 preschool rooms) in 4 states that have different regulatory policies.

Outcome measures: Quality of classroom environments (ITERS, ECERS) and assessment profile of early childhood programs.

Ages at baseline and follow-up: Not applicable.

Main findings: Findings confirmed prior evidence regarding the importance of ratios, teacher training, and group size for high-quality classroom processes, but demonstrated the more significant contribution of teacher wages and parent fees. Both structural and process measures of quality varied with the location of the center in a state with more or less stringent child-care regulations. There was a significant contribution of teacher wages and parent fees to the quality of classroom processes. For every age group, classroom quality was most strongly associated with teachers' wages. Wages, in turn, were most strongly correlated with parent fees and teacher training for infant and pre-school rooms.

The sensitivity of child-care quality to the regulatory context of child care was suggested regarding the contribution of site and, to a lesser extent, of central-level regulatory compliance to the quality of classroom processes. There was positive association between observed care and the location of centers in states with more stringent regulations. Teacher training, teacher wages, and parent fees, as well as adult-to-child ratios (for infants) and group size (for toddlers), significantly predicted the quality of classroom interactions in younger age groups. For preschoolers, only ratios and wages predicted classroom quality.

Reference: Phillips et al. (2000).

Note: 3.1.

65. Article: "The Prediction of Process Quality from Structural Features of Child Care" (No Project Name)

Location: United States (California, Colorado, Connecticut, North Carolina)

Study: The study aimed to identify structural characteristics of center care that are associated with observed center quality from a large multi-state project.

Design: Analysis of data collected at the center level using hierarchical regression models.

Sample: Stratified random sampling of 100 child-care centers in each state; (n = 400); 224 infant/toddler classrooms and 509 preschool classrooms were observed.

Outcome measures: Process quality was measured using the Early Childhood Environment Rating Scale (ECERS), the Infant/Toddler Environment Rating Scale (ITERS), the Caregiver Interaction Scale (CIS), and the Teacher Involvement Scale (TIS). Data on structural characteristics related to caregivers, classrooms, wages, centers, administrators, and economics were also collected.

Ages at baseline and follow-up: Not applicable.

Main findings: For infant/toddler care, the adult-child ratio, teacher wages, proportion of infants and toddlers, and parental fees were significant predictors of ITERS scores in the final model, while adult-child ratio, teacher wages, and proportion of infants and toddlers were significantly related to CIS. For preschool, ECERS scores were related to better ratios, higher wages, and proportionately fewer infants and toddlers at the center, higher center costs to produce child care, and the state-by-sector interaction. Significant teacher's background variables in estimating CIS total score included BA degree or some college and experience, as well as adult-child ratios. Prediction of process quality from structural measures varied somewhat according to age group. The structural measures included in the hierarchical regression models predicted process quality more strongly in preschool than in infant/toddler classrooms. In infant/toddler classrooms, process quality was higher with moderately experienced and better paid teachers and more experienced directors.

In preschool classrooms, process quality was higher in classrooms with teachers with more education, a moderate amount of experience, and higher wages. Better adult-child ratios, lower center enrollment, and a lower proportion of infants and toddlers and subsidized children also predicted higher process quality for preschoolers. Teacher wages were strongly related to process quality in both infant/toddler and preschool classrooms. Higher quality was found in states with the most stringent regulations and in nonprofit centers. However, sector differences varied across the states. In general, the sector differences were strongest in the least regulated states. The study found that the overall process quality in rooms where infants and toddlers were cared for was substantially lower than in rooms where older children were cared for. The levels of overall process quality required to support children's development were not being met by most of the child-care centers in the sample.

Reference: Phillipsen et al. (1997).

Note: 3.1.

66. Observing Mother and Child Behavior in a Problem-Solving Situation at School Entry (No Project Name)

Location: United States

Study: The study examined the relationship between ratings of mother-child interactions in a problem-solving situation at school entry and child's academic achievement in grades 2, 3, and 4.

Design: The data collected at the time of school entry (see below) and the academic performance at grades 2, 3, and 4 were analyzed using factor analysis and regression models. Interactions between the different measures collected at school entry were also examined.

Sample: The original sample included 342 children-mother pairs; the sample was the entire KG entry population of a small-city school district, excluding 7 children who were accompanied by fathers. 181 children were followed up at 4th grade.

Outcome measures: Academic performance (Iowa Test of Basic Skills) at grades 2, 3, and 4. The measures used at school entry included: child cognitive ability (vocabulary and pattern analysis subtest of the Stanford-Binet Intelligence Scale), gross and fine motor skills, family demographics, and the mother-child interaction during two semi-structured problem-solving tasks.

Ages at baseline and follow-up: At KG entry (mean age 5 years), followed up at grades 2, 3, and 4.

Main findings: There was a moderate relationship between the rating of mother-child interaction and academic performance at grades 2–4, which explained 17–24% of variance in the academic scores. However, when ability and demographic data were included in the model, the mother-child interaction accounted for only 1%. Although the rating of mother-child interaction is a significant predictor of academic performance in grades 2–4, the results indicate that school achievement measures, family demographics, child ability measures, and mother-child interaction ratings all share a considerable amount of overlapping variance.

Reference: Pianta and Harbers (1996).

Note: 3.2.

67. Predictive Validity of Early School Screening

Location: United States

Study: The study assessed the predictive validity of an early school screening procedure. The screening procedure included Stanford-Binet Intelligence Scale, language skills, perceptual-motor skills, early school behavior scale, and task orientation.

Design: Two cohorts of participants were followed through the first 3 years of school.

Sample: All children in a city school district who entered KG during each of two consecutive years (Cohort 1, n = 424; Cohort 2, n = 351).

Outcome measures: Retention, special education placement, teacher nominations of behavior and emotional problems, and performance on standard achievement tests.

Ages at baseline and follow-up: KG entry and grade 2.

Main findings: Some measures (e.g., fine motor and cognitive skills, maternal education) were consistent predictors of many forms of school difficulty. The screening procedure correctly predicted 80% of the cases across the set of outcomes, while it was more accurate in predicting children who did not show any form of school problems.

Reference: Pianta and McCoy (1997).

Note: 1.3.

68. Mother-Child Relationships, Teacher-Child Relationships, and School Outcomes in Preschool and Kindergarten (No Project Name)

Location: United States

Study: The study examines associations with child-mother and child-teacher relationships and early school outcomes.

Design: Analysis of data on child adjustment to schools and their relationships with mothers and teachers using hierarchical regression analyses.

Sample: 55 preschool (4 years old) children with at least one risk factor in one small school district.

Outcome measures: KG adjustment rated by their KG teachers. Pre-academic skills (the Boehm Test of Basic Concepts, language, and concepts) also rated.

Ages at baseline and follow-up: Mother-child and teacher-child relationships and pre-academic skills were assessed at 4 years, and school adjustment was assessed after KG entry.

Main findings: Overall quality of child-mother interaction predicted teacher-reported adjustment in KG, and quality of both child-mother and child-teacher interaction predicted children's performance on concept development. The mother-child relationships have stronger association with child outcomes than do the teacher-child relationships.

Reference: Pianta, Nimetz, and Bennett (1997).

Note: 3.2.

69. Meta-Analytic Review of Home Visiting Programs for Families with Young Children

Location: United States

Study: Meta-analytic review of home-visiting programs.

Design: Meta-analysis of 60 home-visiting services. Program efficacy was measured by weighted mean standardized effect calculated for each outcome group, and the relationship between program and impact was explored within each outcome group.

Data source: 60 studies.

Outcome measures: The study grouped outcomes as follows: (1) child outcomes (cognitive, social/emotional, prevention of child abuse); (2) enhanced childrearing practices (parenting behaviors and attitudes); and (3) maternal life course (education, employment, reliance on public assistance).

Ages at baseline and follow-up: Not applicable.

Main findings: In general, children in families who were enrolled in home-visiting programs fared better than did control group children. Within the set of child outcomes, three of the five average effect sizes were significantly greater than zero, although modest (cognitive, socio-emotional, potential abuse). Within the set of parent outcomes, three of the five average effect sizes were significantly greater than zero. Two of these included the more direct measures of parent mediation of child enhancement: parenting behavior and parenting attitudes. The effect of home visit dosage is weak at best. The results of program design features analyses were inconclusive. No one program feature emerged as a significant influence on effect size across outcomes.

Reference: Sweet and Appelbaum (2004).

Note: 3.2.

70. Chicago Child-Parent Center (CPC) Program/ Chicago Longitudinal Study (dataset)

Location: United States

Impact Evaluation: The Chicago Child-Parent Center (CPC) Program (n = 989 children) provides comprehensive education, family, and health services; it includes half-day preschool at ages 3 to 4 years, half- or full-day KG, and school-age services in linked elementary schools at ages 6 to 9 years. The comparison group (n = 550) consisted of children who participated in alternative early childhood programs (full-day KG): 374 in the preschool comparison group from 5 randomly selected schools plus 2 others that provided full-day KG and additional instructional resources, and 176 who attended full-day KG in 6 CPCs without preschool participation.

Design: The study analyzed longitudinal data from the 15-year follow-up of a large nonrandomized matched-group cohort to determine the long-term effectiveness of a federal, center-based, preschool and school-based intervention program for urban low-income children.

Sample: Sample size; treatment, n = 989; control, n = 550. Assignment of treatment was not random, the entire cohort of program participants was included in the study. The control group was selected randomly from 7 KGs and 6 child-parent centers (without preschool exposure). The treatment group was matched on age of KG entry, eligibility for government-funded programs, neighborhood and family poverty.

Outcome measures: Rates of high school completion and school dropout by age 20 years, juvenile arrests for violent and nonviolent offenses, and grade retention and special education placement by age 18.

Ages at baseline and follow-up: Baseline, ages 3 or 4; follow-up, 18- and 20-year-olds.

Main findings: Relative to the preschool comparison group and adjusted for several covariates, children who participated in the preschool intervention for 1 or 2 years had a higher rate of high-school completion (49.7% vs. 38.5%, p = .01); more years of completed education (10.6 vs. 10.2, p = .03); and lower rates of juvenile arrest (16.9% vs. 25.1%, p = .003), violent arrests (9.0% vs. 15.3%, p = .002), and school dropout (46.7% vs. 55.0%, p = .047). Both preschool and school-age participation were significantly associated with lower rates of grade retention and use of special education services. The effects of preschool participation on educational attainment were greater for boys than girls, especially in reducing school dropout rates (p = .03).

Relative to less extensive participation, children with extended program participation from preschool through second or third grade also experienced lower rates of grade retention (21.9% vs. 32.3%, p = .001) and special education (13.5% vs. 20.7%, p = .004).

Reference: Reynolds et al. (2001).

Notes: 1.3, 4.1.

71. High/Scope Perry Preschool Program Study 1

Location: United States

Impact Evaluation: A 2-year preschool education program for 3- and 4-year-olds living with low-income families. Teachers had bachelor's degrees and certification in education, and each served 5–6 children. They used the High/Scope educational model in daily 2.5-hour classes and visited families weekly. In this model, teachers arranged the classroom and daily schedule to support children's self-initiated learning activities, provided both small-group and large-group activities, and helped children engage in key experiences in child development. Teachers studied and received regular training and support in their use of this educational model.

Design: A randomized controlled trial in an urban poor setting, following 123 children from age 3 to 40.

Sample: A sample of 123 low-income African American children who were assessed to be at high risk of school failure. 58 of them were randomly assigned to a program group that received a high-quality preschool program at ages 3 and 4, and 65 to another group that received no pre-school program.

Outcome measures: Short- and long-term effects on education, economic performance, crime prevention, family relationships, and health.

Ages at baseline and follow-up: Ages 3 through 11 and again at ages 14, 15, 19, 27, and 40.

Main findings: High-quality preschool programs for young children living in poverty contribute to their intellectual and social development in childhood and their school success, economic performance, and reduced commission of crime in adulthood. The program group had higher median annual earnings than the no-program group at ages 27 and 40 ($12,000 vs. $10,000 at age 27 and $20,800 vs. $15,300 at age 40). The program group had significantly fewer lifetime arrests than the no-program group.

Differences between the program and control groups include highest level of schooling completed (65% vs. 45% graduating from regular high school); intellectual and language tests from their preschool years up to age 7; school achievement tests at ages 9, 10, and 14; and literacy tests at ages 19 and 27. At ages 15 and 19, the program group had significantly better attitudes toward school than the no-program group. Significantly more individuals of the program group were employed at age 40 (76% vs. 62%), and at age 27 (69% vs. 56%).

At age 40, more males from the program group raised their children. Return on investment for the Perry Preschool program was $244,812 per participant on an investment of $15,166 per participant—$16.14 per dollar invested. Of that return, $195,621 went to the general public—$12.90 per dollar invested and $49,190 went to each participant—$3.24 per dollar invested. Of the public return, 88% came from crime savings, 4% came from education savings, 7% came from increased taxes due to higher earnings, and 1% ($2,768) came from welfare savings.

Reference: Schweinhart et al. (2005).

Notes: 1.1, 1.3, 3.1, 4.1.

72. High/Scope Perry Preschool Program Study 2

Location: United States

Study: The details of the program are described above.

Design: The study estimated the rate of return and the benefit-cost ratio for the Perry Preschool program, accounting for locally determined costs, missing data, the deadweight costs of taxation, and the value of non-market benefits and costs. It improves on previous estimates by accounting for corruption in the randomization protocol, by developing standard errors for these estimates, and by exploring the sensitivity of estimates to alternative assumptions about missing data and the value of nonmarket benefits.

Sample: See Study 1 description.

Outcome measures: See Study 1 description.

Ages at baseline and follow-up: See Study 1 description.

Main findings: Estimated social rates of return generally fell between 7 and 10%, with most estimates substantially lower than those previously reported in the literature. However, returns were generally significantly different statistically from zero for both males and females and were above the historical return on equity. The benefit/cost ratios after adjusting for compromised randomization ranged from 5.4 to 9.8.

Reference: Heckman et al. (2009).

73. Parents as Teachers Program (PAT) Study 1 (This annotation is included to give context to Study 2.)

Location: United States

Impact Evaluation: IE of PAT implemented with a different approach in two programs: (1) Salinas Valley program for Latino families and (2) a program specifically targeted to teen parents. Salinas Valley Program offered monthly home visits for as long as families choose to remain in program, up to the child turning 3. Home visits conducted by a trained parent educator covered lessons from the national PAT curriculum. Program participants received an average of 20 visits (28–50 min/session) over 3 years. Voluntary group meetings in English and Spanish were held, but less than 15% of the families attended. The control group received age-appropriate toys, and significant developmental delays or other problems were referred. For the teen program, PAT service was offered in monthly home visits and group meetings through children's second birthdays. At home meetings, the national PAT curriculum was delivered. On average, 10 visits were conducted during the 2-year period (duration per session not stated). Participation at group meeting was low, averaging 2–3 meetings over 2 years. Another program group received comprehensive case management service, with face-to-face contacts provided as often as requested or at least quarterly. Case managers provided referrals or arranged for required specific services. Finally, a third group received both services.

Design: A randomized control trial of PAT program targeting different beneficiaries.

Sample: Randomly assigned families to the program (n = 298) and control (n =199) group for Salinas Valley program; PAT program only (n = 177), case management only (n = 174), combined intervention (n = 175), and control (n = 175) for the teen program.

Outcome measures: Parent knowledge of infant development; parent attitudes and behaviors; child development (cognitive, communication, social development, self help and physical development); child health and health care (immunization, use of health care services).

Ages at baseline and follow-up: Baseline at less than 6 months. Assessments of child development were conducted at ages 1, 2, and 3 years.

Main findings: The study found small and inconsistent positive effects on parent knowledge, attitudes, and behavior and no gains in child develop- ment or health outcomes among the treatment group compared with the control group. Among subgroups, Latino children in Spanish-speaking homes benefited more, with significant gains in cognitive, communication, social, and self-help development. The teen PAT demonstration indicated that those who received PAT along with comprehensive case management service benefited the most. In Salinas Valley, people who received more intensive services enjoyed more gains.

Reference: Wagner and Clayton (1999).

Note: 3.2.

74. Parents as Teachers Program (PAT) Study 2

Location: United States

Qualitative study: The study looked into a program that did not produce the expected outcomes on children—although it had small and inconsis- tent effects on parents' knowledge, attitudes, and behavior (Wagner and

Clayton 1999)—and conducted a qualitative investigation on why it did not work.

Design: The study collected 3-year longitudinal case studies of 21 families, interviewed parents and home visitors, and analyzed videotapes of home visits. Another 60 mothers participated in focus group discussions.

Sample: 21 case study families, 60 mothers for focus group discussions. (The study does not explain how these families/mothers were selected.)

Outcome measures: Not applicable.

Ages at baseline and follow-up: From birth or shortly after birth for 3 years.

Main findings: Bottlenecks found in the investigation were:

- Mismatch of perception of how home visitors saw their own role and the expected role (home visitors saw the provision of social support as their primary responsibility, although the program focused on parent education). The emphasis was on helping mothers feel good about themselves and not enough emphasis was placed on expected goals for parent-child interaction.
- Not enough articulation of the behavioral implications when giving parenting information.
- Demonstration by the home visitors was not recognized as modeling by parents and had little influence.
- Home visitors were not comfortable being cast as experts, although families perceived them as experts and wanted to learn from them. The intervention needed to accept and support parents while actively helping them to adopt behaviors that have been demonstrated to promote healthy development.
- The home visitors lacked the ability to detect possible developmental problems. This could be due to insufficient training or to the visitors' strong bond with the mothers having blinded the visitors to the children's problems.

Recommendations:

- The goals need to be sufficiently precise so home visitors and parents can actually reflect on their achievement.
- The PAT curriculum provided a wealth of information about development, but the program needed to more directly state what it was trying to do.

- Staff needed to be adequately trained to recognize indictors of atypical development.
- Home-visiting programs need to incorporate the reality that some parents cannot or will not follow through on what the program provides and need additional strategies to ensure successful child development.

Reference: Hebbeler and Gerlach-Downie (2002).

75. Project CARE

Location: United States

Impact Evaluation: Child development center (center-based) included half-day (mandatory) or full-day child care; teacher-child ratio was 1:3 for infants, 1:4 for 2-year-olds, 1:6 for 3–5-year-olds. The teachers received intensive training for the program. The program emphasized both cognitive and socio-emotional development. Special focus was placed on language. Family education program provided weekly home visits for the first 3 years. (Average home visits were 2.5 for home-visits-only group and 2.7 per month for home visits and center care group.) For 4- and 5-year-olds, weekly or biweekly visits were made, averaging 1.4 for home-visits-only group and 1.1 per month for home visits and center care group). Home visitors tried to help families deal with concerns through problem-solving strategies; they demonstrated and described developmentally appropriate activities for their children. Home visitors were trained using the same materials as the daycare teachers. Monthly parent meetings were also conducted as an information source and as a support group.

Design: A randomized control trial of different treatment (center care plus family education; family education only; control).

Sample: High-risk families randomly assigned to three groups (educational daycare plus family education, n = 15; (2) family education only, n = 24; (3) control group, n = 23, at baseline.

Outcome measures: Children's cognitive skills (Bayley, Stanford-Binet test, and McCarthy scales); Home environment (HOME); mother's attitude toward child-rearing.

Ages at baseline and follow-up: Baseline at 6 months through 54 months.

Main findings: On each test after the 6-month assessment, scores of children in the educational day-care plus family support group were greater than those in the other 2 groups. No cognitive intervention effects were obtained for the family education group. Group effects were not obtained for measures of either the quality of the home environment or parent attention. Home visits alone were insufficient to affect either children's outcome or parents' behavior. Control group children who did not attend daycare scored about 1 SD below the educational daycare group on cognitive skills at 54 months.

Reference: Wasik et al. (1990).

Note: 3.2.

76. Nutrition and Early Child Development Program

Location: Uganda

Impact Evaluation: An integrated child-care package that mobilized groups of parents and caregivers at the community level was evaluated. Child fairs facilitated by "animateurs" (local workers) were held every 6 months and served as an important service delivery and communication channel through which communities could access integrated health and nutrition services for their children. Community support grants and innovation funds provided financial assistance for ECD projects with matching community contributions in cash or in kind. A national support program for child development focused on supporting national level activities, such as participatory monitoring and evaluation; micronutrients program; ECD curriculum development; information, education and communication (IEC); and advocacy for children's rights. And communication campaigns were conducted through multiple media (radio, community events, local workers, and so on).

Design: Experimental, difference-in-difference comparison between the program and control communities. The study measured "intent-to-treat" effect on child nutrition.

Sample: Randomly selected (using stratified sampling) 2,250 households in 50 randomly selected parishes (subdistricts). Households were assigned to 3 groups of 750 each: group A, which received all ECD services as well as the experimental delivery of albendazole at child health days, or group B, which received all the core ECD services, or the control group.

Outcome measures: Child weight (height was also measured, but analysis focused on weight); family's knowledge, attitude, and practices covering healthcare-seeking behavior and child care.

Ages at baseline and follow-up: Not applicable, baseline conducted in Jan.–Mar. 2000, follow-up in Jan.–Mar. 2003.

Main findings: There was significant improvement among the youngest children (less than 12 months old) in the project communities and a smaller improvement in this age cohort in the control group. In contrast, nutritional status apparently deteriorated for children relative to the baseline period in some of the other age cohorts for reasons that are not clear. This decline occurred in the treatment group as well as in the control group. In terms of child-care practices, the project sites adhered more closely to the guidelines on exclusive breastfeeding than did the control group, and had better content of complementary feeding, according to parents' reports.

Reference: Alderman (2007).

Notes: 3.2, 3.3.

77. Nutrition and Early Child Development Program Study 2

Location: Uganda

Impact Evaluation: See Study 1. The study focused on early stimulation and parenting practices.

Design: See Study 1.

Sample: See Study 1.

Outcome measures: (1) Mothers' caregiving attitudes and behaviors: behaviors that support learning and development, daily routines and caregiving, and daily experiences including play; (2) fathers' involvement (behavior and attitudes) in caregiving; and (3) attitudes toward parents' role in a child's learning and development. The assessment of behaviors that support learning and development was based on aspects of caregiving adapted in part from the HOME inventory.

Ages at baseline and follow-up: Same as Study 1.

Main findings: Compared to the baseline, the program mothers were more likely than the control group to involve their child in their own daily routines such as housework and agriculture. Program mothers also reported greater involvement in learning activities (counting, naming, and drawing) at final assessment compared to the baseline. In addition, the program mothers reported greater agreement with their role in promoting children's preparedness for school. The results provide some support for the aim of changing fathers' attitudes toward their involvement in children's development. Attitudes toward father involvement beyond traditional aspects of physical caregiving were improved by the project. However, changes in actual behaviors were limited.

Reference: Britto, Engle, and Alderman (2007).

78. Uruguayan Household Survey

Study: The Uruguayan household survey covers around 18,000 households each year in urban areas. Survey items include socio-demographic characteristics of the households, school attendance, and highest grade completed for all individuals. Since 2001, the project has collected retrospective information on preschool attendance in the context of a rapid expansion of preprimary classes.

Design: Retrospective analysis of household surveys. Analysis compared school progression of siblings with different exposure to preschools, as most of the heterogeneity in preschool exposure and school attainment comes from household characteristics.

Sample: 23,042 children in 5 years.

Outcome measures: School attendance and years of schooling among children aged 7–15.

Ages at baseline and follow-up: Not longitudinal. Children 7–15.

Main findings: By age 15, children with preschool had 0.79 more years of education compared to their siblings without preschool exposure. Preschooled children had a 27 percentage point higher likelihood of being in school at age 15 than those without preschool exposure. Children whose mothers had lower education appeared to benefit more from preschooling.

Reference: Berlinski, Galiani, and Manacorda (2008).

Note: 3.1.

79. Responsive Feeding Study (No Project Name)

Location: Vietnam

Study: An observational study in rural Vietnam, as part of a prospective randomized community intervention trial of a nutrition project run by the NGO Save the Children.

Design: An observational study, not an impact evaluation, that studied relationships between caregiver behavior during feeding and children's acceptance of food. Observation and coding was done using video recording.

Sample: The original study included 240 children 5–25 months of age. For this study, children were randomly selected to participate at either 12 or 17 months, (n = 91).

Outcome measures: Children's food acceptance at 11 or 17 months. Caregiver behaviors were assessed using 3 variables: person feeding, verbalization of caregiver, and physical actions of caregiver.

Ages at baseline and follow-up: Not applicable; children were observed at 11 or 17 months.

Main findings: Positive and mechanical/direct verbalization by the caregiver was significantly associated with the odds of a child accepting the offered bite. When verbal comments were positive, children were 2.4 times as likely to accept the bite compared with when no verbal comments were given. When verbal comments were mechanical/directive, children were less likely to accept the bite. Physical actions of the caregiver were correlated with accepting bites, though in an inverse fashion. Force feeding was also positively associated with acceptance. Children who fed themselves were more likely than children fed by a caregiver other than the mother to accept the bites.

Reference: Dearden et al. (2009).

Note: 3.2.

80. Nutrition and Preschool Intervention (No Project Name)

Location: Vietnam

Impact Evaluation: Intervention used Positive Variance Inquiry for 2 years (1999–2000), funded by the Save the Children organization. Project implemented in 5 communes and targeted 0–36-month-olds, identified successful child-care practices of poor families who have well-nourished children. Nutrition component included growth monitoring and a monthly nutrition education rehabilitation program conducted by local health volunteers, targeting severely malnourished children. Two communes were followed up with an ECD project for 2 years (2002–03) targeting 4–5-year-olds. ECD component strengthened existing service through material support and teacher training on child-centered teaching models, as well as separate mother and father information sessions, and established a small local library for parents.

Design: Quasi-experimental IE but no control group with no intervention and no baseline data for cognitive development. Baseline available only for height: compares nutrition-only vs. nutrition plus ECD interventions. Generalized linear models (GLM) were used to estimate effects, and generalized estimating equations (GEE) were used for assessing the effects on proportions.

Sample: Community selection was not random at entry. ECD communities were selected based on lack of access to service. Sample of children for the IE were only selected from 2 communes with similar socioeconomic conditions, nutrition + ECD = 141; nutrition-only = 172.

Outcome measures: Children's height and cognitive test scores using Raven's Progressive Matrices Test.

Ages at baseline and follow-up: No baseline data only after the end line data at 6.5–8.5 years old.

Main findings: ECD interventions had significantly better scores on cognitive skills test than nutrition only; effects are particularly large for children malnourished at the end line. There were no additional effects of the ECD program on nutritional status.

Reference: Watanabe et al. (2005).

Notes: 1.2, 3.1.

Source: Authors' research.

Appendix Notes

CCT = conditional cash transfer; ECD = early childhood development; ECE = early childhood education; IE = impact evaluation; KG = kindergarten (in the studies conducted in the United States, kindergarten typically refers to preschool education provided during one year before primary school entry); SD = standard deviation; SES = socioeconomic status.

Instruments used in the IE and studies include the following:
AIS = Adult Involvement Scale
Bayley Scales of Infant Development
CIS = Arnett Caregiver Interaction Scale
ECERS-RE = Early Childhood Environment Rating Scale Revised
ECOF= UCLA Early Childhood Observation Form
FDCRS = Family Day-Care Rating Scale
ITERS = Infant/Toddler Environment Rating Scale
HOME Inventory = Home Observation for Measurement of the Environment
    (HOME) Inventory Scale
McCarthy Scales of Children's Abilities
MDI = Mental Development Index of the Bayley Scales of Infant Development
PPVT-R = Peabody Picture Vocabulary Test–Revised
PPVT-III = Peabody Picture Vocabulary Test–III
Stanford-Binet Intelligence Scales
TIS = Teacher Involvement Scale
TVIP = Test de Vocabulario en Imagenes Peabody (Spanish version of PPVT)
WAIS = Wechsler Adult Intelligence Scale
WISC-R = Wechsler Intelligence Scale for Children Revised
WJ = Woodcock-Johnson Psychoeducational Battery
WJ-R = Woodcock-Johnson Psychoeducational Battery–Revised
WJ III = Woodcock-Johnson Psychoeducational Battery, Third Edition; Woodcock-
    Muñoz = Batería III Woodcock-Muñoz
WPPSI = Wechsler Preschool and Primary Scale of Intelligence

Appendix References

Aboud, F. E. 2006. "Evaluation of an Early Childhood Preschool Program in Rural Bangladesh." *Early Childhood Research Quarterly* 21 (1): 46–60.

Aboud, F. E., S. Shafique, and S. Akhter. 2009. "A Responsive Feeding Intervention Increases Children's Self-Feeding and Maternal Responsiveness but Not Weight Gain." *Journal of Nutrition* 139 (9): 1738–43.

Alderman, H. 2007. "Improving Nutrition through Community Growth Promotion: Longitudinal Study of the Nutrition and Early Child Development Program in Uganda." *World Development* 35 (8): 1376–89.

Armecin, G., J. R. Behrman, P. Duazo, S. Ghuman, S. Gultiano, E. M. King, and N. Lee. 2006. "Early Childhood Development through an Integrated Program: Evidence from the Philippines." Policy Research Working Paper 3922. World Bank, Washington, DC.

Barker, D. J., J. G. Eriksson, T. Forsén, and C. Osmond. 2002. "Fetal Origins of Adult Disease: Strength of Effects and Biological Basis." *International Journal of Epidemiology* 31 (6): 1235–39.

Behrman, J., Y. Cheng, and P. Todd. 2004. "Evaluating Pre-school Programs When Length of Exposure to the Program Varies: A Nonparametric Approach." *Review of Economics and Statistics* 86 (1): 108–32.

Berlinski, S., and S. Galiani. 2007. "The Effect of a Large Expansion of Pre-primary School Facilities on Preschool Attendance and Maternal Employment." *Labour Economics* 14 (3): 665–80.

Berlinski, S., S. Galiani, and P. Gertler. 2009. "The Effect of Pre-primary Education on Primary School Performance." *Journal of Public Economics* 93 (1–2): 219–34.

Berlinski, S., S. Galiani, and M. Manacorda. 2008. "Giving Children a Better Start: Preschool Attendance and School-Age Profiles." *Journal of Public Economics* 92 (5–6): 1416–40.

Bradley, R. H., R. F. Corwyn, M. Burchinal, H. P. McAdoo, and C. G. Coll. 2001. "The Home Environments of Children in the United States Part II: Relations with Behavioral Development through Age Thirteen." *Child Development* 72 (6): 1868–86.

Britto, P. R., P. Engle, and H. Alderman. 2007. "Early Intervention and Caregiving: Evidence from Uganda Nutrition and Early Childhood Development Program." *Child Health and Development* 1 (2): 112–33.

Burchinal, M., C. Howes, and S. Kontos. 2002. "Structural Predictors of Child Care Quality in Child Care Homes." *Early Childhood Research Quarterly* 17 (1): 87–105.

Campbell, F. A., C. T. Ramey, E. P. Pungello, S. Miller-Johnson, and J. J. Sparling. 2002. "Early Childhood Education: Young Adult Outcomes from the Abecedarian Project." *Applied Developmental Science* 6 (1): 42–57.

Currie, J., and D. Thomas. 1999. "Early Test Scores, Socioeconomic Status and Future Outcomes." NBER Working Paper 6943. National Bureau of Economic Research, Cambridge, MA.

Dearden, K. A., S. Hilton, M. E. Bentley, L. E. Caulfield, C. Wilde, P. B. Ha, and D. Marsh. 2009. "Caregiver Verbal Encouragement Increases Food Acceptance among Vietnamese Toddlers." *Journal of Nutrition* 139 (7): 1387–92.

Doherty, G., B. Forer, D. Lero, H. Goelman, and A. LaGrange. 2006. "Predictors of Quality in Family Child Care." *Early Childhood Research Quarterly* 21 (3): 296–312.

Downer, J. T., and R. C. Pianta. 2006. "Academic and Cognitive Functioning in First Grade: Associations with Earlier Home and Child Care Predictors and With Concurrent Home and Classroom Experiences." *School Psychology Review* 35 (1): 11–30.

Feinstein, L. 2003. "Inequality in the Early Cognitive Development of Children in the 1970 Cohort." *Economica* 70 (Feb): 73–97.

Fernald, L. C., P. J. Gertler, and L. M. Neufeld. 2006. "Role of Cash in Conditional Cash Transfer Programmes For Child Health, Growth, And Development: An Analysis of Mexico's Oportunidades." *The Lancet* 371 (9615): 828–37.

Flouri, E., and A. Buchanan. 2004. "Early Father's and Mother's Involvement and Child's Later Educational Outcomes." *British Journal of Educational Psychology* 74 (Jun): 141–53.

Glewwe, P., H. G. Jacoby, and E. M. King. 2001. "Early Childhood Nutrition and Academic Achievement: A Longitudinal Study." *Journal of Public Economics* 81 (3): 345–68.

Glewwe, P., and E. M. King. 2001. "The Impact of Early Childhood Nutritional Status on Cognitive Development: Does the Timing of Malnutrition Matter?" *World Bank Economic Review* 5 (1): 81–113.

Goelman, H., B. Forer, P. Kershaw, G. Doherty, D. Lero, and A. LaGrange. 2006. "Towards a Predictive Model of Child Care Quality in Canada." *Early Childhood Research Quarterly* 21 (3): 280–95.

Goodson, B. D., J. I. Layzer, R. G. St. Pierre, L. S. Bernstein, and M. Lopez. 2000. "Effectiveness of a Comprehensive, Five-Year Family Support Program for Low-Income Children and Their Families: Findings from the Comprehensive Child Development Program." *Early Childhood Research Quarterly* 15 (1): 5–39.

Grantham-McGregor, S. M., C. A. Powell, S. P. Walker, and J. H. Himes. 1991. "Nutritional Supplementation, Psychosocial Stimulation, and Mental Development of Stunted Children: The Jamaican Study." *The Lancet* 338 (8758): 1–5.

Grantham-McGregor, S. M., S. P. Walker, S. M. Chang, and C. A. Powell. 1997. "Effects of Early Childhood Supplementation with and without Stimulation on Later Development in Stunted Jamaican Children." *American Journal of Clinical Nutrition* 66 (2): 247–53.

Guldan, G. S., H. C. Fan, X. Ma, Z. Z. Ni, X. Xiang, and M. Z. Tang. 2000. "Culturally Appropriate Nutrition Education Improves Infant Feeding and Growth in Rural Sichuan, China." *Journal of Nutrition* 130 (5): 1204–11.

Haas, J. D., E. J. Martinez, S. Murdoch, E. Conlisk, J. A. Revera, and R. Martorell. 1995. "Nutritional Supplementation during the Preschool Years and Physical Work Capacity in Adolescent and Young Adult Guatemalans." *Journal of Nutrition* 125 (4): 1068–77.

Hair, E., T. Halle, E. Terry-Humen, B. Lavelle, and J. Calkins. 2006. "Children's School Readiness in the ECLS-K: Predictions to Academic, Health, and Social Outcomes in First Grade." *Early Childhood Research Quarterly* 21 (4): 431–54.

Hebbeler, K. M., and S. G. Gerlach-Downie. 2002. "Inside the Black Box of Home Visiting: A Qualitative Analysis of Why Intended Outcomes Were Not Achieved." *Early Childhood Research Quarterly* 17 (1): 28–51.

Heckman, J. J., S. H. Moon, R. Pinto, P. A. Savalyev, and A. Yavitz. 2009. "The Rate of Return to the High/Scope Perry Preschool Program." Unpublished manuscript, Department of Economics, University of Chicago.

Hoddinott, J., J. A. Maluccio, J. R. Behrman, R. Flores, and R. Martorell. 2008. "Effect of a Nutrition Intervention During Early Childhood on Economic Productivity in Guatemalan Adults." *The Lancet* 371 (9610): 411–16.

Huffman, L. R., and P. W. Speer. 2000. "Academic Performance among At-Risk Children: The Role of Developmentally Appropriate Practices." *Early Childhood Research Quarterly* 15 (2): 167–84.

Jaramillo, A., and K. Tietjen. 2001. *Early Childhood Development in Africa: Can We Do More and Better for Less? A Look at the Impact and Implications of Preschools in Cape Verde and Guinea*. World Bank Africa Region Human Development Series. Washington, DC: World Bank.

Kagitçibasi, C., D. Sunar, and S. Bekman. 2001. "Long-term Effects of Early Intervention: Turkish Low-Income Mothers and Children." *Journal of Applied Development Psychology* 22 (4): 333–61.

Kagitçibasi, C., D. Sunar, S. Bekman, N. Baydar, and Z. Cemalcilar. 2009. "Continuing Effects of Early Enrichment in Adult Life: The Turkish Early Enrichment Project 22 Years Later." *Journal of Applied Developmental Psychology* 30 (6): 764–79.

Loeb, S., M. Bridges, D. Bassok, B. Fuller, and R. W. Rumberger. 2007. "How Much Is Too Much? The Influence of Preschool Centres on Children's Social and Cognitive Development." *Economics of Education Review* 26 (1): 52–66.

Love, J., E. E. Kisker, C. Ross, H. Raikes, J. Constantine, K. Boller, J. Brooks-Gunn, R. Chazan-Cohen, L. B. Tarullo, C. Brady-Smith, A. S. Fuligni, P. Z. Schochet, D. Paulsell, and C. Vogel. 2005. "The Effectiveness of Early Head Start for 3-Year-Old Children and Their Parents." *Developmental Psychology* 41 (6): 885–901.

Love, J. M., E. E. Kisker, C. M. Ross, P. Z. Schochet, J. Brooks-Gunn, D. Paulsell, K. Boller, J. Constantine, C. Vogel, A. S. Fuligni, and C. Brady-Smith. 2002. "Making a Difference in the Lives of Infants and Toddlers and Their Families: The Impacts of Early Head Start— Executive Summary." U.S. Department of Health and Human Services, Washington, DC.

Macours, K., N. Schady, and R. Vakis. 2008. "Cash Transfers, Behavioral Changes, and Cognitive Development in Early Childhood: Evidence from a Randomized Experiment." World Bank Policy Research Working Paper 4759. World Bank, Washington, DC.

Malmberg, L. E., P. Mwaura, and K. Sylva. Forthcoming. "Effects of a Preschool Intervention on Cognitive Development among East-African Preschool Children: A Flexibly Time-Coded Growth Model." *Early Childhood Research Quarterly*, in press.

Manandhar, D. S., D. Osrin, B. P. Shrestha, N. Mesko, J. Morrison, K. M. Tumbahangphe, S. Tamang, S. Thapa, D. Shrestha, B. Thapa, J. R. Shrestha, A. Wade, J. Borghi, H. Standing, M. Manandhar, A.M. del Costello, and members of the MIRA Makwanpur trial team. 2004. "Effect of a Participatory Intervention with Women's Groups on Birth Outcomes in Nepal: Cluster-Randomised Controlled Trial." *The Lancet* 364 (9438): 970–79.

Marcon, R. 2002. "Moving Up the Grades: Relationship between Preschool Model and Later School Success." *Early Childhood Research and Practice* 4 (1).

Martin, A., R. M. Ryan, and J. Brooks-Gunn. 2007. "The Joint Influence of Mother and Father Parenting on Child Cognitive Outcomes at Age 5." *Early Childhood Research Quarterly* 22 (4): 423–39.

McKay, H., L. Sinisterra, A. McKay, H. Gomez, and P. Lloreda. 1978. "Improving Cognitive Ability in Chronically Deprived Children." *Science* 200 (4339): 270–78.

Meeks-Gardner, J., S. P. Walker, C. A. Powell, and S. Grantham-McGregor. 2003. "A Randomized Controlled Trial of a Home-Visiting Intervention on Cognition and Behavior in Term Low Birth Weight Infants." *Journal of Pediatrics* 143 (5): 634–39.

Mistry, R. S., A. D. Benner, J. Biesanz, S. Clark, C. Howes. Forthcoming. "Family and Social Risk, and Parental Investments during the Early Childhood Years as Predictors of Low-Income Children's School Readiness Outcomes." *Early Childhood Research Quarterly*, in press, uncorrected proof.

Montie, J. E., Z. Xiang, and L. J. Schweinhart. 2006. "Preschool Experience in 10 Countries: Cognitive and Language Performance at Age 7." *Early Childhood Research Quarterly* 21 (3): 313–31.

Mwaura, P., and B. T. Mohamed. 2008. "Madrasa Early Childhood Development Program: Making a Difference." In *Africa's Future, Africa's Challenge: Early Childhood Care and Development in Sub-Saharan Africa*, ed. M. Garcia, A. Pence, and J. Evans. Washington, DC: World Bank.

NICHD Early Child Care Research Network. 1996. "Characteristics of Infant Child Care: Factors Contributing to Positive Caregiving." *Early Childhood Research Quarterly* 11 (3): 269–306.

———. 2002. "Early Child Care and Children's Development prior to School Entry: Results from the NICHD Study of Early Child Care." *American Educational Research Journal* 39 (1): 133–64.

———. 2003. "Does Amount of Time Spent in Child Care Predict Socioemotional Adjustment during the Transition to Kindergarten?" *Child Development* 74 (4): 976–1005.

———. 2005. "Duration and Developmental Timing of Poverty and Children's Cognitive and Social Development from Birth through Third Grade." *Child Development* 76 (4): 795–810.

Olds, D., H. Kitzman, R. Cole, J. Robinson, K. Sidora, D. W. Luckey, C. R. Henderson, Jr., C. Hanks, J. Bondy, and J. Holmberg. 2004. "Effects of Nurse Home-Visiting on Maternal Life Course and Child Development: Age 6 Follow-Up Results of a Randomized Trial." *Pediatrics* 114 (6): 1550–59.

Olds, D. L., J. Robinson, R. O'Brien, D. W. Luckey, L. M. Pettitt, C. R. Henderson, Jr., R. K. Ng, K. L. Sheff, J. Korfmacher, S. Hiatt, and A. Talmi. 2002. "Home Visiting by Paraprofessionals and by Nurses: A Randomized, Controlled Trial." *Pediatrics* 110 (3): 486–96.

O'Rourke, K., L. Howard-Grabman, and G. Seoane. 1998. "Impact of Community Organization of Women on Perinatal Outcomes in Rural Bolivia." *Pan American Journal of Public Health* 3 (1): 9–14.

Pancsofar, N., L. Vernon-Feagans, and the Family Life Project Investigators. Forthcoming. "Fathers' Early Contributions to Children's Language Development in Families from Low-Income Rural Communities." *Early Childhood Research Quarterly*, in press, uncorrected proof.

Paxson, C., and N. Schady. 2007. "Cognitive Development among Young Children in Ecuador: The Roles of Wealth, Health, and Parenting." *Journal of Human Resources* 42 (1): 49–84.

———. 2010. "Does Money Matter? The Effects of Cash Transfers on Child Health and Development in Rural Ecuador." EDCC (2010), 59 (1): 187–229.

Peisner-Feinberg, E. S., M. R. Burchinal, R. M. Clifford, M. L. Culkin, C. Howes, S. L. Kagan, and N. Yazegian. 2001. "The Relation of Preschool Child-Care Quality to Children's Cognitive and Social Development Trajectories through Second Grade." *Child Development* 72 (5): 1534–53.

Penny, M. E., H. M. Creed-Kanashiro, R. C. Robert, M. R. Narro, L. E. Caulfield, and R. E. Black. 2005. "Effectiveness of an Educational Intervention Delivered through the Health Services to Improve Nutrition in Young Children: A Cluster-Randomised Controlled Trial." *The Lancet* 365 (9474): 1863–72.

Phillips, D., D. Mekos, S. Scarr, K. McCartney, and M. Abbott-Shim. 2000. "Within and Beyond the Classroom Door: Assessing Quality in Child Care Centers." *Early Childhood Research Quarterly* 15 (4): 475–96.

Phillipsen, L. C., M. R. Burchinal, C. Howes, and D. Cryer, 1997. "The Prediction of Process Quality from Structural Features of Child Care." *Early Childhood Research Quarterly* 12 (3): 281–303.

Pianta, R. C., and K. L. Harbers. 1996. "Observing Mother and Child Behavior in a Problem-Solving Situation at School Entry: Relations with Academic Achievement." *Journal of School Psychology* 34 (3): 307–22.

Pianta, R. C., and S. J. McCoy. 1997. "The First Day of School: The Predictive Validity of Early School Screening." *Journal of Applied Developmental Psychology* 18 (1): 1–22.

Pianta, R. C., S. L. Nimetz, and E. Bennett.1997. "Mother-Child Relationships, Teacher-Child Relationships, and School Outcomes in Preschool and Kindergarten." *Early Childhood Research Quarterly* 12 (3): 263–80.

Power, G. 2005. "Preliminary Findings from Cambodia MCH Campaign." Presentation at a meeting of the Communication Initiative Partners. Accessed December 9, 2008, http://www.comminit.com/pdf/Thursday_BBC_MCH Final.pdf.

Raikes, H., B. Green, J. Atwater, E. Kisker, J. Constantine, and R. Chazan-Cohen. 2006. "Involvement in Early Head Start Home Visiting Services: Demographic Predictors and Relations to Child and Parent Outcomes." *Early Childhood Research Quarterly* 21 (1): 2–24.

Reynolds, A. J., J. A. Temple, D. L. Robertson, and E. A. Mann. 2001. "Long-Term Effects of an Early Childhood Intervention on Educational Achievement and Juvenile Arrest—A 15-Year Follow-Up of Low-Income Children in Public Schools." *Journal of the American Medical Association* 285 (18): 2339–46.

RTI International. n.d. "The National Institute of Child Health and Human Development (NICHD) Study of Early Child Care and Youth Development." Accessed June 1, 2010, https://secc.rti.org/.

Sammons, P., K. Sylva, E. Melhuish, I. Siraj-Blatchford, B. Taggart, and S. Hunt. 2008. "The Effective Pre-School and Primary Education 3–11 Project: Influences on Children's Attainment and Progress in Key Stage 2: Cognitive Outcomes in Year 6." DCSF/Institute of Education, University of London.

Schweinhart, L. J., J. Montie, Z. Xiang, W. S. Barnett, C. R. Belfield, and M. Nores. 2005. *Lifetime Effects: The High/Scope Perry Preschool Study through Age 40.* Ypsilanti, MI.: High/Scope Educational Research Foundation.

Siraj-Blatchford, I., K. Sylva, B. Taggart, P. Sammons, E Melhuish, and K. Elliot. 2003. "The Effective Provision of Pre-School Education (EPPE) Project: Intensive Case Studies of Practice across the Foundation Stage." Technical Paper 10, DfEE/Institute of Education, University of London.

St. Clair, D., M. Xu, P. Wang, Y. Yu, Y. Fang, F. Zhang, X. Zheng, N. Gu, G. Feng, P. Sham, and L. He. 2005. "Rates of Adult Schizophrenia Following Prenatal

Exposure to the Chinese Famine of 1959–61." *Journal of the American Medical Association* 294 (5): 557–62.

Sweet, M. A., and M. I. Appelbaum. 2004. "Is Home Visiting an Effective Strategy? A Meta-Analytic Review of Home Visiting Programs for Families with Young Children." *Child Development* 75 (5): 1435–56.

Sylva, K., E. Melhuish, P. Sammons, I. Siraj-Blatchford, and B. Taggart. 2008. "Effective Pre-school and Primary Education 3–11 Project: Final Report from the Primary Phase: Pre-school, School and Family Influence on Children's Development during Key Stage 2 (Age 7–11)." Research Report DCSF-RR061, Department for Children, Schools and Families, London.

Sylva, K., E. C. Melhuish, P. Sammons, I. Siraj-Blatchford, and B. Taggart. 2003. "The Effective Provision of Pre-School Education (EPPE) Project: Findings from the Pre-School Period: Summary of Findings." Department for Children, Schools and Families, London. Accessed November 18, 2009, http://k1.ioe.ac.uk/cdl/eppe/pdfs/eppe_brief2503.pdf.

Wagner, M. M., and S. L. Clayton. 1999. "The Parents as Teachers Program: Results from Two Demonstrations." *The Future of Children* 9 (1): 91–115.

Walker, S. P., S. M. Chang, C. A. Powell, and S. M. Grantham-McGregor. 2005. "Effects of Early Childhood Psychosocial Stimulation and Nutritional Supplementation on Cognition and Education in Growth-Stunted Jamaican Children: Prospective Cohort Study." *The Lancet* 366 (9499): 1804–07.

Wasik, B. H., C. T. Ramey, D. M. Bryant, and J. J. Sparling.1990. "A Longitudinal Study of Two Early Intervention Strategies: Project CARE." *Child Development* 61 (6): 1682–96.

Watanabe, K., R. Flores, J. Fujiwara, and L. T. H. Tran. 2005. "Early Childhood Development Interventions and Cognitive Development of Young Children in Rural Vietnam." *Journal of Nutrition* 135 (8): 1918–25.

Index

Boxes, figures, notes, and tables are indicated with *b*, *f*, *n*, and *t* following the page numbers.

Lightning Source UK Ltd.
Milton Keynes UK
UKOW020942240911

179223UK00001B/43/P